THE TALES OF

DOCTOR HARRY

Retired Rural Family Doctor

 FriesenPress

Suite 300 - 990 Fort St
Victoria, BC, V8V 3K2
Canada

www.friesenpress.com

ISBN
978-1-5255-2332-8 (Hardcover)
978-1-5255-2333-5 (Paperback)
978-1-5255-2334-2 (eBook)

1. BIOGRAPHY & AUTOBIOGRAPHY

Distributed to the trade by The Ingram Book Company

TABLE OF CONTENTS

INTRODUCTION

Medicine is a demanding profession. As a family doctor, you must always be aware of what is happening or developing in other narrower specialities that might be appropriate for your patients.

Attending meetings, reading journals, going to conferences, and participating in hospital rounds are a must for family doctors in order to stay on top of a rapidly changing medical world.

Family practice is really a series of unrelated events in the short term, but in the long term there is a continuity since you are attending the same patients through many events over a long period of time – often many decades.

The first part of this book plays out more or less chronologically and covers my early years, my education, and ultimately my years as a doctor, including my thoughts on the profession looking back over my career.

The second part of the book is different.

Why did I put a travel section in the book? Over the years, many people (including patients) have been interested in where we had been and where we were going next and have encouraged – almost demanded – that I write a book about my life including both medical and personal travel.

I have written the travel section not as a travelogue but as a collection of interesting events that occurred during our many expeditions to various parts of the world. A lot of them have a humorous twist.

We have had a lot of adventures, hiking, biking, sailing, cruising, or paddling to some very remote places.

It is my hope that the pictures I have included will provide a glimpse at some of the places we have been

DEDICATION

I dedicate this book to all the patients of all varieties, from prime ministers, CEO's, and celebrities and to those whose lives have been difficult. The MD's and nurses whom I have encountered in my office, the hospitals, house calls and remote locums have all taught me something for which I will be eternally grateful.

PART ONE
RURAL DOCTOR

As the days go by, I often dream of our days walking along a very remote beach on a very remote island in the South Pacific where I was doing a locum for six months. It was referred to as the End of the Earth by some people, and there was a book written about it by that name.

Not a sign anywhere that anyone had ever been there before, just soft, golden white sand stretching for miles, a gentle breeze, a warm sun, and the rhythmic whispering of the waves rolling in and disappearing into the sand, the remnants of each singing as they returned to their origin. It was stony quiet, the occasional gull or albatross soaring on high.

I am a happy man and very calm and content. I am very thankful that I have been fortunate enough to have spent time in that wonderful place.

My wife Marian and I wandered a little further, climbed up a bright orange cliff where we could see for miles along the shore – many bays of white sand, black lava outcropping, and turquoise sea. This was likely paradise.

It was and still is an intense feeling of being a miniscule part of something much larger and grander, but still an integral piece of the cosmos. It is an elation mixed with a sense of unreality accompanied by a calm deep warmth. Contented satisfaction. At the same time there is a parallel sense of excitement at the discovery of that which is beyond our experience or understanding. Perhaps it could be called a temporary psychosis. Does unbridled joy fit into that category? Thinking about this – and a number of other places we have been – has made me feel I should share this by attempting to write down a few thoughts about my lifetime in medicine and the changes I have witnessed.

1. EARLY YEARS

Life began in Toronto in 1935. My mother was a nurse who stayed home after marrying my father. He was an internal medicine specialist who did family practice in North Toronto – the suburbs at the time but now downtown. He worked at St Michael's hospital and seemed to work all the time, so we kids rarely saw him. Fortunately, mother was a champion, always available for triumphs or tragedies. I had two younger sisters, Arlene and Lynne, but I always preferred the dog Max. Max was my best friend and protector (even with my parents). My sisters were not the enemy, but they were very close to each other and involved in girl things that I could never really relate to.

I guess I was sort of a genetic family doctor because besides my father, my mother's father was also a family doctor. My grandfather was a great guy who practiced in Mattawa on the Ottawa River where he was the Canadian National Railway doctor, so he had to take the train down to smaller places. He saw diseases like cholera, typhoid, even smallpox but never got any disease himself. He always had a cigar in his mouth and declared the bugs would not dare to come anywhere near him. He had many stories about winter house calls with horses, cutter, and buffalo robe. The cigars, however, did catch up to him in the form of several heart attacks at the age of sixty and a fatal stroke at age eighty.

My father, a quiet intellectual man who studied classics first – Greek and Latin – then sciences, then medicine, was a workaholic. We seldom saw him, and when he was home, he was often reading a medical text on a little stand even during meals. He practiced until he was eighty-three and became very depressed when he retired and my mother died of heart problems at eighty-six. My father lived to be one month short of ninety-nine.

My father was born in 1901 and remembered the first cars. "Untrustworthy things," he'd claimed at the time, "they will never last." You had to crank start them, and they were not so great in the winter, but in the summer, the rumble seats (outside in the back) were lots of fun even though you were choking on the dust and fumes from the gravel roads.

He remembered the first aircraft as astonishing, actually leaving the ground and moving much like a bird. Impossible until the Wright brothers came along and proved it could be done. It's difficult to imagine the technical expertise necessary to fly, especially when no one had ever done it.

My father graduated in 1929 from University of Toronto as my grandfather had eighteen years earlier. There were no antibiotics then, sulfa came in the late thirties followed by streptomycin and then the amazing penicillin in the early forties. The question was what dose to use of penicillin. In those days they thought one hundred thousand units was a big dose. Now that would be considered minimal.

I had a *parapharyngeal* [beside the tonsil] abscess at age two. As this was before penicillin, the treatment was surgical drainage and required being hung upside down to prevent aspiration or swallowing the pus. I was the first patient with that diagnosis to live in this surgeon's experience I was told.

Although my father worked constantly, he did take me fishing a couple of times for trout. I remember my father – ever the scientist – was researching whether he caught more fish with the head of the worm or the tail.

On another occasion, we had an aboriginal guide, which was very exciting because this man knew everything about the outdoors and fish. We were to have a shore lunch on an island as well. As the time drew near for lunch, I watched wide-eyed as he built a fire first with grass, birch bark and pine needles, then small sticks followed by slightly larger and in the shape of a teepee. When was he going to rub the sticks to get it started? At this stage he poured gasoline over the teepee, stood back a few feet and threw a match onto it. Innocence lost!

As a boy, we had a large backyard with a picket fence along one side. It was really good for testing your balance. On the other side, there was quite a steep bank leading down to the sidewalk. There were lots of climbable trees, and they hung out over the sidewalk so we could be spies, watching people go under. There were quite a few young boys my age around, so there might be a few of us up in the trees at any one time. We never dropped anything on the people walking below. Really!

Of course, there were no televisions then, so we were always exploring, hiding, building forts, climbing fences or garage roofs, skating, and catching frogs and minnows. We would fight at times, but it never meant anything so there were no hard feelings or grudges. We were just like a bunch of puppies really. To give yourself a real scare, you visited the graveyards at night. There were ghosts everywhere.

Our gang were the good guys, of course, bastions of freedom and feared by all the other gangs who wanted to invade our territory. They didn't, of course, no doubt trembling in fear of our reputation.

We lived on top of my father's office, and before emergency departments, people came to the office anytime, so being awakened at night by intoxicated people or other emergencies was not that unusual – and probably good training for my future.

We attended Allenby Public School on Avenue Road just above Eglinton, which was the suburbs then, so there were fields and creeks around with pollywogs, minnows, and all manner of interesting bugs. School was fun. I was in love with my Grade 2 teacher who I guess liked me too. She skipped me to fourth grade. My sixth grade teacher was Miss Buck who always wore suits and kept her hair in a bun, her eyes bulging. If we misbehaved – which of course *I* never did – she would lean over you with her eyes bulging and tell you she would, and I quote, "tear your heart out." We didn't think she would really do it, but it was best to play it safe.

In public school, we won the city hockey championships by virtue of one player on our team who was so much better than the rest of us that we couldn't take the puck away from him. His name was Eric Nesterenko, and he would go on to enjoy a long National Hockey League career. Eric was a friend of mine and he played his first game for the Toronto Maple Leafs while we were still in high school. He scored two goals in his first game, but he was more impressed with the hundred dollars he got paid for the game.

2. AN EDUCATION

When I was about fourteen, we moved out to the country northeast of Toronto just off Bayview near York Mills where the next house was a significant distance away and the roads were gravel. People riding horses past the house was not an unusual event. There was no bus service, and the traffic was sparse. Since we lived on the edge of the Don Valley, I had my first major exposure to nature. I spent hours down in the valley learning about birds, animals, snakes, and plant life, which is still fascinating to me. Nature is constantly changing, so every time I ventured out – even if it was the same place I'd visited before – it would be different. Life is a constant learning experience, which to me is one of the great joys. There is always more to learn.

Living in the country made getting into the city a little more difficult. Hitchhiking was fine for me, but when my two sisters needed a ride, my father was not always available. We went through a series of hand-me-down cars, once I learned to drive, so I could drive my sisters around. A couple of the cars stand out. One was an old Dodge; the doors would not shut, so I kept them closed by tying one door to the other one with a rope inside the car. It worked well until, one day, when going around a corner, the rope broke, and my sister Arlene fell out onto the road. Fortunately, she had no major injury.

Another vehicle was a yellow Buick convertible. What more could a young boy ask for? It was very popular if not too reliable. The top would not always click into place, so I often drove it –even in the winter – with the top down. It was great to be young and alive.

High school in North Toronto during that teenage emotionally fragile time of life was actually quite comfortable for me. I did not like school, but I liked sports, and for that I had to achieve certain marks. Sometimes I accidentally overshot the mark for which I was punished and had to take an extra subject – of course, they called it *enhancement* rather than punishment. I guess it's all in the perspective.

We had some excellent teachers and some poor ones too. A Grade 10 English teacher drew me out into enjoying and understanding the nuances of Shakespeare, Shaw, and the Irish poets. Another English teacher asked me one question all year.

"Hall," he said, "spell *cat.*"

Despite getting pretty good marks, he still made me write the final exam. At that time, if you had over seventy, which I did, you usually were exempted. I don't think he liked me or maybe anybody else either?

At the seventy-five-year school reunion – this was in 1985 when I was fifty – we had to line up if you wanted to speak to a teacher. I got in his long line in order to tell him how bad he was, but while waiting in line and talking to other people, I realized they were all there for the same reason. I thought he would get enough criticism, so I lined up for other teachers I liked and appreciated.

The real reason I stayed in school was for the sports, and we did exceptionally well at North Toronto. We won the Toronto track and field championships every year. In football, we had the same coach every year, Bobby Coulter, and he took the same team through, and we won it all including the Red Feather which was symbolic of provincial championship. I was a flying wing (or wingback), a position that no longer exists by that name. On offence, we played one yard behind the line at either end, so we were multi-purpose.

We blocked, caught passes, and were involved in some running plays, particularly the reverse

We did well in basketball but never won the championship. I recall my shame in one championship game against Riverdale who had an exceptional player who was my check. They beat us, and he scored twenty-six points. Suicide seemed like the best alternative until the next day when the track and field season started. I was a sprinter and jumper (both long and high) and held some records for several years. We also managed to win the TSSAA (Toronto Secondary School Athletic Association) championships in tennis and badminton so school seemed good in those days.

Along the way, the student council of the day decided I should be the next president, so they did a lot of work, and despite my terrifying fear of public speaking, I got elected. The school band was out on the street playing "I'm Just Wild About Harry" a song from the twenties that had been recently re-popularized when it was used by Harry S. Truman in 1948 in his successful presidential campaign. There were several friends with tee-shirts saying the same thing, riding tricycles up and down the rows in classes. It was so much fun that the school administration clamped down on it, and I guess it never happened again. My future first wife was elected secretary, and so began *that* relationship. Interestingly enough, my opposition for president was Eric Nesterenko, and for the hockey fans, the treasurer was Roger Nielson.

Speaking of fear of public speaking, I passed out and embarrassed myself at my first meeting with all the class reps. I started to feel queasy, then sweaty, and then the next thing I knew I awoke on the floor and Ria, my vice president – who would one day end up marrying Roy McMurtry, MPP – was reading my speech. It could not have got any worse. By the end of the year, I could get up in front of the school, but not without discomfort. When I think of opportunities that I had been offered and turned down because of my fear of public speaking, I wonder how different life might have been if I had conquered that fear earlier.

Another sideline during high school was a brief modeling career. In those days Eaton's was *the* store, and one of their forays into public relations was picking a girl and boy from each high school to be an Eaton's Rep. They did all kinds of nice things for us – events, speakers, clothes including a very nice-looking jacket with Eaton's Rep displayed on the vest pocket. In return for all these goodies, we were asked to model their new fashions at occasional fashion shows for young people. There we were on the runway. Imagine! I think we could even get a good deal on the clothes we wore, but I' m not sure of that memory. I did not pursue that career any further.

Tennis was my summer sport, and I actually rose to being ranked third in Canadian junior ranks at age eighteen. I really enjoyed all the different sports, and I do believe more kids would be better off to play a lot of different ones rather than narrowing down to one (usually hockey). Not many kids make the National Hockey League, and so many quit when they realize they won't make it and they are left with nothing – or maybe they take up golf.

Interestingly we were out at a concert not long ago when an old high school teammate (a former football quarterback) whom I had not seen since, came up to see me.

"It was fifty years ago that I threw you the pass that won the Toronto championship," he said.

He then proceeded to tell my wife Marian that I was even better on defence.

"Nobody ever got by him."

Makes your head swell for a few minutes. I was a Toronto high school all star one year.

One of the things I noticed in sports was that there was a camaraderie, even among long-term rivals. I guess it emerges out of common interest and mutual respect.

MEDICAL SCHOOL

I was lucky enough to get into pre-med at University of Toronto. It was basically a bachelor of arts in two years with no degree, but it shaved some time off entrance into medicine proper. It was at a time when they wanted us to be more well-rounded, so we had a variety of subjects. English (the heaviest with biggest failure numbers), psychology, philosophy, anthropology, zoology, physics, and chemistry.

A couple of interesting things happened. Since I was playing university football, we had practice every day all fall, which cut significantly into study time. I also had a long commute home every day. I was still hitchhiking up Bayview, but the rapid development of the area had produced a lot more traffic by then, and if I was there at almost the same time every day, the drivers got more comfortable with picking me up.

When exams came around, I was ill-prepared, but I learned something amazing to me. In philosophy, the exam was one question based on one book. I think the idea was to expand on the theme of the book. I didn't know it at all well, so I decided to take the opposite premise. I expected to go down in flames. To my astonishment, I got an excellent mark, and the professor was so impressed that someone had taken an opposite approach that he embarrassed me by reading portions out to the class. An epiphany! At university level, you don't have to just memorize and regurgitate, you can object if you can back it up.

Another consequence of my university football career was that I received a major concussion in football training camp up on Lake Couchiching at the Ontario Athletic Leadership Camp. The coach was Bob Masterson, the ex-NFL All Star from the Washington Redskins, and he said it was the hardest hit he had ever seen. I was unconscious for quite a while and spent three days in Toronto General Hospital. This was 1954, and there were no CTs nor MRIs then. For quite a long time after, every time I would leap to catch a pass, I was dizzy and wasn't sure where I would land. It also knocked my marks down for a year or so. I guess now they probably would have kept me out of sports (certainly football) for a while. We went on to win the Yates Cup symbolic of the Ontario Quebec university football championship. There were only four teams then, Toronto, McGill, Western, and Queens. We then went on to beat University of British Columbia in the first East West game – now known as the Vanier cup. That was 1954, and we were inducted into the U of T Athletic Hall of Fame in 2014.

Another football injury, the result of clipping, resulted in a torn lateral meniscus (knee cartilage) which was an off and on problem for the rest of my life until a knee replacement at age sixty-eight.

We also were on the U of T tennis team, which won the interuniversity championship in 1953 with a record number of wins, a feat for which we have been nominated for the Athletic Hall of Fame also. These things take time it seems. I noted one induction last year for a 1925 event.

The following year, in first medical year, they needed a *rabbit* for an *EEG* (electroencephalogram, or brainwave test) so I volunteered. After it was over, the professor asked me if I had ever had a head injury; so concussions *can* do significant damage, and of course now are suspected as one source of dementia. I am keeping my fingers crossed on that score.

One of the interesting sidelines around that time is what I refer to as my operatic career. The Metropolitan Opera in those days had a travelling show that toured a few cities each year. That year *Aida* was the show. For the triumphal scene they needed a lot of extras – animals, dancers, gymnasts, and of course, soldiers, so who better than a football team. We were invited (even paid) to march on the stage as the music played, dressed as the soldiers of the day with spears and shields. We were standing behind the stars as they sang, and the strength of their voices was incredible. They actually shook the stage, and this was Maple leaf Gardens. Since I was there, I thought I must be part of it, so I made the smallest possible little peep that I couldn't even hear myself, but it satisfied me enough to say I had sung in the Metropolitan Opera. Since then, if I sing, my wife laughs, and the dog disappears.

Following pre-meds, in my first medical year, we had a more or less even mix of pre-meds like myself, and students who had taken a different route, mostly in science degrees. Several had master's degrees already.

There was certainly some slogging to do in medical school; the basic sciences, anatomy, physiology, bacteriology, pharmacology were more memory work than anything else, but all necessary.

The demonstrators, professors, and faculty were a varied lot. We had J. C. Grant of *Grant's Anatomy*, a rather stern, no-nonsense fellow. We had Dr. Ham for histology, and Dr. Best – of Banting and Best insulin fame – who was very knowledgeable but rather pedantic. There were also many lesser lights, some of whom were interested in you as a person. To others, you were a necessary evil to get by in their search for the Holy Grail of full professorship, which was proof that they were superior to everyone else. To achieve this, some of these individuals saw students as stepping stones on the way to their rightful recognition.

On our first histology exam (microscopic anatomy) I thought I had done quite well. My mark was zero and a comment that he could not read my writing. Horrors! I didn't think it was *that* bad, but it didn't matter what I thought. He would not back down so it put a little pressure on me for the rest of the year to get a passing mark. I really had to be almost perfect plus write clearly. It was very demanding. Maybe I should have been a pathologist after that?

The whole process became much more "real" and important and interesting when we started to see patients. It was still rather intimidating because I realized how little I knew in the grand scheme and how much there was to learn.

Some classmates were very good at getting old exams and figuring out what was likely to be on the upcoming exams, but I was interested in knowing as much as I could about all aspects of medicine not just what was to be on the exams. Actually, it sort of fit my philosophy of trying to do it all. I have an insatiable curiosity and hate to miss out on anything.

One time, the university president had a dinner to which two students from each faculty – medicine, law, engineering, etc. – were invited. I'll never know why I was one of the two from medicine to be invited; the other was basically our gold medalist. I certainly wasn't number two, but I wasn't at the other end either. I guess we will never know. Our gold medalist, who was a good friend, was so smart that competing with him was not an option.

Back then, if you were a med student, you learned whether you passed by getting the *Globe and Mail* on a certain date and looking for your name therein. One year they left a significant number out – letters B to G, in fact. Imagine their anxiety until corrected the next day.

In 1958, before the start of my final year I got married to Gigi Nyberg, former high school student council secretary.

I delivered seventeen babies in my fourth year as a medical student, but most delivered only one or two. I was just lucky to be in the right place at the right time.

Another time I was watching the anesthetist in a face down case with the chief of neurosurgery, a man who always enjoyed terrifying students. A face down case in neurosurgery is when the surgery is on the back of the head. When the anesthetist stepped out of the room for a minute, the intubation tube fell out of the patient onto the floor with a thump. The surgeon looked down at the anesthetist and there I was, I was sure I was going to be decapitated. Fortunately, the anesthetist came through the door at that moment, so all was saved.

At the conclusion of my final year of med school – 1959 for me and my cohorts – the dean appeared on the steps of the medical building with white gloves and read out the names of those who graduated. Your sympathy for those who failed almost overcame your joy of passing yourself. Of course, as you got closer to graduation, you became more confident so that when you graduated you knew everything. Well, maybe not quite *everything*.

OTHER ASPECTS OF UNIVERSITY LIFE

It was a wonderful, intense, busy time of life. The opportunities of university are many, so many clubs for various interests, so many sports. There are so many different people from different backgrounds and interests and so many events, you can't take it all in, and I wonder if they are still there. Do they still have the annual engineering vs medicine snowball fights? We always won of course, but I have forgotten how we decided that.

Fraternity life gave you sort of a home base in university. They were a bunch of guys who had your back –and were known to have a few parties – and the frat house was a great place for lunch with friends.

Sports were a major interest for me. Besides football, we also won the intercollegiate tennis championship and played basketball and water polo at the inter-faculty level.

A member of the University of Toronto squash team invited me down to play squash one day. I had never played squash but had played a lot of tennis. He barely beat me. The coach of the squash team happened to be watching and invited me to be on the University of Toronto squash team. I guess it was sort of a backup team because we played local Toronto clubs, not the other universities. The only reason I won a few matches was that I could serve a tennis serve, so it landed right in the corner. On the bigger courts, I didn't do so well, and I never got comfortable with those back-hand corners.

3. INTERNSHIP AND RESIDENCY

After graduation in those days, a rotating internship for a year was mandatory after which you could enter specialty training or go into practice.

Family practice residency I don't believe had even started, and we had no experience with general practice. In the hospital, the stories were often quite derogatory about general practice as the "elsewhere general" where they really didn't know what was going on but were fortunately saved by the brilliant doctors "at our own hospital." You never heard good stories, so it was painted as if anyone with any intellect would pick a narrow specialty. The dregs would be left as family doctors. I am not sure if that has changed a lot. I have had specialists say to me at meetings that they don't know how we could keep track of what is going on in all areas of medicine, but we must.

A retired cardiac surgeon and neighbour thought he would do general practice as something to keep him busy. I asked him if he would do obstetrics, prenatal.

"Oh no," he said, "the nurse would look after that."

What about diabetes, hypertension, or gastrointestinal disturbance problems? Again, he didn't seem to keen. He seemed to get the idea that maybe general practice wasn't just "listening" which he felt he was good at. He only tried it for two weeks.

As a family doctor who has done everything short of major surgery – where I would assist on our own patients – I saw myself as the quarterback of the health team who deployed specialists, if and when it was appropriate, but stayed very involved in all aspects of the patient's mental and physical health, from delivery (birth) until death.

The internship year at Toronto Western Hospital was a very busy year, and of course, I got paid virtually nothing. I believe it was fifty dollars a week. You had free room – in our case it was a house across the road from the hospital with three of us in what had been the living room and dining room. It was fumigated three times during the year for cockroaches. Food, fortunately, was free after eleven at night (leftovers) and the cashiers doing the meals were very kind, understanding and may have accidently underestimated the cost of your meal occasionally. The work was long and inclusive and I loved it. Taking responsibility and doing work that mattered.

Working in Emergency there was interesting. One day the chief of surgery came in having cut off part of his toe in a lawn mower. It seemed like a good one to refer to one of the staff surgeons.

Another time a fleet of ambulances appeared at the door without warning. They wanted doctors to take to an accident at Bathurst and Front (downtown Toronto) in rush hour. Two street cars had collided in the intersection as the crowd emerged from the opening ball game. I jumped into the first ambulance for the wildest ride I have ever had down Bathurst Street in rush hour. Everything was more or less stopped. With sirens blaring and lights flashing, we were cutting around cars, streetcars, and people. We were up on the sidewalk on both sides before we got there. There were a number of people with minor injuries, but only one man lost part of a leg.

My first scrub in for surgery was as second assistant to the chief of surgery. The chief resident was first assistant. It was a long involved abdominal perineal cancer operation. When it was over, the chief asked me if I would dictate the operative note. I said yes, of course, after all he was the chief. Fortunately, the chief resident told me he did the identical operation the day before on another patient. He suggested I get out the previous note, change the name, and use it as a guide. What a relief!

The next case was a mitral stenosis as the assistant to the surgeon. Mitral stenosis is a narrowing of one of the valves that separate the chambers of the heart. The surgeon had to put a finger through the atrium (left atrial appendage) to break down the stenosis. Around his finger was a suture, the tension of which I was controlling, too loose would mean massive bleeding, too tight would cut off circulation. At least he didn't ask me to dictate the note.

On one occasion I was assisting in the operating room for forty-two hours in a row (all emergencies, mostly trauma). Imagine if I had to make any quick decisions.

One day, as I was going to get on the elevator, the operator dropped to the floor in front of me. He had no pulse and was not breathing – and this was in the days before CPR. I gave him a very hard punch in the middle of his chest and his heart started up again. He was in the hospital for a while with acute myocardial infarction and cardiac arrest. Following that, I always had wonderful service on that elevator

The urology service was very busy and there were some good surgeons. One of them made rounds (daily post-operative visits) very quickly despite a large patient load. His secret lay in how he entered the room.

"You're fine, how are you?" he'd say.

"Fine," the patient would say.

And with that, he would be out the door, even though we might have been up all night transfusing the patient.

I always enjoyed obstetrics because everyone was so happy (almost always). Years ago, if someone was young and not married and got pregnant, they usually disappeared for a few months and stayed in the many "homes" in Toronto. A lot came to our hospital so that, by the time I finished my obstetrical stint, I had delivered about one hundred and fifty babies. The chief resident (once he was comfortable with us) allowed us to use forceps whenever we needed to. So we had posteriors, faces, twins, even breeches with after coming heads with forceps. The residents were always available for problems such as placenta previa, postpartum bleeding, or any other emergency beyond our abilities. It was a great experience and a confidence builder.

Following internship what does one do? I became very interested in internal medicine (the fun of diagnosing and treating) more unusual and rare diseases.

FIRST YEAR OF INTERNAL MEDICINE RESIDENCY (VANCOUVER 1960-61)

With my internship over I was ready to start my residency and decided to go first to Shaughnessy Hospital in Vancouver, which at the time, was the equivalent of Sunnybrook in Toronto – but it has taken a different path since. My wife Gigi and I drove out in a Volkswagen bug and found a place to stay, but again the pay was very low.

I had a great year, much more relaxed and more time to look things up at my leisure. During the year, we had regular rounds to discuss patients, and we had some rare cases. One was a sarcoid of the small bowel, the only case I ever saw. Sarcoid is a rare disease that usually attacks lung tissue.

We had two acute intermittent porphyria diagnoses, one in an eighty-four-year-old man, which made it the oldest recorded onset. He had been diagnosed with terminal cancer of the stomach, so he was on drugs like morphine and phenobarbital when he came in, both of which made his porphyria worse. We were able to get him comfortable and home again. Intermittent porphyria is a metabolic disease with acute abdominal pain and urine that turns purple in the sunlight.

The most outstanding experience of my residency year at Shaughnessy had nothing to do with medicine and everything to do with lifestyle. We ventured down to Mount Baker in July. Mount Baker is a gigantic dormant volcano in Washington State, just across the US border a few hours away, and it boasted great skiing. Remember that, at that time, Whistler in British Columbia was just an idea; a ski resort wouldn't open to the public there until 1966. And so, it was Mount Baker for us.

The nearest lodge was Church Mountain Lodge which lay in the valley after nineteen miles of switchbacks, a beautiful log lodge with a big stone fireplace. There was no accommodation at the top of Baker. In my youthful entrepreneurial enthusiasm, I rented the whole lodge for the winter. I didn't have a dime, but the owners named Baker, Laree, and Newt were such nice people they were agreeable. She was a wonderful and inexpensive cook. There were twenty-seven beds, so a little effort was required to form a ski club of the doctors from the Shaughnessy Hospital and Vancouver General Hospital. The understanding was that they pay up front, no refunds. We had four or five fractures the first week, so we had room for more people. As time went on, we were able to take more people because, inevitably, somebody had to work or were otherwise called away.

Mount Baker claims the biggest snowfall in the world, and there was no significant grooming, so you learned to ski deep heavy snow, or you quit. The mountain was steep, and you could climb higher if you wanted to. Glade skiing was wonderful once you were able to master it.

Newt was the local mountain lion hunter – called upon if there was trouble with local livestock – so all the sofas surrounding the big stone fireplace were covered with magnificent skins.

In the spring, we would ski all day in the warm sun then come down for one of Laree's great meals. Newt would take me to his pond (next to the Nooksack river) to fly fish, and we would catch cutthroat trout and rainbow trout as the sun set down the valley in the west. That was heaven or at least heavenly. A magnificent year skiing at Mount Baker cost me nothing.

In June of 1961, we ran out of money in Vancouver. We were able to go down to White Rock, and went crab fishing with a group of doctors. I used a forked stick with the string across the prongs to lift and put the crab in a bag I had tied around my waist. This was done in the tide pools at low tide. We were able to put them in people's freezers and ate nothing but crab for two weeks. Following that, I couldn't eat crab for about ten years.

By this time Gigi was pregnant with our first child and flew home to Toronto while I drove across the country with my youngest sister Lynne. We had no money, so we slept in the car, beside the car, on picnic tables or whatever was available. After arriving in Toronto, Gigi and I drove down to Boston where I was set to take up the second year of residency.

SECOND YEAR OF INTERNAL MEDICINE RESIDENCY (BOSTON 1961-62)

Boston is a beautiful historic city and home to arguably the best medical centre in the world, Massachusetts General Hospital the largest teaching hospital of the Harvard Medical School, as well as New England Journal of Medicine, the Brigham Hospitals, Beth Israel Hospital, Deaconess and New England Baptist.

The post-grad medical system was so intertwined that we had speakers of renown appearing and available to all.

In addition to hospital work, I also did clinic work (outpatients). The patients came from all over the world. We had kings, sheiks, presidents, and prime ministers and a huge variety of all types of people. I had to wear a suit, and I only had one, so I purchased another one for twenty-eight dollars; I leave the details to your imagination. I guess it fit the definition at the time.

Once again, the pay for residents was miniscule, and I was a young married man with a brand-new baby girl; Karen was born a month after our arrival in Boston, on August 4, 1961, which earned her dual citizenship. I was making two hundred dollars a month, and the rent on our fifth-floor apartment was one hundred and thirty dollars per month. There was really no place to take the baby for a walk. A short distance away was a huge Catholic church with a very large parking lot, but it was guarded by monks and priests who would allow no one to walk on their sacred parking lot. An example of good old Christian charity I thought at the time. As a diversion, we still had our Volkswagen bug, so we got around a bit in the northeast mountains and even climbed Mount Washington. I should've taken my skis because there were people skiing on the headwall at the top. The fellows, as we were called, were from all over the world.

Everyone on the staff was a super specialist, limited to a small area. One fellow only did pituitaries, another only syphilis, several only did thyroids. You get the picture. There were no generalists, which was sometimes awkward with inpatients. Different specialists would sometimes write opposing orders. Someone needed to be in charge. Did you ever hear of a general practitioner to sort out priorities and advocate for the patient? A lot of interesting things happened during that year.

We looked after the Kennedy family, and on cardiology I remember reading Joe Kennedy's electrocardiogram one day. He was in controlled rate atrial fibrillation (which is an irregularity of the heart), and in those days, the association with a cerebral vascular accident (strokes) was not recognized. There were no computers to put it all together. You will remember he ended up with a stroke.

Another strange case was a man from New York City, who had lost his voice, and this was a problem since he owned a large rug manufacturing company with branches around the country, and he was not able to communicate with his people, who could not hear him on the phone – no emails or faxes back then either. He had tried every speech specialist (he said) in New York City to no avail, so presented in Boston. I was the first to see him, and I was putting his neck through a range of motion when his voice came back. I wish I knew what I did, but anyway he was very excited and wanted to take me back to New York as his personal physician. Maybe I should have taken him up on it.

We had the British Prime minister as a patient. I was part of a large team that met every day to discuss his situation. Imagine how the British doctors must have felt. He was a really soft-spoken gentleman, not demanding, but he was very aware of all that was happening around him.

The sheiks, when they were admitted, generally brought their whole entourage and took up a lot of space, but money didn't enter the picture. Since they stayed in a private hospital, they could all move in almost like a hotel.

While I was there, a researcher from the Peter Bent Brigham won a Nobel Prize. Nobody even knew him. He had been working away in a lab somewhere in the basement.

Roger Bannister, the first man to run a mile under four minutes – and a respirologist – gave us a talk one day. Many of the writers of textbooks were there and seen frequently at clinical rounds. Intensive care rounds were always outstanding. It was one nurse to one patient, so she knew everything about the patient. The team that went around included physicians and nurses and laboratory people, biochemist, pharmacists, physiotherapists, and anybody else who dealt with the patient. With all that expertise the bedside rounds were superb.

Since so many people came from all over the world, they often had to stay in hotels before being seen the next day. Since they were vulnerable there, as fellows, we would rarely be on call to cover them.

In one memorable week, I saw only five patients. One was a case of thrombosed hemorrhoids, another was acute pericarditis (inflammation of the sack that contains the heart), and three were rupturing aortic aneurisms that all presented with back pain. All three were emergency operations and did well. The vascular surgeons were so busy that they asked that I not be put on the schedule again (kidding).

Another instance where I had some kidding for a while – kidding that stopped abruptly – was a patient where I made an offbeat diagnosis. Cardiac surgery patients were worked up by the medical side before surgery. The patient came in with a diagnosis of mitral stenosis (heart valve narrowing) and was booked for surgery. To me the history was strange for mitral stenosis (remember there were no echocardiograms then) just a chest x-ray and clinical acumen. I could not hear a murmur either, and my hearing was good then, so I committed to a diagnosis of myxoma of the left atrium (a very rare, benign tumor of the heart). There was loud guffaws and kidding from the specialists until the day of surgery. I was actually right. I thought that was a good thing, but some of the consultants weren't so pleased with my performance. I guess a ranking cardiologist didn't appreciate being shown up by a kid from Canada. The next rotation, hematology, was much friendlier. We did a lot of bone marrows, so I actually was comfortable reading them for a while, but as time goes by I didn't have enough volume to maintain my skills.

Overall it was a wonderful year, a great experience. I maintained contact with a couple of people for quite a while, doctors and the Harvard Business School graduates as well. I was encouraged to stay on, but thought I needed to make a little money before continuing.

4. FAMILY PRACTICE

While in Boston, I exchanged Christmas cards with a clinic-mate who was in a small town in Ontario. He said that they needed someone with medical expertise. And because at good medical institutions you could barely survive on what you were paid – and because now I had a family – I felt I had to make some money to carry on with internal medicine. I decided to join him and do general practice in Orillia, Ontario, for a year.

I loved it.

We did everything, except major surgery. I love it so much that one year stretched into the rest of my medical career with a few small detours along the way.

So here I was in a small town, having come from a high-powered medical complex in a huge city. What do I do?

The business of medicine was never mentioned during medical school or residency, so I knew nothing. I joined a group with my classmate and got paid a salary which was much better than I had before. It took me quite a while to figure out how their system worked since I wasn't used to thinking of monetary value for my services.

This small town had about twelve to fifteen family doctors, three surgeons – all of whom hated each other – one internist, and that was it. The family doctors were basically in three groups. We "knew" the doctors in the other two groups were rather dense, behind the times, and ruthless money grabbers.

Early on, I had to decide whether I wanted to practice solo or in a group. The group idea was comforting as I had other experienced people to ask questions of both a medical and general nature, and since I was in a new location, it could form the foundation of a social life at the start. Since I knew nothing about how the group was organized financially, I was happy to be working and getting compensation. After a while, I started to wonder and, allowing for overhead, tried to see if what I was receiving seemed fair. I thought I should possibly look at the fee schedule. I'm sure all groups were different, but ours was very different.

It seemed in the days before insurance, people paid as they went. If they didn't have money, I didn't charge them (despite what Tommy Douglas said), and I'm sure I'm not the only doctor who did that. On the other hand, when the junior members were doing most of the work and the senior members were making most of the money, I began to wonder how *that* worked. It was very complex.

It was a little too complex for my simple mind, so once my classmate and I figured out what was happening to us, we left and joined the other renegades with similar ideas. We then built a building across the street from the hospital. Guess what? Those other guys weren't nearly as bad as we "knew" they were. We would all be independent financially and bill fee for service. I did that for my whole time prior to retiring from my office practice. It was a real pleasure to have your own office built to your specifications, with your own secretary and nurse working directly for you only rather than the clinic – where the staff tended to favour the older doctors they had known for a long time.

Miraculously, three more children appeared; one at a time fortunately. Krista was born in 1964, Marla in 1965, and Erik in 1968.

We moved into our new office building across the street from the hospital in 1969.

In 1971, after a difficult time, Gigi and I separated and eventually divorced.

Along the way, I was opted out for a while, which meant I charged slightly more than the fee schedule and the patient received the money from the government which was supposed to replace what they paid me, or *to pay* me, or to give it to me if they had not paid me at the time of their visit. After a while, I began to realize that sometimes this was to the patient's benefit. A few patients would run up a huge bill because they would just keep the money when it came and then they would say they could not pay me when they saw me. Interestingly I wrote a couple of letters to the federal health minister, Monique Begin, at the time about the problem, and she did not answer my first letter, but after my second letter she answered both letters at the same time, as best she could – and she resigned the next day. I'd like to think I had something to do with it, but probably not. I was accustomed to working a lot, so I just kept doing it. I did everything, anaesthesia, medicine, minor surgery, assisting major surgery, emergency (not a real department then), obstetrics, psychiatry, and hospital rounds. I was basically on call all the time unless I arranged for someone to cover me occasionally.

I met Marian as a nurse in the hospital. She was intelligent, very competent, compassionate, beautiful, vivacious, and fun. She moved from the hospital to the Harvie Clinic, where I worked, then worked for me when we moved into the new building in 1969. We married in 1973. Marian already had two children. Stephanie was born in 1969 and Stephen in 1971. That made us a family of 6 children.

In 2000, after thirty-seven years at my office, I stepped away and decided to work for a time as a medical-surgical hospitalist. I eventually narrowed the hospitalist job down to psychiatric as I had also taken on some nursing homes as well. I also did locums in remote, exotic places. Locums are short-term postings either covering for another doctor who is away or stepping in to address a temporary shortage in a community.

FAMILY AND FAMILY PRACTICE

Balancing work – especially a busy family practice – and family life at home can be a challenge.

I did not want to be the same as my father in terms of family, so I made a point of doing a lot of things with the kids. That became a priority, so we did a lot of hiking, camping, canoeing and downhill skiing. We belonged to a small private ski club with only one hundred and fifty families, so there were fewer rules, and the kids did all kinds of things that they could not have done in the regular resorts. They built trails through the bush, too narrow for adults, huge jumps from which they might go seventy-five to eighty feet. They all also raced a lot. The alpine team at our club were Ontario champs, one year beating all the big teams from Collingwood, Osler, and Georgian. It was quite a shock for them. They had never heard of us. Several kids from that team went on into the ski arena, instructors, ski directors, and makers of ski movies.

Our son Stephen was on the Southern Ontario juvenile ski team for two years. It was a great family sport. We all adapted to whatever mountain we were on – although I can remember the kids sitting on top of a mogul in a big mogul field wondering why it took us so long to get there. Their day will come!

We camped all over North America, all the provinces plus Yukon, Alaska, and thirty other American states. I tried to take a month every summer camping with a soft-top tent trailer which got wet after a few days of rain and blew over once in Saskatchewan. There were many fond memories and adventures. There were a lot of campfires with a lot of songs and a lot of laughter. One thing we did commonly was to start a story and then the next person had to continue it before passing it on to the next and the next. Some extraordinary tales emerged from this freewheeling style. It promoted both imagination and lots of laughs. We hiked, picked all kinds of berries, apples, ferns, mushrooms, clams, and anything else edible. We swam in lakes, rivers and rapids. We had a sluice under a bridge and below a dam beside our house and there were other rapids that we would go to occasionally. It was great fun swishing through the rapids. Some of them were closed eventually, usually because of some tragedy. I would generally hover at the bottom in case of any incidents. We looked at the stars and tried to find the constellations. We played hide and go-seek in the woods and never lost anyone permanently.

My feeling about the kids was to expose them to everything, encourage them in whatever interested them. We did not try to push in any particular direction. The bottom line was that they should be happy with whatever they choose. Money, although a necessity, should not drive everything you do. We did notice that none of them pursued nursing or medicine. Are they happy? You'll have to ask them. It's a personal thing. I guess they are content. We still see them all and they seem to be enjoying life generally. The occasional tiff between them seems to resolve easily. The family has expanded now to include fourteen grandchildren as of 2017.

5. DR. HALL

I saw a great deal over the course of a thirty-seven-year family practice that ran from 1962 to 2000. When you add to that my hospitalist days from 2000 to 2014 and nursing home days that spanned 2005 to 2016, it means I've come away with a few tales to tell. Then there were the locums, but perhaps I'll tell those tales separately.

The stories I am about to share may seem a little scattered and disjointed because, of course, most of them are not related.

—

The usual day consisted of hospital first with hospital rounds and any procedures: lumps and bumps removed, bone marrows, lumbar punctures, and colonoscopies which I did every Tuesday at 7:30 in the morning for ten years until I retired from my office. I found quite a number of cancers which were then referred to appropriate surgeons. It was interesting as the technology advanced, and I enjoyed the challenge of colonoscopy. A colonoscope is a long tube with a light at the end of it so you can see into the large bowel starting at the rectum.

The office usually started between nine-thirty and ten and ran until noon. I intended to attend hospital rounds as often as possible at noon. We had three kinds: emerge, pediatric and perinatal, and grand rounds. Is there any other hospital our size with three major academic rounds per week?

Office was again all afternoon and often not getting home until seven or seven-thirty, but I always tried to get to any events involving the kids, sports, Christmas concerts and the like.

—

There were many deviations from normal. Deliveries were unpredictable, and often time consuming, but a happy delightful part of family practice. Emergencies of many kinds upset the routine and always had to have priority. I always started the day on time, but I was often late as the day went on. Patients never complained to me, only the staff, because they seemed to believe when their turn finally came up I would spend the appropriate length of time with them. I recall one elderly lady who always brought a long list and expanded on each item. After a long time and trying to ease her out of the office she'd asked…

"Is my hour up already?"

—

In the early days of my practice, house calls were done at various hours, but most often in the evening. How many you ask? My record was twenty-one in one day ending at three in the morning. This followed a headline in the local paper which came out about supper time saying that three children had died following mild cold symptoms, and so every parent in town was in panic mode. It turned out there was a devious explanation for all three, and one of them wasn't even local. *Good responsible journalism*, I thought wryly.

House calls were a good thing in many ways. It let people stay in their homes, and it let me have a look at their home environments.

I learned a lot about them. There was a time when I felt I had been in every house in town when the town was smaller. I made house calls out in the country as far as Vankoughnet some fifty miles away especially for palliative patients who could not make it in. Those days seem to be gone largely.

—

A number of years ago I was called to see an asthmatic patient to whom I gave some epinephrine which was standard then. I found out later that he had also called two *other* doctors, after my visit, and had not told them that he had already had two needles of epinephrine. He died from an epinephrine overdose much to everybody's surprise. It's a helpful thing to let other people know what's gone ahead. He did not.

—

Another interesting call was from the police. It seems a farmer was down behind his stone fence and was shooting at cars as they drove by, and the police wanted me to come and give him a needle. I politely refused their kind invitation since as far as I knew he was still doing it. As fate would have it, he later became a patient of mine and was really a kind gentle person. What happened that day?

—

Another pathetic house call was to a couple because the husband had hanged himself in the basement. The poor little guy had tied a rope to a beam then kicked the stool out, but he had put the rope on backwards, so he strangled to death rather than breaking his neck and ending it quickly. His wife was very upset because her bridge club was coming that afternoon and he was upsetting her schedule. Following that little talk, I felt that I had a good idea why he did it.

—

There was one lady whose husband was dying of a lymphoma (lymph node cancer). She took up with another man before her husband died and interestingly the new boyfriend died of the same lymphoma two years later. Was it a coincidence?

—

An older lady, who had an inflamed perineum (area around the vagina) that was not responsive to antifungals and steroids, was biopsied. It was a cancer of the Bartholin's gland (secretory glands near the vaginal entrance) from which she died. It was a first for me and for the gynecologist who saw her.

—

Addictions were always difficult to deal with: smoking the biggest one is very difficult to eliminate. For some reason women, in my experience, seem to have a more difficult time stopping. The various methods and medication for helping have made a significant difference in smokers who now are often feeling like a pariah.

—

The hard drugs, of which there are many, now are often started early. They can be very difficult to deal with since crime is often involved from prostitution to theft and even murder where gangs and the deals go wrong. I recall one young man who was heavily into heroin which he thought was the most wonderful thing in the world.

"Once you try it," he said almost rapturously, "you have to do it again."

And he certainly did. He robbed some stores and he even stole some prescription pads from my office which he used within a half an hour of the theft. Fortunately, the pharmacist was available and aware of his history. Despite many attempts at rehabilitation, which his parents paid for, he eventually died of a heroin overdose.

—

Alcoholism was very difficult to treat. Fortunately, there are quite a number of good programs out there now including Alcoholics Anonymous. I always found I couldn't get anybody to answer my root question when it came to alcoholism, no matter how I phrased it.

"What are you thinking as you take that first drink, knowing that alcohol is killing you?"

I can think of one thirty-seven-year-old woman with two teenage children who was jaundiced, knew she was going to die, and still drank, leaving two teenage children with no support. Her husband had left long since because of her alcoholism. I ended up being a pseudo-uncle for those kids for a short time.

Another alcoholic actually worked for the railroad on the repair crew. He forgot the schedule one day, and his cart was knocked off the track by a train. Needless to say, he was fired, but he continued to drink. He was yellow and had a distended belly and still he kept going until he died. Very sad I thought. Unfortunately, similar stories were not rare.

—

An older brother and sister who had lived all their lives together on a farm and had never had a significant relationship with anyone else stayed the same after their parents died. One day the sister died quite suddenly. The brother died three days later of no apparent cause.

—

Another elderly couple lived in a house absolutely full of newspapers. They were piled as high as they could reach everywhere, leaving only tunnels through them to the bathroom and a small part of the kitchen. The couple stayed mostly out on the porch when weather allowed.

—

Violence is another problem that happens of course under different circumstances and it is certainly more common in the addiction crime world. In practice it was not common but of course alcohol resulting in being drunk, affects people differently. Some people are funny, some go to sleep, but some get violent and want to fight, and it is often a recurrent theme even though they may come out the loser every time. Why? Family violence is often hidden. Usually it is abuse of the female partner. Why do they stay in such a relationship? The abuse is usually verbal and psychological as well as physical. They become accustomed to the belittling and insults, so much that it saps their confidence and leaves them feeling helpless and unable to summon the energy or courage to escape. They may have no financial resources, may be afraid of losing their children and being isolated from them, and, of course, they may have nowhere to turn except the homes for abused women which are not a long-term solution.

I remember one lady with many scars all over but a lot on her face. She had enough head trauma that she had permanent brain damage with significant loss of intelligence. It took outside intervention to get the police involved and her husband jailed.

—

Another mother told us her boyfriend had punched her baby in the face for crying; the baby actually had knuckle marks on his face. When it got to court, the mother denied that it happened. I guess she was fearful of losing her partner who no doubt had apologised profusely and behaved perfectly since. There were a number of people who needed anger control management.

—

One middle aged woman was *apparently* very clumsy and kept injuring herself (falling downstairs, bumping into things, cutting herself) At the same time, however, she was working as a waitress and could handle all kinds of dishes without any problem. One night her husband, who was a massive man, returned home drunk. She shot and killed him with his own gun. She was accused of murder, of course, but it turned out that all the accidents were actually beatings. I had a record of all the injuries, but I also knew him well, so I must rather shamefully admit that I had not thought of that possibility sooner. She was found not guilty.

—

Sexual assault, to my mind, is vastly underestimated in terms of its long-term consequences. In the psychiatric world, it is a very common denominator for a lot of ills, anxiety disorders, personality disorders, borderline personality. The penalties, in my opinion, should be much more severe than they are. They have often ruined a whole life. Many women are never able to trust and relate to men.

I think of one lady (and her sister) who were sexually assaulted over several years by their father. In her fifties she took him to court and he was sentenced to jail in his mid-seventies. Curiously, her sister who had been through the same thing was affected only mildly and was able to lead a fairly normal life although she did divorce. Other women, and I'm sure there are lots, have kept it a secret so they are not branded and somehow feel guilty. I think a number of those who have told me, have done so for the first time in their lives. One lady was seventy-three years old and talked as if it had happened yesterday. It was some relief for her, but her marriage was poor; her husband had never seen her without clothes and she was difficult to relate to.

The other side of this difficult problem is rape resulting in pregnancy and the question of abortion. Two cases stand out in my mind. The first girl's mother was a strident anti-abortionist. She used to carry placards, go to parades until her daughter age sixteen became pregnant. The world looked completely different then, and following the abortion, she was never heard from again. The second girl, a minister's daughter, was sexually assaulted at university. Her father, of course, had a very difficult time with the thought of abortion, but when your daughter is the victim it looks very different than the theory. To be reminded constantly, by the presence of that child, of that event could be a type of torture. You would have to make an effort to remind yourself that the child is not to blame. Abortion was decided. There are lots of people who are against abortion under any circumstances, but I suspect they haven't had close and urgent contact with these types of situations.

—

The unsettling thing about violence, and threats of violence, is that often there is no sense can be made from it, often it is utterly irrational. Within the first year in practice I received a note in the mail with an Icelandic postage stamp on it, telling me that they were going to kill me. I asked the police, who were not concerned. They felt it was just a crank. A little later, another letter arrived with a foreign stamp; this one said that they were very sorry that they had to kill me because I'd always been so good to them. I actually carried a knife with me for a couple of years after that – better safe than sorry, or dead, but I never heard anything more.

—

You never know what you are going to face, and sometimes even mild or mundane symptoms can point to serious problems. One day I had a house call to see an eleven-year-old girl with a bad headache which she had not suffered before. I went to see her and found that she had some neck stiffness. After getting her to the hospital, a lumbar puncture revealed blood. She was sent to Toronto's Hospital for Sick Children with subarachnoid hemorrhage. There was no known family history for such a problem. It turns out she had a berry aneurism (bulging artery shaped like a berry) requiring neurosurgery urgently. She survived.

—

Another lady of about sixty who had quite a lot of angina (chest pain) and some heart problems insisted she did not want anything more done for her heart. She was in the hospital had severe angina and actually died, but she would not let us do anything for her pain. It's very hard to hold back when you know you can do something and your patient won't let you. She was not a regular patient of mine so

I did not know her background and she was not in a frame of mind to discuss anything so the motivation remained unknown.

—

The therapeutic value of venting – getting something off your chest – is often overlooked. As health-care professionals we feel we want to intervene with questions or suggestions, but sometimes it is better to sit back and stay silent. I've been surprised how often over the years people will start to vent, get on a bit of a roll, and finally stop to say they feel much better, and meanwhile, I haven't done anything but listen.

Listening seems to have become a lost art. It's amazing what a moment's silence on your part may bring out. Sometimes people have things that are close to the surface but of which they are fearful or are ashamed to talk about, and all of a sudden, a silent opening presents itself, and they blurt it out to their surprise and often yours as well. Listen, and if you are not sure what is happening, keep listening; the answer or – at least a clue – may well emerge in time. Resist the urge to intervene.

—

Brain tumors are always devastating, and I believe, worse in children. I have had a few such patients who have come through with varying results. One child that comes to mind was nine years old. I drove her down to SickKids Hospital in Toronto myself with her mother. The neurosurgeon was rather reluctant to go ahead because he feared the aftermath. Surgery was done, however; and the girl survived, but was it worth it? She was never normal, her eyesight was very poor, she staggered and was often accused of being drunk, but still alive. She ended up in a nursing home with a lot of very elderly people. It was very difficult for her parents, but especially mother.

Another eight-year-old boy had surgery, chemotherapy, and radiation. –Despite requiring replacement for his pituitary loss,, he is now twenty, attending university, and doing very well. Who knows what path your life will take?

—

Headaches present a conundrum. Migraine can be severe. How far should you go with opiate medication? One outstanding patient of mine, who was subsequently seen by the Sunnybrook headache specialist, was on two hundred and forty milligrams of morphine, three times daily to control her headaches. She was working and driving a bus. This dose was extremely high for anyone.

—

Renal failure (kidney failure) is another major problem, mostly in diabetics and older folks, but some patients can be young and suffer renal failure due to other causes. Once the patients are on dialysis, they are all hoping for a kidney transplant. If there is a reason they cannot have a transplant, they are doomed to a life of dialysis and constant medical intervention. Is that something to look forward to? On the other hand, if you decide you don't want to have that kind of future, we may consider you depressed and want to put you on more medication. If a young person decides they don't want to live like that, should they be allowed, following psychiatric evaluation, to be able to have doctor assisted suicide?

—

Psychotherapy has always interested me, and the rewards over the years were great both for the patient and, secondarily, my own satisfaction. There were different techniques all of which have their value in the appropriate setting. Couples therapy usually went well if both parties were sincere and not hiding something. Family therapy is different, however. The family theoretically is supposed to discuss and discover the real problems and be willing to work on that. Even when it is obvious to you, it may be very difficult for them to see if they have a lot of fixed ideas. I must admit I had difficulty with religious folk who tend to feel that praying more would be the answer to their problems. It can't always be like that, but it is a little frustrating when people won't or can't look deeper into their situation but rely on prayer to cure all problems.

—

Back pain management is another very difficult problem. History is very important. It is very tough to sort out exactly what is happening. Imaging such as x-rays and MRIs are generally useless, so it comes down to the history and physical. If Dr. Hamilton Hall's book *The Back Doctor* does not sort it out, what can you do? Are you to suspect them of being drug addicts? How do you sort it out, and sketch out a plan of attack? There are no easy answers, but it's easier if you know the patient well.

—

A young lady who we'll call Alice (not her real name) was a well-known scattered young lady. She came into the office urgently one morning extremely upset.

She had grown up with her grandparents. Her grandfather was an alcoholic, her grandmother a drug addict, both however were very pleasant people and cared for each other. Alice's mother may have been a prostitute. Alice married a man we'll call Jack (again not his real name) a rather simple but good-hearted young man very much in love with her. They had three children.

Alice got involved with another man and left Jack. Soon thereafter, Jack broke through the window in the middle of the night and stabbed Alice's new boyfriend to death. He then raped Alice, walked out the door, and started to walk down the railway track where the police caught up with him a short time later still just walking. Life was over from his perspective even before the trial.

—

There was a family of schizophrenics who were of great interest to the Hospital for Sick Children and Toronto's Mount Sinai Hospital both of which were doing genetic studies on schizophrenics. Schizophrenia is a mental illness. They wanted to get this family involved because there were four children who were schizophrenics and one that was very normal. The family had agreed to go along with the genetic testing, but when it came time to have the blood taken they refused, but they gave no reason.Unfortunately schizophrenics are often paranoid or at least misinterpret other peoples motivation, There is apparently only one other similar family in Finland.

—

A very unusual event was a virgin birth. The proof was a very robust hymen at the time of delivery. This lady was married but had never had intercourse nor would she allow any pelvic examinations along the way. Presumably her husband had ejaculated somewhere in her perineum and the little rascals found their way. The last time this happened a couple of thousand years ago was a major event, but this time It passed by without anybody knowing except the patient and myself. I didn't notice any unusual stars, shepherds, or wise men bearing gifts.

—

One night while doing psychotherapy with a young man, I fell asleep. The poor fellow had just told me that he had been charged by the police for threatening his mother-in-law with a gun. Amazingly he was not angry with me but felt sorry for me and thought I must be very tired. I felt angry enough with myself for both of us.

—

A young woman in her twenties presented in the office one day. She was a heavy smoker and presented with dizziness of significance so that she was tending to fall in all directions. Unfortunately, it turned out to be a cerebellar metastasis from lung cancer from which she passed away in relatively short order.

The cerebellum is a part of the balance mechanism, so any abnormality there can produce vertigo which most people describe as dizziness. Vertigo refers to the unsettling, disorienting sensation of motion relative to your surroundings – the world seeming to spin around you.

—

A young man appeared one day with a pinkish macular (patchy) whole body rash, which I thought was probably an infectious mononucleosis rash at first. However, it didn't follow the usual pattern, and it turned out to be secondary stage syphilis. There are three stages to syphilis most of which are very rare now. The first stage in men is an ulcer-like lesion on the penis, which might disappear. If it was under the foreskin it might not have been noticed or the fact that it went away meant it wasn't anything to worry about. Right?/ This is usually followed by a lightly spotty pink rash, and the third stage involves either a severe neuropathy with a very strange flopping gait or complete insanity or both. Follow up with contacts is mandatory as well as antibiotics

—

Glomerulonephritis is a kidney inflammation which often presents as *hematuria* [blood in the urine] or very dark concentrated urine with swelling. It often occurred in individuals who'd suffered a recent strep infection and was not rare in the early days of practising in Orillia. They all seemed to get better at least as far as we were able to see them.

—

I have seen only rheumatic fever twice, both times in Australia. It too usually follows strep throat and presents with fever, often sore joints. But the real concern is the possibility of heart valve inflammation, which often leads to heart failure later in life.

—

I have seen hematuria with kidney stones requiring surgery in a two-year-old which is extremely rare. Babies cry so you could not rely on the symptoms, only the blood in the diaper.

I have seen a bleeding stomach ulcer in a three-year-old which is virtually unheard of.

We saw a few of the Thalidomide babies; none of them were actually my patients, but I assisted at surgery on some of them. By the time I was in practice, thalidomide was recognized and was not used anymore. It was a drug used for pregnant mothers to help with nausea and vomiting. It unfortunately resulted in a lot of limb abnormalities including amputations. Interestingly enough I was living in Boston at the time it was recognised in Canada. It was never available in the United States because a Canadian woman by the name of Frances Oldham Kelsey, working for the FDA, would not allow its use there. She became a hero and was awarded the President's Award for Distinguished Federal Civil Service by JFK.

—

Believe it or not, in the early nineties, Bob Rae's NDP Government wanted to stop doctors from performing routine physicals. A number of people wrote in including a patient of mine. She told him that I had found three primary cancers on her that were asymptomatic, both breasts, and uterus. She got through all three well. Would she have fared as well if we hadn't discovered them on a routine physical? Almost certainly not.

—

An elderly lady in her nineties was admitted to the hospital in a semi-comatose state. She became comatose and remained that way for about a month. Her family thougt that she was dying. They took it upon themselves to sell her goods and gave up her apartment. Unfortunately for them, she came back to consciousness and was somewhat angry about the fact that they had changed her housing arrangements. She was left with nothing. Do you suppose she would have changed her will?

—

An elderly man worked in a hardware store for many years. By all accounts a true gentleman, he was respected by everyone, but he began to have a change in his personality, began to swear at people which he would have never done, and then he lapsed into a coma. We sent him down to Toronto General Hospital where they kept him for a couple of months before phoning and informing us that he been diagnosed with severe dementia, that he would die soon, and that we should just tuck him in a corner somewhere. The diagnosisof dementia must have been made with the pre-coma history as well as not finding any known physical cause for it.With the advances in technology would they have found something else now?

About a month after he came back to us, he simply woke up one day and started talking. The first thing out of his mouth:

"You sure think some funny things sometimes, don't you?"

He was able to get mobilized and went home and lived with his wife for about two years before he fell down stairs and broke his neck. So, what happened at Toronto General Hospital that he slipped into a coma, and then got better, undiagnosed by folks looking after him there?. It was very strange.

—

A couple of grisly interventions come to mind. One young man had recurrent urinary tract infections for which we could not find any cause. Anatomically he seemed normal. It turned out that he was sticking a pencil up his urethra (penis) periodically, and that resulted in significant infections.

Another elderly man came in one night with rectal bleeding, and he had a Coke bottle stuck up his rectum. It's hard to think about how that would feel. Would a Pepsi bottle have been better? Always in competition you know.

—

Motor vehicle accidents are often quite messy, but a few things stand out there. One patient of mine was driving his truck one night with his seatbelt on. He ran head-on into a car with three young people in it. The three young people, who were not wearing their seatbelts, were killed and he was in a coma for two days, but he lived and returned to his previous work. I have put together more stories later in the emergency section.

Another very disturbing accident occurred involving a head-on collision between two teenagers – who were both drunk – and a young family of five aboriginals who were returning home from a ball game in which Dad had been playing. The entire family was killed except for a baby who had to be transported to Toronto.

The two drunks, who were not injured badly, were actually *laughing* in the emergency department. Sometimes it is very difficult to control your emotions (anger in this case). The surgeon involved could barely control himself. Coincidentally one of them drowned about a month later.

—

There've been many cases of *pertussis* [whooping cough], German measles, and red measles diagnosed. Measles with complications are often quite serious, and I had one three-year-old patient, a little girl with pneumonia, *encephalitis* [brain inflammation] and congestive heart failure. Fortunately, at that time, a pediatrician had moved in only thirty kilometres away. We got the patient down to him. She however, did not recover totally, and her brain did not return to normal although she was able to function in a less than average kind of way, and later in life able to hold some jobs for a while.

—

A young mother one day came into the office with her baby of eighteen months who I realized suffered from Downs syndrome. I started to talk to her about the diagnosis and what she could expect later on. She was shocked and asked why I was talking about this? No one had ever told her that her daughter had Downs syndrome. Unfortunately, that was only part of the problem because the baby also had the stigmata of *cretinism* [low thyroid function], and we ended up sending the child to the Hospital for Sick Children in Toronto, where at that time, she was only the eleventh or twelfth person who had ever come with that dual diagnosis. The cretin part of the diagnosis is easily treated with thyroid supplementation.

Downs syndrome is a genetic abnormality with usually a typical appearance, sometimes with heart abnormalities and some degree of developmental delay. On the other hand, individuals with Downs syndrome are often quite happy, and I am aware of one man with Downs syndrome who is a greeter and informant at a huge store. There are at least ten thousand items in the store, and he can tell you exactly where everything is.

"Aisle nineteen left hand side."

—

Carcinoid syndrome has turned up twice, a disease which involves excessive bright red flushing, often diarrhea, not related to menopause. It is caused by chemical secretions from a carcinoid (cancer like) tumour.

—

I have seen three cases of patients afflicted with *Clostridium perfringens cholecystitis*. Two of them died. – The fact that one survived was very unusual. This bacterium is the cause of gas gangrene which is so very deadly.

—

I have seen one patient with Prader–Willi syndrome and one patient with a diagnosis of Turner syndrome abnormality in my practice.

Prader–Willi involves a voracious appetite, massive obesity and developmental delay. The patient is usually uncontrollable and will eat anything, even towels etc.

Turner syndrome is a genetic abnormality in females missing (or partially missing) an X chromosome and usually presents as a small stature, very thick neck, and swollen hands. There is no treatment.

One man who was unconscious turned out to have tuberculous meningitis, another remote relic of the past, which I had never seen before and don't expect to see again.

EMERGENCY DEPARTMENT WORK

I worked in emergency on a regular basis for about thirty years and was Chief of Emerge and Family Practice for a couple of years. When I first went to Orillia, there was really no organized emergency department and no schedule for doctors. It is a tourist area, so it is very busy in the summer. A lot of the local resorts or camps made arrangements with local clinics or individual doctors who saw almost every illness in their offices or made house calls.

As time went on, we developed a piece of the hospital that we used for emergency and eventually in the seventies a schedule was made up for the local family doctors. Next we insisted on BCLS, then ACLS and ATLS which are advanced cardiac life support and advanced trauma life support courses. This improved the efficiency along with the emerging technologies which were ultrasound, CT and eventually MRI and a twenty-four-hour laboratory. An increasing number of specialists also helped immensely including psychiatry.

A lot of strange things happened in emerge, some of them never fully explained. In the past we used to work alone twelve to twenty-four hours and weekends were from Friday night until Monday morning.

Recalling some of the strange things which happened in the past, I realize that I could have or would have handled them differently now with all the emerging knowledge and equipment. Myocardial infarction (heart attack) was treated with bed rest up to a month, later with Coumadin (a drug for thinning the blood) and very gradual ambulation. Strokes really had no treatment other than physiotherapy at the time. The evolution of cardio pulmonary resuscitation methods have changed along the way. I guess the stats are still not that great unless it is a witnessed arrest.

I recall having three patients in hospital at the same time that had been resuscitated (heart wise) but their brains never recovered. One was a young man who was electrocuted. He lived about a month. Another was a woman in her forties with myocardial infarction and cardiac arrest. She lived a few months. The third man was a young very active man, but heavy smoker who had a heart attack and arrest. He was in his late twenties and had actually been a hockey referee. His heart recovered, and his brain recovered only a little. He went home with his wife and children, but sadly she could not handle it. He was like a two-hundred-pound fourth child of age two, she said. She was forced to put him in a nursing home where he lived for several years. A hockey fan, he would be taken to hockey games occasionally where he would usually embarrass whoever had taken him with his antics.

It was very difficult to know whether CPR was appropriate when a patient with cardiac arrest came through the door in emergency, and you were not sure of the timing, which is usually the case. Should you do CPR or not do it on a patient? We always did it as a routine unless we were sure there was a significant time interval with no attempt at resuscitation. Sometimes later we regretted that we did. One lady, age fifty, spent time on the chronic floor in the hospital for over a year. She had, had a myocardial infarction with arrest with insignificant brain recovery, and so she was in bed really as in a vegetative state. We naturally asked ourselves, *what would she want? What is best for her? What is best for the family?*

Once again, we are reminded how important advanced directives are. For myself, if something happens to me so that I don't know my family after a month and I have virtually no chance of recovery please, please let me go. I do wish that everyone had an advance directive. We probably should demand them upon admission to hospital and particularly nursing homes. It does require you to think about death for a moment and how you would like it to be handled. People don't like to think about their demise, so they procrastinate, and it never gets done. Perhaps a routine form explaining the options and a tick-off sheet could fill the gap.

I have seen too many demented elderly people, or brain-damaged people. Relatives stop coming to see them because there is no feedback. They are left alone, but we can keep them alive if they will swallow. *Should* we keep them alive? Would they want that? ADVANCE DIRECTIVES! Start them early. You don't know what is ahead. Things are changing, but at the moment, we must keep them alive if we can.

Another young man came in one day with evidence of subarachnoid hemorrhage (a major bleed inside the skull most often from a small berry aneurism) from which he was quickly dying. When I told his wife what was happening, she shuddered.

"Oh no, this is my third husband to die of the same thing."

I was almost afraid to shake her hand. How is that possible?

Another alcoholic patient of mine was brought into emerge in a coma. We were unable to get any signs of response with painful stimuli. As we were assessing him and planning our next move, the nurse came in the door and said we had another patient in the next room in exactly the same condition. When she mentioned his name, our comatose patient jumped off the stretcher, lunged through the scrub room and started to beat on the other patient. *An interesting coma*, I thought.

One Saturday morning about eleven thirty in the morning, a young woman appeared very anxious coming to the emergency department upset. We asked her what the problem was.

"I have called off my wedding," she sobbed.

"Oh really, when is that?"

"At one this afternoon," she said sobbing.

What a lot of courage (but smart) to call it off at that stage. A little counselling would be in order.

There have been many cardiac arrests over the years, many of whom have done well, most often associated with arrhythmias of one kind or another. Knowing your management of the arrhythmias is crucial for working in emerge.

It certainly wasn't always the case, but strokes now, with certain criteria and the use of clot dissolving medication, come with the possibility of complete recovery. This is a real bonus

Infections of all types find their way into emergency. A huge variety from colds to meningitis are seen, and serious ones admitted.

Major trauma is a stressful part of emerge work. In days gone by, we didn't have all of the specialists we have now, and transfer to a hospital in Toronto wasn't as quick and easily arranged as it is today. I have seen all manner of injuries from heads, chests, limbs, organs. Some stand out more than others.

I was thinking of one lady who rode her bicycle in a parking lot with no cars and no helmet. She fell and hit her head. She had an *extradural hemorrhage* [bleeding between the skull and the brain covering] and ended up being sent to a hospital in Toronto. We had done a flap, which is to say we removed a piece of skull to relieve pressure, but forgot to send the bone piece along. It was sort of embarrassing, but luckily she did okay.

The stress in emerge is in the numbers when you are really busy. That's when something major shows up. It's not so bad now because there's more help, and there are shifts and more facilities available quickly.

One of the situations that became a major problem in the sixties was the development of major highways. We had inevitable deaths from motor vehicle accidents because there were no medians and a lot of level crossings. One particular crossing produced at least one death every weekend because it was a major road crossing the highway. When the traffic built up, trying to cross the highway on a Friday night, people would start honking, and the person at the front would gamble. I can remember one weekend we had twelve motor vehicle accident deaths. The median and the fly overs have now eliminated most of the carnage. But it's important to recognize that these sorts of developments evolved, only gradually after lots of blood was spilt.

How quickly things can happen and change our lives forever. South of Barrie on Highway 400 there was a big ditch between the north and south lanes. This was before the barriers were put in. One winter day I was driving south when a northbound car slid into the ditch, spun around, and started sliding towards me. It missed me but hit the car behind me head on. I don't know what happened to the people, but it must have been fatal. It held up traffic for hours.

We saw stabbings and shootings too, of course, and they were always dramatic. It seemed they always happened at night. One particular incident, a patient of mine, was a local policeman. He pulled a car over for speeding on the highway. When he pulled up beside the window, the window opened, and he was shot five times by the driver who it turns out had killed a cop further north. This, of course, required big surgery, a long-term recovery, and counselling. This particular policeman, who was a very calm guy, did very well emotionally and actually ended up being used to talk with other policemen who had been shot.

Humorous things happen in emerge sometimes too. One old deaf man came in one day with some chest pain and we were having difficulty talking to him, but he was in some distress. It was frustrating for everyone.

Finally, he said, "I've got aids–" at which time the nurses were running for cover, at least mentally "–but I left them at home."

There was a big sigh of relief followed by a lot of laughter.

Another interesting incident, and I have actually had this happen *twice*, was while examining a woman's chest.

"Big breath," I say.

Laughter. "Yes, aren't they?"

Adapting to the circumstances can be helpful in emerge. A lady came in with multiple lacerations and had obviously been drinking and was very difficult to control. She was not about to have anybody sew up anything. Since she came from a party, we decided to continue the party with jokes, singing, and laughing. Before long she settled right down, and we could sew up all the cuts without local anaesthetic. She was having a good time.

ANAESTHESIA

For me, anaesthesia lasted only a few years in practice, and as a family doctor, I was happy to give it up when more experienced family doctor anesthetists and fellowship anesthetists appeared. The family doctor anesthetists were very good generally, a lot of them worked emergency as well. They had no overhead, so they were a long way ahead of the rest of us financially. I believe however they missed out on a lot of follow-up on what they started, and they never get the feeling of being an important part of the family constellation. I can recall some scary moments with anaesthesia. As an intern I can remember being the anesthetist for open chests, and a *laryngectomy* [removal of the voice box]. It scares me thinking about it now.

When I first moved to Orillia, we were still using open ether as an anesthetic. I remember dripping it on a mask. You had to know all your signs of their depth and expect some vomiting afterwards. It sounds like ancient history now, but it wasn't that long ago. Or maybe it was. How long is long?

Later in my career, when I did regular colonoscopy work, I used a drug called midazolam and often some narcotic as well. The combination worked well. Midazolam can be used as conscious sedation. During the procedure, you can talk to and direct the patient, but afterwards they will have no memory of it, so it's a type of anesthesia without the need for intubation.

Early in practice, my classmate and I had a little routine going. If a pregnant patient wanted or needed an epidural, I would do that while he was coming to the hospital then he would look after that while I delivered the baby. He would do the opposite for me. This routine worked very well for us, but it would never happen now.It would be considered too risky

PSYCHIATRY

Psychiatry in medical school in the fifties was rudimentary by modern standards, and the drugs available were very basic – barbiturates, chlorpromazine, promazine. The alternative to drugs was often electroconvulsive therapy (ECT) or electroshock therapy as it was known then.

The understanding of mental illness was not based on any chemical or receptor concepts at that time, and mental institutions were full of people often undiagnosed. Schizophrenia was recognized and had many theories as to its causation. The treatment was questionable, but there were many suggested theories and treatments. A number of people spent most of their lives in an institution.

When Valium became available (the first benzodiazepine, a tranquilizer) it was a wonder drug. Since that time, it has become the source of a lot of argument both pro and con. At this moment, it generally seems to be more con despite its usefulness for anxiety. Many people are concerned, I think overly so, about the possibility of addiction.

Depression was the most common mental illness in my experience.

I was in Boston when the first MAO inhibitors, Parnate, Marplan, and Nardil, appeared on the market. They were amazing as antidepressants and seemed to work very quickly. Unfortunately, side effects turned up, and they were practically discontinued as SSRIs and SSNRIs (selective serotonin reuptake inhibitors and SNRI) became more common. I do believe that psychotherapy as well as drugs is indicated. New drugs are coming out, and you can usually find one that fits. Yes, they can have side effects occasionally, but the patient has to remember why they are taking them.

Schizophrenia can mostly be controlled by the antipsychotics, but compliance is the big problem. Once a schizophrenic starts feeling well, it is all too easy for them to become absolutely *convinced* that their medication (which has real side effects) is no longer needed. Hallelujah, they are cured – and so *stop* taking their meds. After a short while, they begin to drift again into their psychosis and are put back on the pills. Invariably it happens again. You would think, after following that routine a few times and having it explained to them *every* time, that they might want to stay on the medication, but of course, this is a mental disorder that affects judgement. That is the main reason for the long-acting injection type antipsychotics. They are very effective and, when tied to some compliance rules, work well.

Bipolar patients are hard enough to treat because of the variation in presentation. They also tend to hold their medication when they feel better, resulting in the same readmissions often to hospital.

Personality disorders and the borderline personalities, with all their erratic behaviours, are still very difficult to treat. A lot of sufferers have had a very checkered past and history of abuse – mental, physical, and/or sexual. They often don't trust people, and it is sometimes difficult to establish a therapeutic relationship that, of course, involves trust. When you hear the stories of their lives, you realize that often they have no experience that we might consider normal. They don't even understand what we are aiming for.

Dementias (Alzheimer's is the commonest one) are brutal. They rob you of everything, all your good times, your achievements, your relationships. They all go, and you are left a hollow body, breathing, existing only if you can still swallow. As the patient sinks deeper into dementia, friends and relatives visit less and less, and so often they go it alone and are practically forgotten. It is very sad! Lots of research is being done, but so far, no significant treatment advances have been made.

Until a reasonable treatment becomes available, one does wonder if a peaceful death would be a blessing. It is interesting to me how some sufferers will stop eating, drinking, and taking their pills. At some level, they are telling us they have had enough. We must respect that. A reminder to once more do advance directives. Write it down, and make sure that at least one other person that you can trust is aware of it.

Psychotherapy, which I enjoyed and found generally very useful, was better for some types of problems than others, and there are a number of techniques. As family doctors, we know the patient, and we are in an excellent position to help them, but it takes a lot of time. You must spend the time. The rewards are great both for the patients and for the doctor. Couples therapy, as I've already said, works well if both parties are sincere in their efforts. Family therapy can be difficult and requires commitment of all those involved.

OBSTETRICS

Obstetrics was a major part of my practice for many years but dwindled as I dwindled.

I delivered between fifteen and eighteen hundred babies, and I wish I had an exact count as I know other doctors have. I delivered babies of babies that I had delivered, which was very rewarding, and I do wonder if I delivered a third generation, but I'm not sure about that

Obstetrics is almost always a happy event once the baby is delivered; often it is somewhat less than happy during labour. There are huge individual differences in pain tolerance. Some mothers enjoyed every minute of the whole experience, while others decided that they would never go through the experience again.

General attitudes and expectations have changed over the decades. Now there are more "timed" deliveries plus a big increase in caesarean sections. Where is this all heading? Will natural vaginal deliveries become a thing of the past, or will there be a rebound in that direction?

It seems that *natural* is rather trendy buzzword at the moment; organic foods, avoiding medication and vaccines while, at the same time, espousing vitamins and supplements of all kinds in doses far greater than required. It's a strange world, but the trends will change again, and who knows what direction is next.

Telling me something is natural does not, in and of itself, impress me. I like to remind people that arsenic and strychnine are natural too. How do you know the natural things don't have noxious elements to them? You don't! Yet folks go along with the latest trend based on no science at all. Being scientifically minded makes me wonder why people don't question a lot of the trendy ideas when they are so quick to question the use of certain drugs that have been very well researched and monitored over decades of use. Patients flock to the internet to look up medications. It is easy to read about side effects and fixate on them to the point that the original purpose of a medication is forgotten. This type of ill-informed fixation can dissuade people from taking medication they might genuinely benefit from. Television programs are also mostly negative when it comes to medications, and so they often do people a great disservice I believe.

But we have digressed from obstetrics.

There are many possible complications of obstetrics, and I've seen them all, some less often than others. There are still stillborn babies. We usually know ahead of time with modern technology. There are still cord presentations, postpartum hemorrhage, eclampsia, abnormal presentations arms, feet, placenta previa and many others.

My last delivery was in Iqaluit. When you work in emerge there, you also deliver the babies that show up. My last one was twelve and one-half pounds with shoulder dystocia (some large babies have difficulty getting their shoulders through the birth canal). The patient had not felt any movement that day. She had had an ultrasound the day before, which apparently said the baby was *small*. There was no fetal movement for a full day. When she came in she was in very active labour but there were no fetal heart sounds. She was unable to push the baby out, and it took a few manoeuvres to deliver. There were no obstetricians or gynecologists in Nunavut. The baby was macerated, and the pediatric resident tried everything but to no avail. The skin maceration suggested the baby had been dead for at least twenty-four hours. Mother was noted to be jaundiced, so the whole story was not known. It was not a great departure from obstetrics for me. I'll try to remember all the good times.

On the gynecological side, there were lots of bladder repairs and hysterectomies. There were cancers of the cervix that was picked up on Pap smears. If cancer was found early they all seemed to do well. I only had three deaths from cervical cancer and they were all between 75-85. Pap smears are not recommended over age 70. I believe they (the experts) should review that.

PEDIATRICS

Kids were almost always fun. The nurse gave the needles, so I was the good guy and almost like an uncle sometimes. In fact, I did get called uncle on occasion and actually was honoured to be asked to make short speeches about a couple of patients at their weddings.

I did not see a new case of polio, but we had a number of cases of post-polio syndrome in older people.

I saw three cases of Wilms' tumors (a type of kidney tumor) over the years; two in my own practice (who did well) and a third in Iqaluit who was sent down to Ottawa so I don't know the outcome of that.

Then there were neuroblastomas. These are another malignancy of either the adrenal gland or the brain in young children. They were inevitably fatal in my experience and they are thought to be a genetic mutation.

I saw some Thalidomide babies with absent arms and fingers. And one time I came across a case of Henoch–Schönlein purpura, an autoimmune disease in children with joint pain, extensive bruising (without trauma), and potential for renal damage.

I also had one case of tapeworm (disgusting critters).

Fear of doctors amongst children was not common, but I found it comes easily. One day when I was working in the emergency, I heard a mother in the next bed behind the curtain tell her son…

"If you don't behave I'll get the doctor to give you a needle."

He was wide-eyed when we went in to see him.

Jehovah Witnesses are very difficult since they will not accept blood products. One night in emerge a young seven-year-old girl presented with a severe post-tonsillectomy bleed. It was apparent that she might die if we could not transfuse her. Her parents said that she understood and would rather die than have blood. I could not agree with that, so we phoned the judge in the middle of the night and were able to take custody of her and transfuse her. The parents were not pleased at the time, but I know that in the long run they were. Actually, another relative of theirs – also patient of mine but an older lady – had lung cancer and her hemoglobin was very low. We gave her a transfusion not realizing that she was Jehovah's Witness, and she felt much better the next day.

"Thank you very much," she said, "I feel much better, but I wish you wouldn't do that again."

Not a word was said while the blood was running.

LONG TERM CARE

I always went to nursing homes to see my patients who had been admitted there, but not on a regular basis. After I stopped doing long term locum's in remote places because of my grandson's illness (more on that later) and was settling into hospitalist work, I was asked to take on a medical director job at the best nursing home locally. They even offered a satellite phone since I had said I liked to be remote sometimes. Not long after that, a second nursing home asked me to look after their needs also. Somewhat reluctantly, I took it on also (one of those mistakes you make).

The first nursing home was run by Simcoe County and really was excellent.

The second clinic was privately run and was crowded – four people in the room with one bathroom in the corner. Imagine four wheelchairs trying to get in the bathroom in the morning, actually fighting over it. Without trying to be derogatory, I was unable to affect any significant changes and was quite critical at times. They did not appreciate my comments even though they were echoed by the pharmacist. They told the nurses not to assist me, which was intolerable. How are you supposed to know what is happening to demented people if nobody tells you? They referred to assisting me as, and I quote: "babysitting the doctor."

At any rate, I was happy to leave that place. They had some good staff, some mediocre staff, and a lot of temporary staff. There were also constant changes at the administrative level as well. The best and most caring head nurse was only there about three months when she suddenly disappeared. Since she had come quite a distance to take the job, and I suspect that conflict with administration was a problem for her too.

Long-term care is quite different than hospital work. This is home for these people, all of whom have a multiplicity of ailments. They are there because they cannot cope on their own at home. A large percentage of them suffer from dementia. All have chronic illnesses of some kind. Some are remediable – others not.

Then, of course, you can't do anything the patient doesn't want you to. Our job is to keep these people as well and as comfortable as we are able because, to be realistic, it's a one-way street the people are speeding down with the occasional acceleration. If only everyone would prepare advance directives while they can, it would be so much easier to make decisions as situations evolve. The family would also *know,* with certainly, the wishes of the patient, and it might well save a lot of strife at a crisis time.

One lady was sent to us from a Toronto hospital, where she had suffered some sort of catastrophe during surgery and did not regain consciousness. She spent years in the home with a feeding tube, and of course, they had to do absolutely everything for her. Most of the family would've been happy to let her go, but her husband was concerned that their son, who was apparently mentally unstable, would commit suicide if his mother died. The lad *did* seem unstable then, so the husband may well have been right. She eventually did die, however; and as far as I know her son didn't do anything.

Often it was the remote relatives who were the most demanding. I suppose a sense of guilt comes into play since they don't see the patient – while the local relatives who have seen the process developing are more understanding. The POA, or power of attorney, has the last say if the patient can't comment. Sometimes the POA lives at a distance, but it's difficult to get a change in court sometimes, so even though they don't have any direct contact with the patient, they can still dictate what is done or not done.

Does that seem unreasonable to you?

They are often acting on what they have read or seen on television; sometimes they act on their own personal prejudices. A ninety-seven-year-old lady wanted to be left alone to die. She did much better on antidepressants, but her daughter, who lived several hundred miles away and was (in her mind) an expert on the subject had POA and made us stop them to the patient's detriment.

Money rears its ugly head in a lot of family feuds. One very demented lady had a son and a daughter. Both lived remotely. The daughter seemed very concerned and caring – the son not so much. I was asked to write a letter assessing her capacity in which I said she was demented and incapable of making major financial decisions. It went to court, and the son turned up with a letter from a geriatric specialist saying that she was competent. The son's plan was to move her out west and isolate her from her daughter who lived in the Arctic. The judge decided in the daughter's favour, which (to my mind) was reasonable. I wondered how the son got that letter saying she was competent when she so obviously wasn't. I really wonder if he took somebody else to this geriatric specialist to pose as his mother. There was no way that she would have passed the tests.

We tried not to send people to the hospital because it's confusing for the demented – it can be confusing and disorienting even without dementia. They don't know anybody, often don't understand what is happening, and are always happy to get back" home". There are, of course, instances when they must go. Fractures are an example of that. Our overall approach was to keep people as comfortable and content as possible for the remainder of their time on this earth.

TERMINAL EVENTS

Is there a place for doctors-assisted suicide or euthanasia? I do believe doctor-assisted suicide is reasonable under certain conditions. Some people feel better palliative care is all that is needed. I am a palliative physician, and I can say that there are still cases where assisted suicide is reasonable – surrounded by a group of rules and restrictions of course.

Euthanasia is different. These are cases where the patient is generally beyond making the decision. Some of the long-term demented people may be psychotic, in pain, or very anxious – therefore suffering. There may be no visitors since they can't relate or don't recognize them. There is no possibility at this time that the situation will improve. Are we doing them a favour keeping them alive? We can control symptoms with medication, but are we helping them by doing that? Are we keeping them going with the wishful thought that a cure is close at hand. Euthanasia is like going to sleep, but you will not wakeup.

6. TEACHING, RETIREMENT, AND LOCUM WORK

In 1977, having been in practice in Orillia since 1962, I felt a strange urge – or need even – to be challenged again. Perhaps a change of some kind was what I needed. In those days, you did not have to have a CCFP (certification of family practice) to practice, and I had actually done two years of internal medicine training, one in Vancouver one in Boston. Having never done multiple-choice exams before made it rather interesting at first, but once I got onto them, they're not so bad, and there were also orals which were awkward but I got through them all right, so I got not only my CCFP, but also myFCFP or fellowship in the College of Family Practice, a number of years later.

In 1978, I was in contact with Holly King who was organizing teaching practices for the University of Toronto Faculty of Medicine, Department of Family and Community Medicine. They had seen the need to teach family practice residents in rural settings, so I would be the first one in Orillia, and for many years I was the only one. There were the usual practicalities –insurance and responsibility, going through the hospital board, etc. – before we could get going. It eventually became quite well accepted once nurses, administration, and other staff got used to it. I had a resident for one month at a time, up to four (and rarely five) per year since patients didn't mind seeing the residents, but they did not want to see them all the time. I had very many complimentary reports since the residents write reports on me just as I had to do reports on them. I remember one described his month as "the cherry on his family practice residency cake". Another fellow wrote me some ten years after his residency to tell me how much I had influenced his life. One year, Ontario's Family Physician of the Year was a former resident. He gave me the credit for his decision to practise in a small city after his experience with me. Originally, he had planned to join a Toronto group.

On top of what they learned, there was a tremendous amount that I learned. Firstly, they kept me on my toes as they had just finished all their medical training and their family practice residency and were in the final year before their CCFP exams. They knew a lot of facts and figures. What they needed was guidance and experience in putting all that knowledge to practical use. They loved procedures and seldom got to do them in the big teaching hospitals because specialty residents picked them off.

They had generally delivered very few babies and were anxious about obstetrics. They had never used forceps, rarely a vacuum. They were keen to try anything. Most of the residents felt they learned a great deal more in the periphery than in the downtown hospitals. I believe with more guided responsibility they increased their confidence tremendously. One of the major benefits for me, personally, was a tremendous exposure (since Toronto is so cosmopolitan) to residents from all over the world, all sorts of countries and religions, that I would never have otherwise been exposed to. A great many of them were first or second generation Canadians, and of course, their parents wanted the very best for them, so they worked hard, and because their parents worked so hard, they were willing to do that to get into medicine. I also had a chance to talk about the various religions, and I thank them for exposing me to at least a little of their experience.

In the later years, our group was asked to take the residents for the whole final year split between two of us. This worked really well, and they all did well on their exams. Occasionally they went back to spend a day in the city, but they all seemed to come back feeling they were ahead of their peers. This was very satisfying for us as well as them.

When asked what my title was, I never had an easy answer. I didn't give it much thought. I guess I was a lecturer, preceptor or something akin to that. One day, they asked me to fill out a form, and the next thing I knew I was an assistant professor. Surprise!

I did have one unsettling experience in teaching. A young lady who was with me for a month, showed up one day with another female student who asked if she could spend the afternoon with me. I was not prepared to look after two for one afternoon. They had to write reports as well and hers (the three-hour unexpected student) was rather desultory. I never saw her again. She had only been there for three hours and only once, so I didn't expect to have to write a report on her, or her to write one on me. Of course, I didn't find that out until much later when I got copies of the reports. I don't know what devious things were going on behind the scenes, but I did not appreciate being part of it. By the time I got the report, I couldn't even remember her name, so I couldn't report her. I wonder if she skipped where she was supposed to be and maybe filled out a report on herself. I hate to see dishonest people in the profession. That one case left a bad taste in my mouth, and it may have been a partial influence on my giving up the teaching in 1997. Age I suppose might have been a factor too.

HOSPITALIST

On December 31, 1999, the day I retired from my office, I was fortunate enough to have my patients covered by a number of different doctors. Driving home that day, I felt a weight lift from my shoulders that I had never noticed was there before. The air smelled sweeter, the birds sung louder, the sky looked bluer. I guess like a horse pulling a sled or a plow constantly, I only noticed a difference when it was gone.

I began almost immediately working in the hospital as a hospitalist. A hospitalist takes the place of a family doctor for those people admitted to hospital who don't have a local family doctor with hospital privileges. The hospitalists would work one week, then hand over to someone else. It's not ideal for the patients, but it's better than no one to look after them or only a specialist. The first five years after my retirement in Orillia, I spent about half my time as a hospitalist.

I did medical and surgical hospitalist for the first several years but then switched to a psychiatric hospitalist.

LOCUMS

A locum consists of taking the place of another doctor who may be sick, disabled, on holidays or unavailable for some reason. The time depends on the situation. It could be anywhere from a week to six months or even longer – though the tax situation gets complicated if you are in other countries for more than six months.

My next move and first locum was to Northern Ontario for a few weeks in the winter of 2000 where I spent virtually all my time in outlying aboriginal communities. The town of Sioux Lookout some 350 kilometres northwest of Thunder Bay was the centre, and the locums were sprayed out across Northern Ontario from there.

Bearskin Airlines did almost all of the transferring of doctors to the remote areas, and those bush pilots seemed to be able to handle anything. They had no problems with snow, sleet, pouring rain, bitter cold, strong winds, and small rudimentary airports. When I was in the air, I was aware that Ontario has five hundred thousand lakes almost none of which are accessible except by aircraft. It almost seemed as much water as land. If you are a fisherman, your imagination runs wild with the possibilities. Roads (with the exception of ice roads in the winter) were virtually nonexistent. It is beautiful, wild country full of animals, fish, birds and plants (lots of which are edible).

The northern lights on those bitterly cold clear nights could be spectacular.

The first community I went to was Pikangikum where we spent nine days. Pikangikum – the nurses liked to shorten the name to Pik – a first nation's community had received considerable press and was known as the suicide capital of the world. At that time at least, it had a high incidence of alcoholism, and fetal alcohol syndrome was not rare. In fact, one of the more responsible people did not drink at all, and he felt like a social outcast. Virtually every day there was a disaster of some kind. One day a thirteen-year-old girl took an axe to her mother's head in bed. Fortunately, it slid to one side with result a large laceration and virtual amputation of her ear but no fracture.

Another day, a very large lady who was known to be epileptic was found unconscious out on the ice on the river in January. She was brought in by snowmobile and put on a stretcher with wheels in the emergency department. She suddenly awoke, tore off her clothes, and stood up on the stretcher. Unfortunately, no one had locked the wheels of the stretcher. It started rolling to and fro. Anyone who tried to get close to her to prevent her from falling was met with a slap to the head. I got a couple of slaps myself. Eventually, as a group, we were able to subdue her physically and chemically.

About the middle of my stay there I found myself on a radio talking to the pharmacist in Sioux Lookout who supplied – by plane of course – the pharmaceuticals for the area.

"Are you alright?" he asked by way of greeting.

"Sure, why?"

"They usually give people the last rites before they sent them up there."

I *think* he was kidding.

The following day we had a young lady who'd been a victim of sexual assault brought in by the police. They had a standard rape kit which appeared to be unopened, but when we opened it, there was virtually none of the sampling equipment necessary. Since it was still sealed there was no apparent answer.

The night before I left, there was an urgent call from the next little town (population 200) about fifty miles away. A seventeen-year-old girl had ingested two glasses of Javex bleach. There were two nurses there that day attending to her. They did what they could, but they called just before sundown to say she was getting *stridorous* [high-pitched difficult breathing] and her blood oxygen levels were down to seventy (normal being in the low to mid-nineties). The head nurse and I were able to get a local pilot with skis to fly us over and land on the river. As we got out of the plane to climb up the bank, the pilot got my attention.

"You have fifteen minutes until I have to leave because I can't fly after dark and have to land on the river back at Pik."

No pressure.

We were able to intubate her with some difficulty because there was so much swelling and blood, and when we did, her oxygen saturation came back up into the nineties almost immediately. We knew the medevac plane from Winnipeg was only minutes away, so we scrambled back down the bank and returned to Pik. We were a little later than we should have been, but we could just make out his cedar branch markings on the river ice. All this was at minus thirty-five degrees Celsius. It was a beautiful evening that night with northern lights flaring. We found out later that the medevac team was over their hours for the day, so they had to stay there and wait for another flight to Winnipeg. I often wondered if she survived. She had apparently attempted suicide before.

Since bringing in alcohol or yeast was illegal, the local people had devised a way of making alcohol beverage from tomato soup and yeast – it' being easier to smuggle in yeast than alcohol. There was so much soup used that Campbell's thought they loved soup and rewarded them all with T-shirts. I wonder if Campbell's ever found out what their soup was being used for. A young fellow came in one day with an old fracture of his humerus (upper arm) which healed at right angles to normal. He said it was an advantage because, if his chainsaw kicked back, the arm blocked it. He wasn't interested in getting it repaired.

There were several churches, a lot I thought, for a population of eighteen hundred when I was there. Each church was apparently competing and downplaying the others. The head nurse showed me an epistle that was circulated by one of the churches shortly before I left, stating that people and especially children should not watch the Teletubbies, popular costumed TV characters that looked like dolls with keys in their heads since the blackone was "the anti-christ".

The morning we were leaving, an aircraft brought in another group of religious people with Bibles under their arms, and one of the men told me "what these people need is more Bibles." He had never been there before, but he knew what they needed. Could he have been a little prejudiced and possibly wrong?

Unfortunately, the people there were given a significant amount of money with the idea in mind that they would develop a sewage system of some kind and a water system. In their wisdom, they decided instead to build a hotel expecting that they could make money with fishermen coming to the area. But that did not work out, and the hotel was used only by the occasional government employee coming into inspect. The hotel, like most of the other buildings in the area, was covered with graffiti.

I would like to think that eventually a water and sewage system would be available to them.

—

Webequie was another First Nation community that I spent a few days in. It was on the Winisk River, which may be the best brook trout fishing in the world. It is just south of Hudson Bay. It was a totally different situation. Alcohol was not evident – at least to me. The women were skilled workers doing the work, making things out of beads, leather, and hides. The men left early in the morning with their snowmobiles and usually a sled as well. If they were lucky, they would come back with a caribou that night, or if they were less lucky they would at least have a sled full of wood for the woodstove. There was a hockey rink, and even at ten o'clock at night, kids were out there happily playing hockey even though the temperature was minus forty. It was a busy, purposeful existence, and people were happy. The nearest village was something like one hundred and fifty miles away, so that the connection with other groups was limited although, apparently, they did go over there by snowmobile to play hockey on occasion. In the summer, most of the men were fishing guides, since the fishing was so superior there for speckled trout in particular. One guide told me he had personally caught an eight and half pound speckled trout.

One morning there were a pack of wolves that came right up to the nursing station, which is where we stayed. They looked like dogs at a distance, but dogs were what they were after as a meal. The head nurse had a dog team which was all tied up behind the station, so they were eyeing them, but fortunately they went away before anything happened, possibly because there were too many close together. We got a good close up picture of one of their nice yellow eyes.

NURSES

Nurses are an extremely important part of a doctor's ability to function properly to the best of their ability. This applies in all aspects of practical medicine, but nowhere more than in the more remote areas such as the north.

Nurse practitioners or nurses with northern training or experience (that are in charge of the various remote nursing stations) seemed to be a controversial subject for a lot of doctors. I found them generally to be excellent, experienced, and not prone to overstepping their boundaries. It actually made life easier because, when I visited some of the many little villages I had been to, all the little things – throats, ears, gastrointestinal problems, even pneumonias – were looked after, and I got to see their problem cases, which of course, was much more interesting. Some cases I saw, for example, were peculiar pains or rashes, chest pains, unexplained shortness of breath, etc.

I thank them for their professionalism, their help through difficult circumstances, and their unwavering cooperation.

ARCTIC LOCUM IN INUVIK

Spring was such a delight for many reasons, migration, leaves budding, plants growing, black flies biting, and most important spring skiing in the mountains.

Following a few weeks of skiing in western Canada and United States, we headed to Inuvik in the Mackenzie Delta for my next locum. Inuvik is above the Arctic Circle, so permafrost was a reality. The buildings, even the hospital, were up in the air. They had become experts at insulating under the floor because it didn't seem cold in the hospital. Heating was primarily from a central depot and sent by insulated above-ground pipes to the various buildings. The sewage also was returned in a similar fashion in these tubes. Inuvik was about three thousand people, and of course, mostly Inuvialuit but a smattering of Caucasians, Chinese, and even some Arabs. The chief of staff was from South Africa and had extra surgical training so he was the de facto surgeon. All the doctors, of course, had to deliver babies and work in emergency.

My first day, there was a call to medevac a man with questionable *status epilepticus* [epileptic seizure that won't stop and is resistant to most treatment] from Old Crow which is on the Porcupine River in the northern Yukon. It was one of the most memorable flights of my life as we crossed the totally uninhabited Richardson Mountains as the sun was setting. They were, of course, snow-covered in March, and the range of pinks oranges and mauves was never ending. In the small medevac planes, you don't fly at thirty thousand feet, so you have a wonderful view of the colours and the mountains. We took some time to stabilize him and then brought him back to Inuvik. Normally Yukon looked after its own people, but old Crow was so remote from Whitehorse that Inuvik looked after it.

During my time in Inuvik, I visited the smaller centres for three or four days at a time. I spent quite a lot of time in Aklavik, which was about seventy-five miles away on the western side of the Mackenzie Delta. It calls itself the muskrat capital of the world. They had a vigorous little business there, making hats, mitts, etc. out of muskrat fur. My wife has a pair of mitts she loves that are fur inside and out. I have a fur hat that I'm not allowed to wear out in public, but it sure is warm and great around our winters at home.

The delta is an incredible array of ponds and rivers, and how people find their way around in it is mind-boggling. When the ice starts to melt in May and June, it develops a unique almost iridescent blue colour similar to the icebergs in the Arctic.

When we were in Aklavik, we stayed in the top of the nursing station right on the river. One night about three in the morning, we heard shouting and hollering. Remember, when you're that far north you see twenty-four hours of daylight by late May. The ruckus was some people coming through with a snowmobile and a boat. The technique was to pull the boat across the snow with the snowmobile and, when you get to the water, you put the snowmobile in the boat, cross the water, then, use the snowmobile again. It worked in June which was the spring breakup.

June was the migration, and the number of birds flying in was unbelievable. There were thousands of ducks, geese, swans, and cranes. The local people of course were out there hunting them, but they did eat them all. I was impressed one night by a fellow I knew who shot a swan. It landed on the ice on the other side of the river. He went home, brought his canoe back, and paddled across the river to retrieve it. There were so many swans flying in he could easily have shot another one – but of course he didn't *need* another one.

The twenty-four-hour sun was something everyone should experience. I could read easily at one in the morning with no lights. In fact, a lot of people put aluminum foil on their windows to try to get some sleep. The sun just sort of sits at ten o'clock and follows the horizon in a circle.

Aklavik had a family that was most interesting, medically speaking. There were nineteen members of the family who had died in the last three to four years of a gastrointestinal malignancy. It was mostly of the stomach. This was certainly worthy of investigation. I was involved with two of them. One died during my stay.

On his last day, he wanted to share a caribou head with his family. I don't know the significance of that, but it was important to him and his family who all gathered in his room. He died the next morning. With such a strong family connection, investigation was underway when I was departing. No cause had been found, but chemicals in the water were suspected.

—

Near the end of May, we needed to make a visit to Fort Good Hope which was further south down the McKenzie River, and from there to Colville Lake which was north again and inland between Great Bear Lake and the Arctic coast.

To start we took the little Cessna plane with Annie our pilot, who was four foot something, and was quite cavalier.

The other pilots said, "Are you sure you want to take that one? It's been acting strange lately."

"Oh sure," said Annie, who had to put foam on her seat so she could see out.

We were no sooner in the air than there was a great banging noise outside.

"What's that noise, Annie?" I asked.

"I don't know," she said. "But it's not the engine."

I guess it didn't matter if the wings fell off? We continued to fly south above the Mackenzie River, map in hand. As we got closer to Fort Good Hope, the river was starting to break up and the water was totally black. One of those amazing sights I will never forget was flock after flock of snow geese below heading north silhouetted against the black water. It reminded me of that scene with the flamingos in the movie adaptation of *Out of Africa*.

When we landed in Fort Good Hope, the nurse met us with the charts for Colville Lake. I went to Colville Lake where there was to be nineteen patients seen and a local person to help orient us. The nurse could not come with us that day for some reason, so Marian had to help out. While we were on land, the pilot climbed around on top of the wings looking for the source of the noise we had heard. No luck!

So, we took off again, the noise was back, and Colville Lake was quite a distance. The lakes on the way up to Colville Lake were all trampled by caribou, but they were just gone so we missed them. Colville Lake was an idyllic little spot with seventy-five people on the side of a beautiful little mountain lake. The inhabitants were, I gathered, the last remnants of a branch of the Dene people. They all looked the same, short with square faces and huge shoulders. Although there were no trees around, the entire village was made of log cabins. The person who was supposed to help us was too ill to help, so once we found the right building, we found there were actually thirty-eight people who wanted to see us. Of course, we didn't know where any equipment was for immunizations, Pap smears, etc. The pilot had said she had to leave in two hours. It all looked a little daunting at the time. We soon learned the reason for the huge number of people who wanted to be seen; they knew the snow geese were coming – though I don't know how they knew – and they were all, including the oldest, heading out hunting and camping the next day. They wanted to be sure they were okay to go. Finally, the nurse called from Fort Good Hope to find out what was happening. She talked to somebody and sent the rest home; since we were already late, and she had dinner waiting for us. The names of these peoples were, of course, interesting. The aboriginal names were very different. One in particular stood out for me. This massive man with huge shoulders had the name of Hyacinth.

—

After dinner, we walked down to a church that had been built 1865 and painted with dyes and colours from local plants. It also had stained-glass windows. Even though it was ten at night, of course, the sun was still fairly high, and the colours in this old church that had stood for a hundred and forty years were indescribable, like nothing you have seen before. The light on through the stained-glass windows seemed unreal. Apparently, some people were interested in *restoring* the church, but they could not get paint even close to the originals. Pictures I took did not capture the colours, really quite disappointing because I will probably never see them again.

In Fort Good Hope the pervasive tentacles of residential schools had done their damage. I spent some time talking to a man who was suing the government and the Catholic schools for how the abuse affected his life, his family, and his relationships. An intelligent man, he had attended university and had, a total distrust of governments. And who could blame him?

"They have not followed through on any of their promises," he said. Is it any better now?

To return to Inuvik, we first had to fly south to Norman Wells and catch a plane north again to Inuvik. (As a side note, the aircraft that took us from Fort Good Hope to Norman Wells had, shortly thereafter, crashed killing all aboard.)

Back in Inuvik, I talked to another very intelligent Inuvialuit who had been invited to be a deputy Minister of Inuit Affairs in Ottawa and who felt he would take the job. Again, there was great bitterness about the residential schools and the long-term apparently irreversible damage that had been done to all aboriginal societies everywhere.

We wanted to see Tuktoyaktuk before we left Inuvik, and we knew that at some stage before long the ice road would suddenly be closed, so we rented a truck for Saturday only to have a blizzard which meant they wouldn't let us leave. Sunday morning, we were there bright and early. The blizzard was gone, but the road had not been plowed.

Fortunately, it was four-wheel-drive and very high off the ground. We started out battling two-foot drifts in places, which was not too bad until you got beyond the trees of the delta.

When there were trees, at least, I had some idea where we were on the road or where the road was. But now there were no tracks, for no other vehicles had tried it since the blizzard. Once past the trees and out on the Arctic Ocean, I had to guess where the road was. In places, I could see banks where the plows had been before, but lots of places with all the drifting we really were guessing. It was one hundred and eighty plus kilometres to Tuktoyaktuk, and we did not see another car the whole way. About twenty kilometres from Tuktoyaktuk, we saw the plow coming, and from there on it was easy.

It turns out that there had been a northern drum festival on Saturday night, and we were to have dinner with the nurses and the local police, so we really missed out, but what can you do in a blizzard in the Arctic where visibility was zero and nothing to relate to out there. Tuktoyaktuk was the northern trailhead for the Trans Canada Trail (now called the Great Trail). Folks had dug an area in the permafrost so that people could use it to keep food, frozen caribou etc. The area also features numerous pingos, which are shaped like little volcanoes formed by the freeze/thaw cycle. It is a strange mixture of sand and ice that got forced up. The strength and strange ways of nature!? One day I'm sure we will understand all these mysteries.

Some interesting characters can turn up in remote areas. Lots of people ate local plants, roots, and berries as well as fish and caribou as staples. One man's job was preparing muskox horns for carvers. Doesn't everybody have a backyard full of muskox horns?

The world can seem a very small place at times. One day I was talking to this very pleasant Inuvialuit lady who had had some addiction problems that she was dealing with.

"They took my first daughter from me, and she was adopted, and I just found out where she is."

When she described what she'd learned about her daughter and where she ended up, it turned out her daughter had been a patient of mine.

Another lean black-haired man in his eighties lived alone thirty miles from Aklavik at the junction of two rivers. He ate caribou, fish, and berries (occasionally some roots and occasionally rabbit). He ate fruits and vegetables only if he was in town and his relatives made him.

"Why would anyone eat *those* goofy things?"

We were there in Inuvik in 2000, and we used telemedicine quite a lot, particularly for orthopedic and medical situations. The connecting site was almost always Yellowknife and rarely Edmonton.

When I think of the North, I think of sleds and dogs, so we went mushing for a few miles and got our musher's license. We had to manage the team on our own for this. The biggest problem was the Arctic hares, which could grow up to fifteen kilograms. When the dogs saw them, they tended to forget that they were pulling you back there. We had to remind them pretty quickly or we would be on a slalom course through little trees. In the delta there were some good-sized trees – I suppose because of all the water.

CHATHAM ISLANDS IN THE SOUTH PACIFIC (SEPTEMBER 2000)

Our next adventure to New Zealand's Chatham Islands started in September of 2000. I first had to spend a few days on the North Island (Hawkes Bay) orienteering after getting my license in Auckland.

We had been a little concerned before we went about the remoteness and the different medical system. They had private and public systems that seemed to complement each other quite well. If the people wanted faster service or certain doctors they went private. The drugs were different, and the ones that were the same as ours had different names, example there was no Tylenol, they used paracetamol, and for vomiting during pregnancy they used nothing.

After my orientation at Hawkes Bay, we flew out to the Chatham Islands from Wellington. We stayed in a house about seventy-five feet from the four-bed hospital.

There were three nurses, two Kiwis and one American. Two of the nurses were also midwives. I was the doctor, the pharmacist, and the secretary – meaning I actually had to learn to type (it *had* to be better than my handwriting).

Since there was no veterinarian on the island, I was occasionally called upon to do some minor repairs to animals also.

The Chatham Islands are an archipelago of ten islands of volcanic origin a thousand kilometres southeast of Auckland, New Zealand. Some people had referred to them as (and there were books written about them that used this term) *the end of the Earth*. South was Antarctica and east was ten thousand kilometres to Chile through the so-called roaring forties because, except for the tip of South America, the massive storms at that latitude were not slowed or held up by land at all. Of the ten islands only two were inhabited. One was Chatham Island, where we were staying, and the other was Pitt Island, which was about twenty kilometres south across the notorious Pitt Strait. The other islands had various rare birds, plants etc. One small cluster of island (called Forty-fours) had five thousand nesting pairs of royal albatross – of course, no one was allowed near it. Another island (Little Mangere) had the famous black robins which were down to nine birds at one stage and might have gone extinct were it not for the efforts of conservationists and one particular bird called "old blue" who, reproduced much longer than she was expected to.

Black swans were a gorgeous addition to the lagoon. They had red beaks and showed a lot of white when in flight.

The vegetation was entirely different than ours, and there were many colourful species growing wild all over the islands. We grew seventeen kinds of vegetables in our garden. The soil was very fertile once we eliminated the weeds.

There were a number of ocean currents that intersected there which affected the weather but also produced some unknown sea vegetation according to a couple of biologists that were studying them.

There were at least eighteen species of birds on Chatham and Pitt Islands that were found nowhere else in the world. We were very fortunate to see most of them. The magenta petrel was once considered extinct – having not been seen for about forty years – until one was seen on the Chatham Islands. They were nocturnal and lived in caves. There was about six or eight then, and they had a team of conservationists that were studying them and trying to preserve them. We were lucky enough to see one heading out to sea one evening.

On the topic of conservation, there were several conservationists who were trying hard to protect the rare species. One of their main jobs was killing cats that had gone feral countless generations ago thanks to the early explorers who also left sheep, pigs and goats all over the southern hemisphere. The cats, of course, killed everything, so they were the main hazard. They were very wild. They arched their backs and hissed when they saw us.

The two inhabited islands had a total of seven hundred and fifty people. Pitt Island had fifty absolutely beautiful people. They all looked like movie stars. Don't forget, the population there was about fifty percent Māori and there were some descendants of the Moriori, the original inhabitants of the island. The Māori, who were much more aggressive, came out from New Zealand and decimated the Moriori. There was actually a statue of the last pureblood Moriori who died quite a few years ago.

The capital of the Chatham Islands is Waitangi, and in 2000 it had a population of three hundred situated at the mouth of a river on an eight-kilometre curving beach where my wife Marian would walk every morning. Occasionally she would see someone else on the beach, sometimes on horseback. The island was surrounded by magnificent beaches, the best anywhere in my opinion, and in our six months there we never saw another person on any of the beaches except the one in Waitangi. Since everyone on the island was my patient (they had no choice), there was no problem going or travelling anywhere you wanted. We always asked permission, of course, but we were never turned down.

The islands were about forty-four degrees south – as far south as Orillia is north – so not really tropical although there were some palm trees.

There was no crime on the island. No one locked their doors if they even closed them. There was one policeman. Occasionally one of the temporary well-paid fishermen might get a little drunk and drive off a road or something similar.

There was one grocery store which, of course, had to charge outrageous prices and one other building which served as bank, post office, café, police station, courthouse, and jail.

Since I was the only doctor, I was responsible for both islands which meant flying over to Pitt occasionally when emergencies arose. I recall my first trip over. One of the fishermen caught his hand in the cable on a winch.

The runway over there was a grassy field with quite a significant slope which slowed the plane down quicker landing, and I guess helped with the takeoff too. The wind was constant and quite strong from one direction, so they didn't need cross runways. The wind was a major source of power, and a lot of the farms had windmills. Coal was used as well. At any rate, on our first trip I took along some suture, gloves, local anaesthetic etc. and ended up repairing his hand while sitting in a mud-covered Jeep on the side of the runway.

Chatham cliffs

On another occasion, we flew over with the head nurse and her boyfriend, my wife and I and a visiting Dutch pediatrician. At the end of the day, the aircraft could not return to pick us up. The nurse was desperate that we could not go back, which left the seven hundred people without a doctor. There had been a major storm for about three days so that even the fishermen had not gone out. She managed to convince a fellow by the name of Chip known to all as the "cowboy of the sea" to come over and get us. He did, in his twenty-five-foot aluminum fishing boat. On the way back, the seas were three to four metres. We were constantly falling off the edge of waves and dropping a few feet with a slap. Chip was quite blasé through all this, with a cigarette in his mouth and one foot on the wheel, except once in a while he would see something coming and would quickly make a few manoeuvres. Everyone was vomiting, except Marian and me. We finally did make it after what seemed like an eternity (probably one and half to two hours). Of course, there were no seats to sit on, and the floor was slippery from all the fish; there were also no life preservers (none visible anyway) so we grabbed on to something and tried to hang on. We also knew the waters were thick with sharks, so swimming wasn't a good alternative. Sharks were quite common in the archipelago, and the group of islands called the Forty-fours were so bad even the fishermen didn't go near. There were, on the island, a number of people who had experienced shark attacks, at least two of whom had lost an arm and others, fingers.

One *paua* [abalone] fisherman told me about being followed by a shark for a while. He was concerned about escaping when he found a narrow little channel that he could get through but was too small for the shark. He thought the shark would probably wait for him at the entrance, so he waited until the tide was running out at full force and came bursting out as fast and violently as he could. The shark, which *was* waiting, was so surprised that it withdrew, and that fisherman lived for another day. Virtually all the diving fishermen have seen sharks watching them. Maybe it would make you think about a desk job?

One of the amazing things about the crossing of Pitt Strait was a mollymawk which was a species of albatross with a wingspan of close to two and a half metres. It followed us all the way across about three metres above and to one side of the boat without flapping its wings even once in the twenty kilometres. They were amazing to watch as they rode the wind currents occasionally tilt one-sided then the other. They liked to follow fishing boats hoping for bits and pieces. There were also storm petrels which were smaller birds that flew just above the water. They looked as if they would get caught by the next wave any second but, of course, they never were.

The local people made a big deal of us being Canadians who had just spent some time in the Arctic, and they were wonderful to us, frequently bringing us fish, lobsters, paua and lamb. Paua was delicious, and we ate a lot of them. There were multiple recipes, but sliced thin and fried very lightly with onions, garlic, and butter was a favourite. One day, on returning home, there was a lobster on the kitchen counter that was close to a metre from tail to antennae. It was so big that we could not get it in the very large pot that we had, so we had to cut it up to cook it.

Because the food was so expensive in the store, we ordered our food from New Zealand, and it was delivered by ship once a month when we first went there, but up to twice a month by the time we left. We would just go down to the dock and claim ours when the boat came in. Of course, all the trade names were different, so it took some getting used to. Sanitarium was a brand name for a lot of things including cereals.

Since I was the only doctor between New Zealand and Chile and on call twenty-four seven, I not only dealt with local people, but looked after the ocean people too. We would have injured fishermen from the big trawlers of many different origins and would occasionally have to discuss cases with the ship's nurse on a radio telephone the policeman had. The nursing station also had a radio telephone for me to use when we were travelling around, but it was very unreliable. Sometimes I could hear the fishermen talking to each other out on the ocean but couldn't get a call from the hospital. I told them generally where I was going, and they would get the nearest farmer to hunt me down.

One day while walking along a beach, a farmer appeared on the bluff above me, saying they needed me urgently at the hospital. A young man was using an outboard motor alone in the lagoon. I guess he made a sharp turn and fell out. The boat continued to run in circles and kept running over him causing massive lacerations and bleeding. The lagoon was so shallow that he could not escape it. I'm not sure how he got away because he was alone. He had massive bleeding from multiple huge lacerations most of which involved a lot of muscle. We had no laboratory, no blood for transfusion, and one of the nurses had no trauma experience so was quite squeamish. There was no hope of sewing up the wounds, so the best we could do was wrap them up, apply as much pressure as we could with bandages, tensors direct to the arms, hands and legs. We started two or three intravenous, ran a lot of saline (all we had), and monitored his blood pressure and urine output while we awaited the air ambulance from Christchurch eight hundred kilometres (and about five hours) away. A little morphine helped to settle him as well. He made it to Christchurch, but he was there a long time with extensive nerve and muscle damage. I last heard he was improving but faced months of rehabilitation.

There were a couple of interesting sailors that came into the clinic. One was a seventy-eight-year-old retired Australian physician who wanted to cross the roaring forties to Chile, which was ten thousand kilometres of open water. He had a younger crew, both in their sixties. They knew they would have eight gales a month and figured it would take two months to make it. Their sailboat was thirty-six feet long, but they did have a lot of electronic equipment, which he showed us. He had sailed for Australia in his younger days as part of the Australian team. He had actually been involved in that disastrous race quite a few years ago when a lot of boats capsized and there was significant mortality. They said they would let us know if they made it. We never heard from them. Speculation!

Another man came in with his wife one day; He was having chest pain. He was in his forties and he was about to take off in his small sailboat also to Chile. He had a lot of experience sailing, having been going around the world for the last seven years. I was concerned about his chest pain and only convinced him not to go by asking what would happen to his wife if something happened to him mid-Pacific? We managed to get him back to New Zealand where he was found to have quite serious heart disease.

Chatham Island whale skull and beach

On the islands we had no diagnostic equipment. We had an electrocardiogram which was normal in his case but no *troponin* [a blood test for heart attacks] and no bloodwork at all, no enzymes no electrolytes. We could send blood to New Zealand two days a week whenever the plane was going in, but that was the extent of our laboratory capacity. Remember, those clinical skills a long time ago? Fortunately, when I needed them, they seemed to resurface.

On the island feral animals were common – these are domesticated species that have gone wild. We mentioned the cats, pigs, goats, and sheep. There were also rats (not so much feral simply invasive), inadvertently introduced by the same explorers and their ships. There were also wild cattle and the bulls were territorial, so when we went wandering, we had to keep an eye out for them. While I was there, the ministry decided there were too many wild bulls, so they had a chemical brought in that would knock them out (with a tranquilizer gun) enough that they could be gathered up and sent to New Zealand for slaughter. They were very concerned about the drug they were using, however, because it was fatal for humans, so we spent some time learning about antidotes. Prior to that, the farmers would occasionally shoot one; and they said the meat was absolutely wonderful.

One day while crossing a farmer's fields, we saw a group of cattle uphill from us. We tended to be cautious because we knew bulls were in with the cows. Without warning the herd started to charge down the grade directly at me. I stood as big as I could and waved my arms trying to look fierce. They tended to go to one side or the other except for the last two. The one on the left wanted to go to the right and one on the right want to go to the left, so they were sort of leaning on each other as they pounded closer towards me. Fortunately, about six metres away they sorted it out. I got out of the field quite quickly. Interestingly the farmer who owned those cattle was attacked and injured by the bull about a week later. That bull found itself in the freezer shortly after. The lesson learned was to always have an exit strategy and time to execute it.

New Year's Day was a big day on the Chatham Islands. In the morning the men had a wild boar hunt, and biggest boar wins. That year, the biggest one was about two hundred pounds. The kids fished for eels in the river. In the afternoon, they had horse races complete with the white and red officials, and they had a good track with stands. They didn't have starting gates, so they just tried to get them approximately equal before they started. One enterprising farmer even imported a jockey from New Zealand. Bets were placed with the fellow who sat in a jeep at the side of the track. Actually, Marian won a few dollars. Remember, there were only seven hundred people that lived on the whole island, and some of them were temporary fishermen who volunteered for the isolation money. Most of the farms, which were mostly sheep, were ten thousand acres or more; and fishing, primarily for paua (abalone), was the other source of income. Most of the abalone was shipped to Japan where apparently it was worth a lot of money even back then. We were told seventy dollars per kilo. The most active paua fisherman, who hired a number of staff, apparently made regular flights to Japan in his own plane. Theoretically it was all supposed to be all free diving for the paua, and there was a quota, but the fisheries officer wasn't too bothered by the free diving rule because he said they just got to their quota sooner, so scuba was used sometimes.

Some of the farmers were escapees from the urban rat race, an accountant, a hotel manager, a CEO of a business, and some other less prominent jobs but the same *get away from it all* attitude.

As well as the beaches, there were many gigantic cliffs often orange and sometimes with a lot of vegetation and exotic flowers, a great variety of colours in amongst the lava and occasional limestone outcroppings. Another beach we visited quite often had a lot of forty-million-year-old fossilized shark's teeth which made excellent and unusual jewellery. The beach was at one end of a huge lagoon which apparently was only open to the ocean two or three times a year because of sand bars, wind, tides and ocean currents.

In the medical office, which was part of the hospital, it was mostly routine procedures. For obstetrics, first pregnancies were usually sent out to New Zealand about one month before their due date, so there weren't that many deliveries on the island, but the midwife – I guess just because she wasn't doing enough – always wanted me nearby when she was delivering.

One young man from elsewhere claimed to have had only one sexual affair, with one woman, but managed to get gonorrhea, chlamydia, and syphilis. His HIV test had been negative so far. Some people are just unlucky, although, at the time, I suppose he thought he was lucky.

New Year's also attracted some tourists, which were virtually non-existent there because nobody wanted them. They arrived for "the real millennium" which is to say the start of two thousand and one. You will remember the Chatham Islands were the first place on Earth to usher in the millennium because they were in that little dog leg on the International Date Line.

There were some magnificent bronze statues on poles of the different stages of man placed at the site – actually on Pitt Island – that would've been the first place to see the new millennium. They were done by the Polish-born sculptor, Woytek, and they were magnificent in the setting on top of the cliff and they would have been seen by one or two people a year, if that.

You may recall some headlines in the late nineteen nineties about some eighteen sperm whales that beached themselves in New Zealand. That was actually on the Chatham Islands. We visited what we called sperm whale beach several times. There were gigantic bones lying around, and some of the skeletons were up to fifty feet long. Some of the skins were still on, after a time it didn't smell too great, but it was just another amazing site. One of the large skeletons had a small skeleton inside, obviously pregnant.

For me, a huge thrill that will last forever happened one day quite unexpectedly, and I'm not sure I can describe it well. We were out for a hike in a farmer's field at one of the corners of the island. The land was gradually sloping upwards but that is not unusual, so didn't arouse any special expectation. It was midafternoon as we topped a little knoll, and there below was the crashing surf on this small circumscribed sand beach surrounded by bright orange sandstone cliffs which had some fuchsia-coloured daisy-like flowers growing on them. Rolling down the slope was grass blowing in the wind and extending out in front was a turquoise sea with the sun shining down on all this. It was staggering. I wept! It was beyond description the feeling that came over me. This was heaven, I thought, and there was absolutely no sign that anyone had ever been there before. Actually, another time when we were out there, we found a lamb, who, would not leave her mother, who was lying there dead, so we had to tell the owners when we went back. We told the lady of the house where it was, which was down near this beautiful area and she said she had not been down there for ten years. Needless to say, we revisited that place a lot more subsequently. Just around a bend from that beach was a bright orange promontory that was covered with ancient – possibly millions of year's old – exquisite fossils of many sizes and species. I took some pictures but never followed up enough to find out what they all were. Those were "film" days and expensive, so you didn't take enough pictures.

The other islands of the archipelago were quite dramatic in their names, which describe them well; Castle which had eleven-hundred-foot cliffs, Ship, Pyramid, and they were all beautiful from anywhere we looked. We were sad to leave the Chatham Islands and the wonderful people and incredible natural experience, but we had to be out within the six-month limit, or we would've had to pay taxes in New Zealand as well as Canada.

TASMANIA AND EASTERN AUSTRALIA (SPRING OF 2001)

We spent the next five weeks on vacation in Tasmania and eastern Australia. As always, there were a few things that stood out.

In Tasmania, we rented a car but had no reservations, so we drove north from Launceston along the northern coast in a westerly direction. It did seem busy, and when it came time to think of accommodation there were none. A major windsurfing competition was being held there, so all the accommodations were full. and everything was crowded. We were finally able to find a place on a fifty-six-thousand-acre farm in the very northwest corner of Tasmania. The directions to get there were to "turn right at a stone gate and drive until you see lights." That was twenty-two kilometres before we saw a light, but the wildlife was amazing, lots of kangaroos and wallabies plus a Tasmanian devil and a quoll (a carnivorous marsupial not unlike a possum) which was very rare. I wasn't even sure what it was until we looked it up. This farm was divided up into several sections each with a manager. There were nine thousand milking cows that got milked on the automatic milking machines that rotate and do fifty cattle at the same time. What a production. We stayed in what used to be stables, but had been resurrected rather well, but still it was surrounded by a wall. Looking out the door, there were wallabies everywhere.

Spring lambs were a big item also, and they were a little more rotund than the average. The farm was owned by a European conglomerate that visited about once or twice a year. There was a very posh rosewood and mahogany dining room which seemed a little extravagant, but it's what we used while we were there. Watching a sheep being sheared was fascinating and the "good" guys could do it in less than a minute, and they just kept doing it all day. The bewildered sheep got shaved and thrown onto a swing door, and after looking stunned for a few seconds wandered off to see their mates. They packed the wool in large wooden crates, and it was then graded and exported.

We tended to look at medical facilities along the way, out of interest with an eye to future possibilities. One place that we stopped invited me into a room, then went out and locked the door. They needed doctors and were phoning their association to find out how they could keep this one they had captured.

Victoria Island south of Melbourne was on a very large bay and had a lot of animals that we walked in amongst. There were kangaroos, wallabies, wombats, emus, Tasmanian devils (caged) other smaller mammals, marsupials, and ostriches. The emus knew where a bag of peanuts might be, and if you were not fast enough, they would be in your pocket before you could stop them. A very large (six-foot) kangaroo grabbed me with his arms, and I don't know what he had in mind, but I was happy to get away from him, at least I think it was a him. Maybe I'm attractive to female kangaroos?

We were lucky enough to see a duck billed platypus in a river.

Along the south shore to the west were the "twelve apostles" a group of large limestone stacks located not that far off shore. We thought sunset would be the time to see them so after our dinner we drove down there. There was no traffic, but when we arrived there were two to three hundred people hanging off cliffs and some walkways all with cameras ready. It was beautiful, the orange sunset disappearing between the *apostles*.

The next morning, after passing through a very dense, twisting one-lane rainforest road with nobody else around, we finally made our way to Sydney and our flight to Brisbane. We arrived at about ten o'clock at night. The airport was shutting down. We couldn't rent a car, so we wandered around looking for any signs of life. There were none. There was a phone to call a taxi but no answer. Eventually (after almost an hour), a taxi driver showed up who was looking for someone else, so he drove us to a motel. We hadn't noticed an atomic attack, but the absolutely empty airport in a major city at ten did make you wonder.

The following morning, we rented a car, drove to the Gold Coast and Surfers Paradise which featured a beautiful beach with, you guessed it, lots of surfers. The beach, in my opinion, was not as good as Chatham Islands, but the surf was better. I guess I expected to see great surfers on huge waves like Hawaii. Most of the surfers didn't last more than five seconds, so I guess it's like going to a major ski resort, most of the people there are beginners.

Finding your way to the Great Barrier Reef was a must in Australia. Being out there for a day in the comfortable water makes you forget about sun. Marian got a severe burn as we spent about five hours total snorkeling. There was an incredible variety of sea life from turtles of all sizes and fish and corals of all colour imaginable. Our guide was quite excited about some little fish he found in a secluded little area in the coral. They were extremely rare, he said, and they would spend their whole life in that one little area maybe three to four feet in diametre. The birds, animals, lizards, and snakes in Australia were so different to us that it was truly fascinating. We have a huge list including koalas, kookaburras, and platypus that we were lucky enough to see.

HOME AGAIN

Returning home always feels good. It had been our first Christmas away from the kids and grandkids and Grandma Marian especially didn't want to do that again. We felt good about the fact that they all got together at one of our daughter's homes for Christmas.

Back home felt good for a while, but then something happened, some uneasy feeling told me I would feel better if I was working a little, so I started nosing about ads in the journals and deciding what looked interesting, which of course is different for different people. I am very interested in flora and fauna of all descriptions. I'm also very interested in the culture and spirituality of aboriginal people. I believe we have lost our roots and need to get back to reality and our connection to the earth, including our ancestors and the spirituality that comes from that connection. The aboriginals still have that unless they have been drawn or torn away or adversely influenced severely by all the missionaries and other colonial forces.

A locum in Nunavut seemed interesting, so I made contact and arrangements were made. Each place I went, I had to get a license, but there was a pattern to it in the different jurisdictions. There were some differences; for instance, New Zealand wanted our original marriage license. Why we don't know. We sent it to them. They then lost it and said it had never been sent even though they signed for it by registered mail. They then demanded it again, and fortunately, there was some other piece of paper from the wedding that satisfied. Incidentally, we never did get back our original. British Columbia was big on police records, local, provincial, etc. Why, who knows?

IQALUIT, NUNAVUT (SUMMER OF 2002)

Iqaluit (population five thousand) on Baffin Island is the capital of Nunavut, which is one fifth of the landmass of Canada and had, at that time, a population of twenty-seven thousand. Except for a paved circular road, the roads were all gravel and dusty. There was a lot of garbage everywhere – pop cans, cigarette boxes, plastic bags and the like. The houses looked like they had been dropped from the sky in random fashion. The newer parts were developed neatly. If people even own the property, certainly no one pays attention to it. You walked directly to wherever you were going, whether that takes you behind houses and through yards. There was one road that went north that was called "the road to nowhere". It was about six miles, and it just got you out of town on a road. The other road ran east along Frobisher Bay to a tiny community that had featured the original Hudson Bay outpost in the area in the seventeenth century.

One time I was out for a walk on the road to nowhere and heard a clicking sound behind me. On turning around there was a caribou probably twenty feet behind me, crossing the road, wondering what kind of animal I was. By the time I got my camera out, he was probably one hundred feet away and he just kept going in the same direction in a straight line no matter what he came to. I watched him for about a mile. The country was virtually all rock, rolling off into the distance. There were bones, mostly caribou, all over the place. Between the rocks, were low spots with ponds or creeks that had some grasses and sedges and bounteous wildflowers in the spring, which was July and August. You could walk any direction you wanted as far as you wanted.

In July, there was still ice on Frobisher Bay, and the tide was thirty feet (second only to the Bay of Fundy) so when the tide went out at break up, it left eight-foot icebergs lying around on the sea bottom. They used flat bottom boats to resupply. When the tide went out, the boats settled on the sand, and the trucks drove right out to them. There was no deep-water harbour in Iqaluit, but the airport was quite busy and had a huge airstrip. It was one of the few in the world that space vehicles could land on in an emergency.

The hospital had about thirty beds but was going to be extended. It was manned by family doctors, one surgeon, and a pediatric resident from Ottawa. Occasionally there was a pediatrician, and pediatrics was a major part of practice there. There were advantages to having been a family doctor who did everything because everything was needed and there were no high-powered specialists across the road. Virtually all major referrals were sent to Ottawa, but there were visiting specialists who showed up periodically, ear nose and throat and ophthalmology.

Most of the population was Inuit, and despite living in houses in Iqaluit in the winter, a lot of them moved out on the land in the summer. There had been the same sort of abuse there that had happened in so many places at the hands of government and religious organizations. There was still significant bitterness about it, and indeed, some of the stories I was privy to as the doctor made you wonder if psychopaths and sadists attacked these vulnerable people. Obviously, that does not apply to everyone, many of whom had done a great deal to help the native people, and they were well intentioned.

I worked twelve-hour emergency shifts and when I did I stayed in the department which was quite well-equipped for being so remote, but I was also responsible for delivering whatever babies were to be delivered during that shift. I spent a good deal of time talking to the nurses at the various outposts about managing patients or sending them in, all by aircraft, which was generally from elsewhere. A lot of the aircraft came from Edmonton. Occasionally a doctor was required to go on one of these flights to the little communities. Regular visits also were made – an average of about once a month – to look after medical problems the nurses had saved for us to see.

The nurses in these small communities had all had extra training because they really were practitioners and were generally excellent and worked well as part of a team. They used the phone appropriately for advice or to tell us what problems they were sending in.

One night I was on a medevac mission to Pangnirtung on a beautiful fjord further up Baffin Island. We were told it was fog bound which was common in that area but that around the airport was clear to about five hundred feet. The pilot decided he would fly through the fog at five hundred feet hoping to hit the clear spot. The fjord was surrounded by mountains. As we were going through the fog after only a mile or two, I was certainly writing headlines as time crept by and still no airport. Suddenly the pilot veered what seemed like almost straight up, so we emerged from the fog. What a relief, but we still weren't there. They were allowed three tries to land after which they must return to base. The second time he thought he would circle down gradually to where he knew from the topography the airport was, again going down, down through the fog hoping for an opening. As advertised, at about five hundred feet above sea level, we could suddenly see the airport, a sharp turn to the right and we were on the ground. No problem! These northern bush pilots were remarkable. I actually made fifty-seven flights in one year in fog, snow storms, and landing on postage stamp runways. They could do it all.

Alcohol was a problem there also, as people have literally been deprived of their aboriginal skills and were left in unfamiliar surroundings without the skills for the new world they found themselves in.

There were, however, people there who lived a solitary life. Sometimes a small family, that lived miles from the nearest village and lived almost one hundred percent on the land. Occasionally they showed up in the remote villages for a few staples.

Midnight Qikiqtarjuaq

I chanced to visit Qikiqtarjuaq at the end of July early August. It was on a small island off the north shore of Baffin Island and manned by two very competent nurses. One was an Aussie. Most of the icebergs around were still small, but there was one huge one sitting out about a kilometre offshore. It had been there for the better part of the year I was told. They thought it must be stuck on the bottom. If they were ninety percent underwater there must be an awful lot of it under there. I was offered a chance to go to look at it one night by boat by one of the locals. Unfortunately, his motor wouldn't start. The very next day a psychiatrist who was sent up periodically to see if the

Royal Canadian Mounted police were doing okay was watching the iceberg when it fell apart. The sea was a cauldron for a few minutes until it settled with its new equilibrium. If we had been out there, we would undoubtedly have been swamped and probably drowned.

There were about ten fishing boats in Qik, as the nurses liked to call it. The head nurse, her husband, and I convinced one of the fellows to take us up one of the fjords to the Coronation Glacier where it empties into the sea. It was about a two-hour ride with a seventy-horsepower outboard in survival suits. He said no one had been up that fjord in two years and since there were only ten boats in that harbour, I'm sure he would know. We passed a number of icebergs on the way down. There were some huge ones as we moved closer to the glacier. He was astonished how much the glacier had gone further up the fjord. He estimated it had shrunk one hundred to two hundred metres in two years. The water was full of seals which were tempting for him, but he did not shoot any because he couldn't bring them back. I suppose he probably would've been happy to leave us and bring back the seals. There were several rivers falling into the fjord. It was really difficult to estimate how high the glacier was because you don't dare get close to it in a little outboard. We landed a little distance from it and climbed up the rocks along the side which maybe gave us a better idea of the thickness right at the sea. As a guess, I would say it was two hundred to three hundred feet thick, and I could see it sloping as it got further up the valley. This one was said to be about fifty kilometres long and was part of the Penne Ice Cap.

On the way there, there was a wall of large pure white gulls, probably Icelandic. I guess our bright orange suits were too much to resist, and we made such excellent targets. Those fellows were big and excellent marksmen too, and we were a moving target in a motor boat. I guess you can picture it from there.

During the past winter, three polar bears had terrorized the community for a while. I didn't ask how they solved the problem. There happened to be a trail of ninety-two kilometres that came from the Pangnirtung fjord through Auyuittuq Park to Davis Strait, close to Qik, which separated Baffin Island from Greenland. While I was there, they had to close the trail because of polar bears. These were huge animals. I had a chance to see one in Alaska (may have been a world record) that had been stuffed. It was mounted standing, and it was over eleven feet tall. What a sight! I never did see one alive in the wild while I was working up there. I did later on another visit.

Flying back from Qik to Pang on the way back to Iqaluit we flew over mountains that I considered the most rugged looking, steep and sharp-pointed mountains I had ever seen. They're probably not the tallest, but they were interspersed with the glaciers and the turquoise lakes making them a spectacular sight.

Before heading from Iqaluit to Qikiqtarjuaq I chanced to see three German men in emergency. They were intent on mountain climbing on the Pangnirtung Pass (now called Akshayuk Pass). Two of them were doctors. The third was quite ill and unable to accompany his friends. I learned later that one of them had a major fall with multiple injuries that required helicopter evacuation.

I arrived back in Pang then flew back to Iqaluit. I was slated to return home the following day when the chief of staff asked me if I would accompany a child with meningitis who was being sent to Ottawa Children's Hospital of Eastern Ontario and would be leaving in an hour on a Lear jet. I scrambled to get my belongings together and had a ride in a Lear jet. I think it was called "sky services" down to Ottawa. There were two very competent nurses on board, and the child was actually getting a little better as we travelled so it gave the three of us a chance to talk. They encouraged me to think about joining them for occasional excursions anywhere in the world. The only disadvantage I could see was that you might go to a lot of places, but you wouldn't really have time to see them, so I have not pursued that avenue.

WESTERN AUSTRALIA (FEBRUARY 2003)

Western Australia was our next venture into the unknown. We arrived in Perth to be oriented. Medical records there were all electronic and prescriptions also. Some hasty typing practice was required. They had a hybrid private–public system as well, and they seemed to complement each other quite well. They had a lot of drugs on special lists, so if I wanted them I had to phone the government and tell them the magic word they wanted to hear about why I wanted to use a certain drug. I'm sure things have changed considerably now, but an example then was a severely bipolar patient who had been on lamotrigine. He showed up in our remote area. In order to get it for him again, I was forced to say he was epileptic.

As one specialist said to me, "at first it feels awful, but after a while you get used to it. What else can you do to get what you need for the patient?"

Arguing or explaining to the person who answers the phone would be an exercise in frustration. They had their rules, and deviation would have been unthinkable.

After my orientation in Perth, I started out in a place called Three Springs about two hundred and seventy kilometres north of Perth. When we drove there, after driving up the coast to see the Palisades, we did not see a building or a car for the last hundred kilometres. Where were we? Three Springs was a very nice tidy little town of about nine hundred with a gigantic nine-lane Olympic-size pool. Now we know why the Australians are so good at swimming. They also had tennis courts and lawn bowling.

We also noticed that the road into Three Springs from the west was paved in one strip down the middle.

We drove over this road a number of times to Eneabba, one of the satellite offices. The theory was we would drive on the pavement until another car came and, if ever that should happen, we would put one wheel on the gravel until we passed them. Most of the farms were ten thousand to twenty thousand acres with their houses in the middle so you couldn't see them. It wasn't as if they had to plow the snow on their two-mile driveway. Another reason we drove in the middle was we had a better chance of seeing the kangaroos before they bounced in front of us. We never did hit one, but one hit us one night running into the side of the car. He got away, so I guess he didn't do too much damage to himself. The next two towns southeast were Carnamah and Coorow. They were satellite offices that I visited weekly. Coorow had five hundred people and fifteen tennis courts, similar to the swimming expertise, and they played all year. Australia was a very sports-oriented country so cricket, tennis, Australian rules football, rugby, and soccer were watched very intently. The pros made a lot of money. Cricket was very popular.

It's interesting the different things I saw in Western Australia during my tenure there. Iritis (inflammation of the iris) was quite common. Of course, being the only doctor, as usual, I phoned the specialist or their chief registrar at the teaching hospital for urgent consultation. If I needed urgent transfer, flying doctors would show up eventually, though never as fast as I would like for the patient. No doubt, they had to make decisions about which order to pick people up. They covered a vast area, so they got caught short of coverage sometimes.

In the town of Three Springs, we had no rain. In fact, there was barely a cloud in a month, and the temperature was quite hot. One day Marian, who went to the pool almost every day, came walking slowly back from the pool. I believe it's the first time I ever saw her walking slowly; the temperature was forty-five degrees Celsius. The soil was very red, and they treated summer like we treated winter. They couldn't grow crops then, so their growing season, for crops like wheat, was the same as ours. They planted in April and May. Interestingly, they often didn't plow before they seeded, depending on how the ground was after the previous year.

Parrots, parakeets, and cockatoos were very common. The pink headed gala was the Western Australia equivalent of starlings in our country, and they often came in bunches. They were normal birds for people there, but we never got tired of looking at them. There was such an assortment of strange flora and fauna that we were constantly surprised by a new bird, lizard, or animal. They had a golf course but, sorry, no grass.

WAGIN

Our second major stop in Western Australia was Wagin. They had a huge sheep statue at the entrance to the town of about twenty-five hundred . Being again the only doctor there for a month kept me busy. I went to visit Dumbleyung another satellite community. It was next to Dumbleyung Lake where the world speedboat record was set. It was almost completely dried up when I was there at first, but when a little rain finally came, the lake filled up, and the reddish-brown fields turned green overnight.

In a sheep area, there were various jobs of course. The shearers tended to have trouble with their backs because not only did they hold the sheep by themselves in an awkward position, but they did the whole sheep in less than a minute, followed immediately by another and another all day. A lot of them wore back braces. It tired us watching them. Another sheep related job was a crotcher, and I leave it to your imagination what he did to the male sheep.

Following our Wagin episode, we took a couple weeks off and flew to Uluru (Ayers Rock) and the surrounding unusual rock formations. It was very impressive standing alone in the middle of the desert. It was considered a sacred object by the aboriginals who, therefore, do not like people to climb on it. We had decided not to climb on it out of deference to them but couldn't have anyway because there was such a strong wind. When we were there, no one was allowed. Currently a few people each year fall off and die. We saw three dingoes (which look similar to wild dogs) around there as well. The flies around the area were severe and were all over us, so take a hat with netting if you are ever visiting.

I did not see any snakebites but the red back spider had a very significant bite which *could* be serious – but usually required only some anti-inflammatory medication.

Driving to Alice Springs from Uluru took us a day, very flat very red with occasional mesas and the strangest vegetation you can imagine that grew in inhospitable hot dry climate. They tended to be short and have quite thick leaves. Adaptation never ceases to amaze me. Alice Springs was basically an oasis in the desert with a river running through it, which I'm sure must have water in it sometime during a year, but not when we were there. There were, however, a few oases hidden away here and there, and the aboriginals knew where they all were. They knew how to find water in the desert. Certain types of plants told them how deep the water was below the surface so that they knew they could dig down to it. A common aboriginal technique was to burn the low-lying bush over an area because, when it began to sprout again, the animals came back to the new growth and it made hunting easier. More recently, the government decided maybe that was a good idea, so letting fires burn in remote areas was, tolerated. I remember one fire we flew over three weeks in a row, that was still burning and gradually getting larger. It was probably fifty miles from the nearest settlement, so no attempt was being made to stop it. Western Australia was huge and sparsely populated.

Our next stop was Pemberton in the southwestern tip of the province, a very pretty place with rolling hills, reddish soil, lush vegetation, and some very large trees so logging was practical there. We stayed in the outskirts, and of course, I was the only doctor there. I was doing a locum for the doctor who was on holidays. Invited over to her home for dinner, we found that her husband raised small lobster-like critters called marron (*Cherax tenuimanus*). They were like giant freshwater crayfish for which there was an international market evidently. He had merely scooped a pond off the side of the river and separated it by screens. There was trouble because some people felt the effluent was poisoning the river downstream.

Every morning upon arising, there would be a large group of large red kangaroos on the lawn munching away. When people stirred, they would gradually disburse. We saw the occasional dingo there as well. I have not mentioned the bird life up until now, but it was extensive, and , it all sounded new to us. There was one group of magpies that we frequently heard in the morning, and it was quite beautiful almost like a carillon when they got together deep and melodious. It's not what you expect from our magpies.

Following Pemberton, Lancelin was our next stop, said to have the biggest sand dunes in the southern hemisphere. I don't know how they're measured, but I suspected the ones in the Namib Desert might be larger and certainly redder. The local children used small boards like surfboards to surf the sand dunes. We had fun trying it briefly – very briefly.

We were living in the doctor's house directly across from the bay, which was part of the Indian Ocean. It was a very cute quaint little home that she had brought from elsewhere, and she had it full of antiques. It's quite common that homes were raised a little, and you could often see the ground between the floorboards. One night we had a major storm with howling winds, the house was creaking and groaning, and I swear the whole bed was moved for a short while. We wondered if we were in Kansas. In the morning we found all the outside stacked chairs were scattered all over the neighbourhood. We were told it had been the worst storm in about fifteen years.

The sky in Australia was very clear, and apparently, the atmosphere was a little thinner. There was no air pollution. The stars at night were very clear and we could see the constellations easily, for example, the Southern Cross, the Australian triangle, and the tea kettle. We spent quite a bit of time at night looking at the stars.

Termite mounds were common and fascinating. On the outside, all was calm, but make a nick in it and the activity within was incredible. Another trick we had to learn was to stamp our feet when hiking to scare away the snakes because, unlike in Canada, virtually all of them were poisonous.

We took a flight one day up the west coast to Sharks Bay and Monkey Mia where Marian fed some wild dolphins. They somehow had become accustomed to being there, in the open ocean at almost the same time every day. Also, we saw a lot of thrombolites in Shark Bay which were the first forms of life on earth. They lived on nitrogen and produced oxygen.

The next stop was Kununurra in the northern tip of Western Australia, a truly exotic destination. Before going there, we were told many times how beautiful it was. There were some doctors there (approximately eight to ten) and visiting specialists came occasionally. It was very remote, so some foreign-trained doctors who were more surgically oriented than most Canadian doctors were the local surgeons. One was Irish, the other, I believe, South African.

Circumcision was a usual event amongst young aboriginal men. It was usually a ceremony. One unfortunate young man did not want to be part of the ceremony, so he decided to do it himself. With knife in hand, he began to cut some of his foreskin off. It hurt much more than he anticipated, so he stopped. The bleeding, however, did not stop, so he wrapped it in a rag. After a while, he decided to have another go at it, with the same result. After one more try, he didn't know what to do. It became infected, and by the time he came to the hospital, it was a real mess, and he was in agony. He was very embarrassed. It took some unusual plastic type surgery to try to restore him to a normal situation.

Perth, the only city of any size in Western Australia, was about three thousand kilometres away, so there was great excitement when news came through that an internist was moving to Broome, a coastal town known as the pearl capital of the world, and only one thousand kilometres away. This was practically next-door.

Kununurra was a pretty little place with spacious palm trees and parks. It was very close by a large rugged reddish rock formation, one of many that pop out of the desert. The Ord River ran through it and provided irrigation for a lot of fruit and vegetables for Australia. Upstream was a large dam which had produced a huge lake (Lake Argyle) that had drowned a lot of aboriginal hunting land much to their disapproval. They actually had started fish farming in the lake, catfish, which they couldn't sell by that name, so they rebranded them as silver fish. They sold much better by that name.

In this lake and the river were freshwater crocodiles – only little fellows, up to ten feet. People didn't worry about them, children swam in the area, and so did we. There was a dam wall that served as a bridge at Kununurra, and downstream of the Kununurra Dam Wall was salt water including saltwater crocodiles up to twenty feet; these creatures were not nearly as sociable as the freshwater crocodiles. How do they know enough to stay separated from each other? A "salty" was found on top of the bridge one day. Hopefully he figured out which side of the bridge was his.

We took a canoe trip by ourselves down the river one day from the Argyle Lake Dam Wall down to Kununurra and saw magnificent red rocky cliffs and birds of all description. There were herons, darters, stilts, huge bats, (not sure if they were fruit or fox, they both stink equally), hawks and eagles. The flora was also totally different. We saw a few crocodiles, and we did swim in the river just to see whether it really was safe or not. Naturally, being a gentleman, I allowed Marian to go first.

Since a lot of land had been flooded by the two dams, there were a lot of strange looking dead trees in the water. The sun setting through them made quite a dramatic picture.

On the road from Kununurra to Wyndham, which was our next locum, there was a road going west. It was called the Gibb River Road which, after fording a few streams, brought us to at El Questro, a one-million-acre ranch where we stayed overnight. These were real Aussies! And we spent the evening around a campfire, listening to their tales (mostly of their adventures with their snorkel equipped Toyota Land cruisers). The cruisers were virtually the only vehicle we saw in the "real" outback. They went anywhere, and they prided themselves on their off-road exploits through desert and rivers.

The next day we took a ride in an open-air helicopter. There were no windows or metal structure in front or beside us. The seatbelt was the only thing holding us in. We flew out along some of the ridges and mesas. All the land was red as usual.

After landing, we also observed one of nature's unusual adaptations, archerfish that spit from below the surface of the water as high as five feet to knock down insects that they then pick off the surface of the water.

WYNDHAM

Our last stop in the northern end of the province was in Wyndham, which was at the confluence of five rivers where they joined Cambridge Bay which was totally salt water. They had a small hospital, and there was one other doctor there. The diseases were generally the same, but there were some differences. I saw a case of rheumatic fever, which I hadn't seen in years, and some syphilis which I also hadn't seen in years.

Everybody it seemed had heard of the flying doctors. Part of the duties was to visit the isolated aboriginal communities, so I was one of the flying doctors for a few visits to Oombulgurri and Kalumburu where I did prenatal visits, pediatrics, and routine medicine. I may have done some trauma work while I was there if it was relatively fresh.

Aboriginals in Wyndham

Kalumburu, which was on the coast, was bombed by the Japanese during World War II. Apparently, it was mistaken for an airfield.

We also noted on our flights there was a large bushfire which was larger each week but just left alone because it was at least fifty miles from any settlement

View from the bastion

In Wyndham, I also met the most impressive person I have ever met, an aboriginal who was sensitive, poetic, and philosophical. I was able to spend a couple of hours with him. When we first met, he presented me with a short story he had written the day before. It was a love story about two young people. Unfortunately, I seem to have lost it because love stories are everywhere, so I wish I could remember what was so special about it. It was so sensitive I had to fight back tears. This man had a worldview that was remarkable. We discussed people in general, religion's place in the world, politics. He had a grounded philosophical approach despite his being brought up in an aboriginal area (the equivalent of a reserve here). He was very aware of the prejudice of a lot of different kinds of people towards others they don't know haven't met or won't take the time to try to understand. As a bright man, he had had political opportunities, had travelled, and was part of a world organization of aboriginal peoples. The political route he felt got nowhere, so he had abandoned it and was building a sort of shrine which consisted of huge fifteen to twenty foot statues of aboriginal people, their life, and association with earth and its other inhabitants. He was hoping it would be meaningful to the aboriginals themselves and that it would represent something perhaps others would be able to connect with. He pointed out that the few acres where he was doing this was in the middle of Wyndham, which was surrounded by several churches all with individual teaching and all at variance with each other. He seemed to be trying to reach a common ground that all peoples could be comfortable with. I saw him as a visionary and hoped he could have some larger effect as time moved on, a ripple effect that hopefully got larger and larger rather than dwindling. Perhaps he could inspire other people of similar thinking. Perhaps he already has? Me!

DEASE LAKE, BRITISH COLUMBIA (JUNE 2004)

My last remote locum, in June of 2004, was at Dease Lake in north-western British Columbia on the Stewart–Cassiar Highway (Highway 37) about two hundred kilometres south of the Yukon. The highway ran parallel to and joined the Alaska Highway near Watson Lake. The population was about four hundred and there were three small villages within a two-hour drive that I covered as well.

When we arrived, there was a major forest fire about twenty to thirty kilometres away, and the town was full of firefighters from all over. The air was full of smoke which took a few days to disperse.

They normally had one doctor, an Australian who had been there, I believe, for almost five years. He got married there on a ledge in the Grand Canyon of the Stikine courtesy of the local helicopter pilot. He had one child, and he was taking a little time off to be with his wife and daughter who were staying in their sailboat anchored off the coast of Maine. There was another locum doctor there as well, on and off, while I was there.

We did travel regularly to three other settlements. The traffic on the highway was nonexistent. I would travel half an hour without seeing another car going either direction, and it was summer.

One of the areas we went to was Telegraph Creek, 120 kilometres west, which was located on the Stikine River just below the Stikine Canyon. It was probably only fifteen hundred feet deep, but so narrow that flying in a helicopter there were areas I wasn't sure we could make it through. The sheer walls, with occasional mountain goats, disappeared into the roaring rapids and swirling eddies below. When I was there, a total of twenty-six people had made it through in kayaks up until then. I didn't ask about the others that tried. The drive out there was nature filled. Some people have compared it to the Serengeti although, of course, the animals were totally different. The last twenty kilometres went along the edge of the canyon and single file most of the way. Don't look down! The town was very old and mostly aboriginal. The Tahltan people were great, hard-working people with a good sense of community, good sense of humour, and tremendous respect for their elders.

One young person said, "We never make a major decision without consulting them."

Because they were so isolated before the road came through, they had less trouble with the school system than most – at least it was barely mentioned compared to most aboriginal communities.

When the sockeye salmon were running, everyone was there, all the elders were there smoking the fish. Any who had moved away, came back for the salmon run, a real community effort and celebration.

Wildlife was very plentiful in the area, and we saw lots of it on the gravel road out there including moose, bear, deer, fox, wolves, lynx, and even a wolverine which was a first for me. Even a lot of the native people had never seen a wolverine. We did not see a cougar. Apparently, they had moved further north and into this area relatively recently. Despite spending time where the local people told me there had been a mother and two cubs, they stayed hidden. They were probably behind the nearest bush laughing.

There were some mines in the area – jade and gold. A lot of the men worked there and generally they had to fly in and would work three weeks to get a week off or some similar arrangement.

There were some really interesting people that lived in the area. One fellow lived eighty kilometres from the road in a cabin on a little lake. He came out once a year for supplies, and arrangements he had to make. He was friends with all the animals; he knew them all and had names for them. He was aware of their likes and dislikes, even the local grizzlies. He had occasional contact with another man living in similar circumstances about fifty kilometres away. They sort of looked out for each other a little by radio. This fellow was quite intelligent but had a little too much time to think about things, uncensored and unquestioned, so in a year he had developed some pretty strange ideas, at least by our way of reasoning, anyway. However, he was very content back there and had no intention to come back to civilization.

Another very large good-looking Tahltan man with a beautiful wife was a big game hunting guide. He claimed that Canadians couldn't afford his services so all his customers were wealthy Americans. They paid something like twenty thousand dollars a week which included eating, hunting, setting up camp, looking after the trophies etc. promising access to all manner of wildlife. Stone sheep were sort of a specialty because they were so hard to see and get to. Actually, we saw some on the road one day, a rare opportunity. They used horses to transport their equipment through the mountains.

His teenage son, who was helping him, appeared in the office one day clearly jaundiced. He had hepatitis A. It must have been very hard to be sure the drinking water was always pure, those mountain springs looked so pristine.

Someone was always on call, so I had occasional busy time, but generally it was quite light compared to what I was accustomed to for so many years in Orillia. When the Australian doctor came back to start again, he realized that he had been in Canada five years and had to undergo exams if he wanted to stay. What to do? He was fearful, but wanted to stay, he thought he might be able to go back to Saskatchewan without the exams. I never did hear what he ended up doing.

Another wonderful evening, I finished in the clinic about midnight. It was late August or early September, so we had some darkness at least. I came out last alone to see the moon rising in the east, the northern lights dancing above me. They eventually formed a corona on the horizon which lasted maybe fifteen minutes. All this time, there was a wolf pack howling not very far away, that long haunting baritone – they always sound closer than they probably were. It is a moment that has stayed in my mind ever since.

You wonder how people can live in such rugged situations their entire lives with none of the comforts that we have. Their homes are small – wooden of course – often covered with antlers. They were heated by burning wood, so there lots of wood piles around. They did have, in Telegraph Creek, a small cemetery just as you drove in and one of the wooden gravestones read: little Joe one hundred and five years. Next to it was one that read: mrs. joe. It's a long healthy life. They actually could grow some vegetables on the north side of the canyon as the slope decreases because it faced south, and they made full use of a short growing season while the snow and ice were gone.

Virtually everyone hunted. . Game had always been plentiful and still was. In the background was Mount Edziza, named after one of the elders whose trap line extended that far. A beautiful extinct volcano it had snow on it all summer. Right next to it and accessible only by a small aircraft was the Spectrum Range which was appropriately named for the range of colours in the rocks – reds, greens, blues, yellows, and white. It was spectacular to see them both and a herd of caribou on the lower slopes of the volcano. On the way there, we flew over a small lake that the pilot claimed had produced a sixteen kilogram rainbow trout. It was about a day's hike to get to it once you flew into the adjacent lake.

ATLIN LAKE

While we were in Dease Lake, we were able to get a few days off, and made a trip via the Yukon and Alaska into northern British Columbia and Atlin Lake. This was a beautiful clear lake about almost fifty kilometres long with virtually nobody on it. We were able to go for a long, evening paddle in our canoe, down far enough to see the Llewellyn Glacier across the lake, magnificent. The following day we arranged with a local artist and guide who knew the area well to take us down to the end of the lake and hike into the Llewellyn Glacier. He told us one time while skiing on the lake by himself, he was approached and surrounded by a pack of wolves. He took off his skis, waved them around wildly as he shouted as loud as he could.

They watched him for a while then wandered away. Maybe they were concerned they might get rabies from this erratic wild animal?

The Llewellyn Glacier was about 240 kilometres long, started in Alaska and ranged through into northern British Columbia; it is generally considered the source of the Yukon River. It was about a ten-kilometre hike to get there with no real trail. We spent some time walking on the glacier which was quite uneven. Fortunately, we had crampons on our feet and learned how to walk up and down the hills on the glacier. There were lakes and rivers and holes where the water ran down into the glacier. They were rather scary when you got near one as you didn't know how far down it was going.

The fellow who took us in made a habit of making a pile of rocks where the glaciers started on the way in so that he knew exactly how much it was regressing, which was very significant. The ten-kilometre hike out became a test of our endurance, but we made it. Strange how it's farther on the way back. Luckily it was still almost twenty-four hours of sun. There was nowhere to eat when we got back, so he invited us over for "the best smoked salmon you've ever had" in the morning. He was right. We sat on his deck, jutting out from his home all by itself, halfway up the mountain, which overlooked Atlin Lake and the glacier in absolute silence. We could understand why there was a colony of artists living in this very remote area.

STEWART, BRITISH COLUMBIA, AND HYDER, ALASKA (2004)

While working in Dease Lake, we were asked to go to Stewart, British Columbia, for two weeks while the two doctors – man and wife – had a little break. We drove down the Stewart–Cassiar highway and turned off to Stewart which, is at the end of a long fjord and surrounded by mountains. We were there in August, but in the winter, they have very heavy snow on the road, often closed by avalanches. On the way in we passed the Blue Glacier. This is said to be one of five in the world according to our daughter Karen who was with us at the time. Stewart was a pleasant smallish village. The main attractions were just across the Alaska border at Hyder and above it at the Salmon Glacier and Happy Valley.

Hyder was small, featured wooden sidewalks and looked (by design) about two hundred years old. There was a sign that read: home of ninety-nine nice people and one old shit. It was also a common place to watch the grizzlies fishing, which was fascinating! When we were there, one mother was trying to teach her cub how to do it. He was a slow learner and slow mover. Mother would give him a salmon, and he would drop it and did not succeed in catching one himself while we were watching. The grizzlies seemed to set their sights on one fish and would chase it up and down the river, stepping on others until they got it. They bit it in the back, took it up on shore, and started to eat it. Partway through they decided it was time for a fresher one. Leaving that one onshore, only partly eaten, they headed back in the river for another one. Likely either eagles or wolves would descend upon the half-eaten fish. The grizzly, if he saw them, would come bounding back after it. He wants them all.

Beyond Hyder was a road (more of a trail at times) up the mountain to where you got a magnificent view of the Salmon Glacier, and we drove past that (possible if you dare), and after a couple more glaciers, we came to a wide-open valley which used to have a mine.It was.known to the locals as happy valley and was their own secret, special place. The mine was now in ruins and the site was just full of wildflowers. When we were there, there was nobody around just mountains, glaciers, wildflowers, and rushing rivers. It was beyond words.

DEASE RIVER (2004)

The Dease River in northwestern British Columbia was a one-day canoe trip. We started at Dease Lake, which was over sixty kilometres long with only two people living on it, and the river ran north from there. Lack of landmarks meant it was difficult to assess where we were. We'd been told the trip wouldtake eight hours, but we made it in about four – probably because we didn't know where we were. It was a beautiful trip with a few gentle rapids. While we were on the water we saw several moose, many ducks, including redhead ducks (*Aythya aAmericanna)ericana*) which was a first for me.

HAIDA GWAII

After our locum at Dease Lake – since we were already in northwestern British Columbia – it made sense to visit Terrace, Prince Rupert, the Queen Charlotte Islands (now called Haida Gwaii), the inland ferry channel, and northern Vancouver Island.

We drove south on the Highway 37, going a whole hour once without seeing another vehicle. We saw where a mudslide eight feet deep had obstructed the highway totally near Terrace. There were lots of fly fishermen as usual on the Skeena River which we followed to Prince Rupert which was a quaint, neat little town. We ate at Smile's Seafood Café, where the waitress was so pleasant and smiling that she must have either owned the place or been having the best day of her life. Perhaps she was manic-depressive in a manic phase – she was very happy, whatever the cause.

The ferry *Queen of Prince Rupert* took us to the Queen Charlotte Islands, docking at a place called Skidegate. On the way across, we saw a two-storey house with a double garage, outside stairs, a deck, and another out building and several large tanks, maybe propane, going the opposite direction. From a distance it looked like they were doing it on their own, but as we got closer, we saw they were being towed on a barge by a tug with a really long line. We drove to Queen Charlotte City to our lodging which was our home base for the week. We booked a flight to the south for a couple of days ahead and then went for a paddle on the Tlell River. It was so beautiful with huge amounts of moss and lichens everywhere, including some called Old Man's Beard – or Woman's Long Hair – that hung from the trees. There were many little Sitka black-tailed deer (*Odocoileus hemionus sitkensis*) and a few fawns.

Next day we drove to Massett and went beachcombing and found a number of agates and later browsed a lot of native crafts – especially masks – in nearby craft shops.

We decided to see if we could drive across the island without GPS using only local advice. There were no signs. It was strictly, "turn right at the big tree and left at the creek…" etc. The roads kept getting narrower and rougher. Then they stopped suddenly. Where were we? We were part way up a mountain. We could see the ocean, but that was no help, so we turned around and tried to find our way back. Was that where we turned? Those trees were starting to look a lot alike and they looked different from the opposite direction.

Still, we survived!

We flew to south Moresby Island. We saw great views all the way – the mountains and the entire archipelago including Hot Spring Island where Bill Reid was buried. The plane landed in a little bay at Rose Harbour, and the owner took us over in his outboard that wasn't working too well. We saw some bald eagles, guillemots and puffins on the way.

Ninstints (or SGang Gwaay) was a very special place, a UNESCO World Heritage Site. It is a sensual, spiritual place with an ambience like no other. It's palpable if you stand quietly by yourself in the presence of the totems.

Another day we drove to Moresby Camp to gain access to the Cumshewa Inlet. There were a lot of *shroomers* looking for pine mushrooms. We put in our big blue canoe and saw lots of birds, cormorants, glaucous gulls, red necked loons and sapsuckers. We paddled south through Carmichael Passage and saw no sign of another person. It started to get a little windy and rainy, waves whipping up. Since this was ocean, we headed back sooner than we probably would have. There were several pristine sand beaches, and we stopped for a snack on one of them. It's always wonderful, to me at least, to find places that appear pristine and untouched. The silent, secluded warmth in the sun offers a place to dream and let the world drift by.

On the way down, we'd noticed a small rock island covered with seals and decided we would get closer for pictures on the way back. As we approached the island, most of them dove in and swam towards us. I guess they had probably never seen two grey haired critters in a canoe. They were as curious as we were. They followed us for several miles, diving then resurfacing with a snort as they continued to surround us.

The next day was our day to leave by the ferry again. There were gale warnings (first of the season) and a small craft warning. As the day wore on, it was upgraded to storm warnings: this is the highest level of warning.

In other words: "The ferry will *probably* not be going, but stay in touch just in case."

Late in the evening, they decided to go anyway. Since it was over-night, we had a cabin which was on the seventh deck. The waves were four metres high, and we rocked and rolled a lot. It was very hard to even think about sleeping. We just had to hang on to something and hope we didn't get thrown too far. The higher you were above sea level, the more action. It suddenly calmed once we got behind some islands as we approached Prince Rupert.

At Prince Rupert we met up with Marian's sister, Helen and Peter, Helen's husband) with the intention of taking the ferry down the Inside Passage together.

Since I had my canoe with me it was very expensive to take it on the ferry if you kept it on your car, but only seven dollars if you put it with the transports, so I got in line with the canoe on my shoulders and put it under one of the transports. I guess I looked a little strange, lined up in a row of transports.

The Inside Passage happened to be cloudy and rainy almost the entire the way, so visibility was limited but much better once we landed. We passed by Bella Bella, but it didn't stop there – Port Hardy, Port McNeil, Telegraph Cove all had their interests. I mentioned the cove earlier and we also saw whales.

There were many cultural centers and Native crafts for sale as we drove down the island. Some of their masks were super but expensive.

7. REFLECTIONS ON A CAREER IN MEDICINE

With age comes gradual (and sometimes acute) deterioration. The inability to do things that were taken for granted is inexorable but discouraging. To maintain a positive attitude is not so easy.

As a doctor I saw a lot of people who had come to grips with age and impending death; they were generally content, some even looking forward to it. I understood how those with chronic problems, conditions which would never improve and only deteriorate might well feel that way. If you are satisfied that your responsibilities have been attended to and that your death is not hurting anyone – and in some cases may even be relieving them of a heavy burden of responsibility – then it may be reasonable to look forward to it. It looked as though having a strong faith and a certainty about heaven was very reassuring as well.

Should we question Heaven? Is it a physical place where you arrive in the new body? If so, what age is the body? What age are your parents, grandparents and forbearers who arrived there before you? What are their physical attributes? Are there streets of gold? Is it winter with snow or skiing? Is everyone going to different places depending on their view of heaven? If so you may not see your friends and relatives.

If it is a spiritual place – with no physical side to it – how do you recognize your loved ones without their bodies? There would be no physical contact, no need for any physical body maintenance, but what would we be *doing* forever? We could philosophize I guess but if there is a God that is central to the afterlife what would that God demand or expect?

If you find it difficult to follow a religious tradition (and there are many to choose from) you are left to sort it out on your own. In the long run we all must decide for ourselves.

As you age, you know the inevitable is getting closer. How can you prepare yourself for that? Keeping busy, involved socially, and physically active can delay and distract, but at some stage we must deal with it. I am eighty-three years old, but I'm still fearful of death. It is so permanent (unless you are a Hindu). I am not ready to let go of this beautiful world, my family, acquaintances, activities, and my contact with nature.

And that contact, that may just be my salvation.

The earth is the beginning and the end of us as humans, both individually and collectively. We are part of the earth. For a few years we are gifted with *life* where we are upright; we eat, sleep and are active both physically socially, and then we slip back into our origins. It would seem that the closer you have been to nature both physically and philosophically, the easier the transition. You could become comfortable with the idea that you will be part of nature in a slightly different way. The aboriginal people of the world have always felt that way. We in our progressive colonial world have lost track of that and now pray in buildings and worship statues that we have built ourselves. How or why did we lose track?

There have been many treatises on lack of nature syndrome, and anyone who has spent enough time in nature has probably had an emotional experience that could be considered spiritual. It could be different for different people. A good starting point is to get where there's absolute silence – no artificial lights. Sometimes in an unexpectedly beautiful place, a sudden turn in the trail or a pause while paddling at sunset, you will have an epiphany. You must find your own, but it's worth searching for. It lets the little concerns of the day recede into their rightful significance instead of overwhelming us. The peace you can derive from such experiences can last and last. Refreshing it occasionally gives us a sense of tranquility.

It seems that, at some stage, we must retire. It is frightening for me although a lot of people look forward to it. I think they could not have enjoyed their work as much as I have. For me it was the feeling of satisfaction I got from knowing I had done my best and made a real difference in the lives of my patients, even if some of them took it for granted. That is the real joy of family practice. We might not make as much money as specialists, but I know our rewards are greater. The happiness surrounding delivering babies, the personal satisfaction of the difficult diagnosis, and the exhilaration of exceptionally good results.

You learn so much if you take the time to listen and not just about aches, pains, and symptoms, but about the myriad skills, hobbies, and interests of your patients. If you don't take the time, both you and the patient are losing what's available.

As you cut back and give up your office practice, you don't have the daily contact with peers, and you begin to wonder if you could be missing something. Even if you read all the journals and attend courses, you don't have the volume of patients, and you start to second-guess yourself. Your worst nightmare would be to get caught unaware of some new change that, if you had only known, would have made a significant difference to a patient. For that reasons, it's better to get out while you are still on top of your game. I retired May 2016.

What about self-image? Can I be a no body? Will my brain shrivel up like a prune or dried apple? Will I get caught short moneywise? How long do I need money for? Will the RIF last? Is there any other way I could make a few dollars if I get pinched? Perhaps I could capitalize on some of my many hobbies.

Hopefully, if you have enough interests and drive, you can find a productive place for your energy – perhaps you could collect your thoughts and experiences and write a book about them.

What about a new career? Philosophy was always an interest.

Spirituality is an area where you could spend the rest of your life trying to understand it all. Maybe that is too broad and likely never ending?! Is that okay, or is it important to reach an endpoint, a conclusion, an answer to all those questions? Is there a beginning, and an end? Is that possible? We really are just tiny grains of sand in the cosmic ocean – of really no consequence in the grand scheme of things. But *is* there a grand scheme? Who knows? Besides, does it matter? How would we know? Should we try to find out? How? Perhaps we are out of our depth before we even begin. We have no baseline.

I don't want to leave this world alone, in misery, having forgotten all the wonderful events in my life, acting like a fool perhaps, and perhaps not recognizing my family who may (and I wouldn't blame them) have stopped coming to visit because they realize I don't know them anymore. To me, that is worse than death, and I hope someone will be kind enough to put me out of my misery if I am in that situation.

If there is a heaven or paradise who will be there? Many groups believe that, they, and they alone, are going. They can't all be right.

Sometimes I wonder if we are in heaven now. Is it not perfect enough? That may depend on your idea of perfect. Everyone is entitled to their own ideas. Can we all be right? Or wrong? Perhaps if we are good people, in this life (whatever *good* means), we will be satisfied, happy, and content. Is that heaven? If not, what are we expecting?

I do believe that a connection with all things natural, under right circumstances, can lead to a sense of transcendence. This may come unexpectedly and lead to a profound peace. If everyone could experience this feeling, there would be no more wars or hatred.

There is no religion that is any better than any other. They all have histories of violence towards others. Let's not forget the Crusades – or the Canada's residential school system for that matter. There is no race or nationality that is superior to anyone else.

Many years ago, at the time of the separatist enthusiasm in Québec, we were met at a campground in Québec with considerable rudeness from the staff – mostly university students – even though I could speak French reasonably. When we got to our campsite with our six children, who could speak no French, we were met by a bunch of French-Canadian children who could speak no English. Left to their own devices, the kids were playing with each other and having a great time even though they couldn't speak to each other. It appears that they hadn't learned the appropriate prejudices yet from their parents. It told me a lot about interpersonal relationships and prejudices.

Has life been successful? What does that mean? Is it measured by numbers? How many patients you see in a day? How much money you have in the bank or size of your home? The car you drive? The people you associate with?

It is an individual thing. I feel sorry for those who measure their success in numbers, for there will always be somebody richer and living in a bigger house.

Did your job bring you real joy? Was there a sense of satisfaction? Was there a challenge? Was there opportunity to learn, to broaden your view of the world, to understand other people's point of view? Were you respected by others for your achievements and social conscience? If so and you are loved by your family, you are a success. If you have had a balanced life (work, play, family), then you are a success by any standard. You will *feel* it, not measure it.

PERSONAL LIFE

I have been talking mostly about my medical experiences. There is, of course, a parallel personal life since graduation – there has been another side of everything. As of 2017, ours is a family of six children and fourteen grandchildren.

Life is so complicated now that I've lost track of what marriage is. Some people live together, but don't get *churched* for years if ever. Some get married and don't change their names. I know one couple where the husband took the wife's name. We have been churched for forty-four years, and we knew each other for some years before that.

We have been very careful not to show favouritism, so the kids get along very well – perhaps with the occasional tiff – and we seem to have provided a good role model for them. Our thinking is that, since all are different, we ought to expose them to everything and encourage them in whatever they are interested in. We did not try to push them into anything. The result is that there are no doctors and no registered nurse (Marian is an RN). Did we *discourage* them? Not consciously though maybe they were aware of the workload.

Family activities were always very important, so we spent a lot of time outside hiking, skiing, exploring, and camping all over Canada and through thirty US states including Alaska. I tried to take a month every summer for camping until the ten years difference between youngest and oldest became more difficult to manage. The two boys and I took canoe trips with two other doctors and their sons every year for probably ten years.

Come to think of it, I don't know why I was still carrying the canoe when they were teenagers. Just stupid I guess.

As the kids moved out, and I retired from the office we were *free* (whatever that means) to do what we wanted, so we did the locums and travelled a lot. We have been to over seventy countries and all seven continents and enjoyed and learned something everywhere

– though we didn't hit the Middle East (and it is not on our list). Marian and I worked together for many, many years and so we were together twenty-four hours a day. It worked out well. Now that I have retired, my wife apparently likes me to be around all the time. I take that as a good sign, but maybe she just has a really long list of things to be done.

CHANGES IN MEDICINE

Over the years, almost everything has changed (except gross anatomy) from tests to procedures and especially drugs. We should note that neuroanatomy, while it hasn't changed, is much better understood now. At graduation in 1959 the antibiotics were penicillin, sulfas, tetracycline and streptomycin. There was great excitement in 1961, when I was already in practice, at the appearance of ampicillin, which would kill some gram-negative bacteria as well as gram-positive bacteria. What a breakthrough! There have been many, many breakthroughs since.

On the flip side, we have also seen the evolution of bacteria that have now grown resistant to antibiotics. This is something that did not happen many years ago, and when it first started, it was only penicillin-resistant staphylococcus mostly in large hospitals. Because of the evolution of antibiotic-resistant bacteria, a lot of very expensive research is required to develop new drugs. This is mostly done privately by the drug companies. Lots of drugs never make it to market for various reasons, significant side effects being the commonest. In order to cover their expenses and have money for new research, new drugs are often very expensive. The government, most often under the guise of safety, attempt to put off the general usage of new drugs as long as possible, and we often have to fill in special forms to have them made available. It seems like a little more harassment. Now there is a large number of antibiotics and even antivirals and antifungals that are useful, but the research must continue.

In 1959 chemotherapy for cancer was virtually nonexistent. It now has made huge strides in treating malignancy and regimens of surgery and/or radiation and/or chemotherapy are getting better all the time. New drugs are coming on board as well. It has become a very specialized field, and family doctors are much less involved now unless they are remote and give treatment to people who are unable to access cancer clinics easily. In those cases, we do what we are asked to do.

Mental health, as a discipline, has developed tremendously from the days of indefinite institutionalizing. We now have a field rich with professionals of all sorts, from counsellors, social workers, psychologists, nurses, family doctors, and psychiatrists, and all may be seeing the same patient at times. Where once choices were virtually limited to barbiturates and ECT, there are now a large number of tranquilizers, hypnotics, anti-psychotics, and antidepressants. From the early MAO inhibitors with their rare but risky side effects to the tricyclics and their many side effects to the newer SSRIs and SNRIs and new MAO inhibitors we have a large selection. It is almost always possible to find one that fits. ECT is still used in resistant cases.

Antipsychotics were, years ago, limited to promazine or chlorpromazine, but now there is a rapidly growing list of effective drugs that can keep psychotic people functioning reasonably well. I remember well in 1961 when Parnate, Nardil, and Marplan were introduced and the dramatic effect they had on depressed people. It was something we had never seen before although we did realize that *some* people got over the depression spontaneously. The suffering and loss of usefulness and effect on all one's surroundings from depression is pervasive. The longer you are depressed, the greater the chance of suicide. . I believe mental illnesses can be much worse than the physical ones because, with most of the physical ones, you have an expectation of improving with time. The mental illnesses don't always afford you that luxury. When insurance companies first started covering people, they would not cover mental illness if you can imagine that. They did not consider it an illness.

The treatment of asthma has changed tremendously since the sixties when epinephrine and oxygen were the only treatments. Isuprel was a favourite for a while. Then aminophylline was thought the most useful drug but the toxic levels were close to the therapeutic level that it fell into disfavour for a while. Nowadays we are much less fearful of steroids (such as cortisone), and lots of studies confirm that they don't wreak any long-term harm to children. They have been a mainstay of treatment for some time now, usually in inhaler form – bronchodilators the common long and short acting are the other mainstay of treatment.

Heart attacks were treated with Coumadin and up to a month of bed rest and then the patient had very gradual ambulation. Now upon presentation in emerge, the clot-busting drugs are used. Angiography is followed immediately by bypass graph or angioplasty and stents. There are often intermediary medications if possible, plus the various tests – stress tests, cardiolyte tests, etc.

Heart failure has come a long way from digitalis and mercurial diuretics, which were given by injection only. I remember the miracle of chlorothiazide coming along in the seventies – an oral diuretic, just amazing. Beta blockers were wonders for the treatment of angina when they first showed up, but the doctor had to be very careful that there was no heart failure because it would make it much worse. Now of course, it is a mainstay in the treatment of cardiac failure. So many other drugs have made a huge difference to cardiac events and hypertension: the diuretics, the beta blockers, the calcium channel blockers, ACE inhibitors, and the arc drugs. As I look back, it has been a kaleidoscope of changes that are still changing ever more rapidly. I can remember doing a research project in Boston on the incidence of deep vein thrombosis in Crohn's disease. To do this, we had to get out all the charts of people with Crohn's disease searching for evidence of deep vein thrombosis and make sure the evidence was ample. We had no Dopplers back then; it took hours and hours. Now with computers and better recording, it could be done in a short time. The result is a lot more research can be done, and everything evolves more quickly.

Diabetes has become even more prominent, and Type 2 diabetes in older obese people is almost epidemic. There are now many choices of medications, and the insulins keep improving in quality and type, so virtually all can be handled now. Insulin pumps are expanding in use as well.

Another rapidly advancing field is genetics, and new discoveries and treatments are emerging every day.

Imaging has gone from plain x-rays with contrast use for gallbladders and kidney to kidneys imaged through IVP and cystoscopy. Now we have ultrasound Dopplers, we have nuclear scanning for many other organs as well. CT scans, PET scans and MRIs are finding out more things and improving our knowledge base.

It makes you wonder how we got along before all these amazing advancements. Of course, we could not diagnose with such certainty, but were *probably* better clinicians. We spent time debating heart sounds and committing patients to major cardiac surgery based on clinical findings history, EKGs and chest x-rays. The amazing thing is how seldom they were wrong even with those limited tools. The skills of those clinicians are something rarely seen any more. Imagine basing major diagnoses based on the X and Y waves in the jugular veins seen by flashlight at the bedside?

The surgical specialties have also seen major changes in technique and equipment. Scopes of all kinds are revolutionizing surgical investigation and treatment. More and more surgical procedures are being done through scopes, and more sophisticated instruments are being used through them. Now even some difficult procedures are being done this way. By the time I finish writing this, there will be even more changes. Very fortunately for us, our large neighbour to the south does a tremendous amount of research, and their people expect nothing less than the best, so that is what they have. They have the best of everything, and it is available immediately. But it costs a lot of money. If you can't get (for whatever reason) insurance you may not be covered at all, or you may be bankrupt but healthy. I'm sure medicine will continue to advance ever more quickly as long as the Americans are on top of the heap – before the Chinese take over that is (by then they will be totally capitalistic).

THE FUTURE

What is ahead for us in our lifetime – for the earth, the people, the environment, and the practice of medicine?

The future overall looks rather a dull gray at the moment, with all the disasters of all kinds, both natural and man-made.

It should be mandatory for children to spend a significant period of time living in a different type of society. For them to learn that nobody is better than anyone else. Some people are born more intelligent, just as some might be born with bigger feet, but it's all genetics. It's not that you did anything to be born more intelligent. Lucky that's all- the genetic lottery. Other people might be better than you at everything else, sports, arts, culture. It doesn't mean they're superior, just lucky.

The environment must be important to all, and as such, it must be attended to by all. It is beginning to look like countries may actually work together as we change our power needs and methods of producing or capturing it.

The future of medicine is a little fuzzy, especially with regard to family practice, which seems to be fragmenting before our eyes. It was always a challenge to be a general practitioner and stay up to date, but you had to. That was simply an expectation. Hospital rounds three times weekly were also a major source of information, and of course, journals and academic conferences were a source of new knowledge, but also often a source of reassurance. Science is advancing so quickly, is it still possible to stay on top of things? Yes, I think so, but you also need a certain volume of patients in order to gather the necessary experience. Just reading the journals is not enough.

Advancing specialization, even in small areas, has significantly cut into the role of the family doctor. When I started, I did everything, except major surgery (where I was expected to assist). As time went on, more and more specialists took over more and more of the things we previously did.

I am fearful that, in the big cities where most family doctors don't have hospital privileges, more and more of them will lose their expertise and their knowledge because they aren't using it enough. Limited practice within family practice is becoming more common, psychotherapy, anaesthesia, emerge. Anaesthesia and emerge have become a popular combination. There is no overhead, but also there is no follow-up, so no opportunity to learn what becomes of your actions. I see too many new graduates who gave up obstetrics immediately or emerge or house calls. I am often stopped by ex-patients who are not very happy with the direction of family practice. The time in appointments is very limited often limited to one complaint, and they often say I only see the side of the doctor's face because they are busy typing on their computer, patients are seldom examined, instead tests are ordered and referrals made. What happened to eye contact; it was supposed to be important when I went to school. The doctors must take time to listen to their patients' legitimate problems, even if they don't understand why they should worry so much about things. How do the older folks with several diagnoses deal with the one complaint rule of some doctors?

Nurse practitioners have had their status elevated, as have pharmacists – and of course everyone is an instant authority on everything having looked up on the internet. When it comes to evaluating medication, they seem to consider only the side effects – as does the press which does a great disservice to people scaring them so much. People often won't take their medications until the next hospital admission. Pills don't work well in the fridge.

Will comprehensive family practice survive? It seems that it is mostly found now in small areas with few specialists. Does it matter if family practice in a comprehensive matter devolves into limited practices of various kinds?

I believe it matters a great deal.

The comprehensive family doctor looked after everything and deployed specialists as they felt necessary. They were your doctor literally from birth to the grave. They got to know you very, very well over a lifetime and understood all sides of your personality. The doctor was in a perfect position to understand your reactions to various interventions in your life and to give advice appropriately. You trusted them and their advice. They were your advocate and helped to guide you through the medical system, which governments are constantly changing (frequently in a politically motivated manner).

The good thing about our system is that everyone is covered. Despite politicians' admonitions to the contrary, we still have very long waits for almost everything. We have no private medical system and no comprehensive pharma-care system, which every other developed country in the world has. I laugh when politicians say that our medical system is the envy of the world. If their eyes were actually open and not clouded by preconceived ideas, they must see the deficiencies. These politicians need to take a look at some other countries and compare them to ours. It has already been done, of course, but I think they like to make up their own stories, and they don't look very carefully.

ADVICE FOR YOUNG DOCTORS

Would I give advice to new family doctors? Only if they ask for it, which lots wouldn't because, of course, when you graduate you know everything. But if they wanted my advice, here are a few things that could be useful.

1. On a personal note, probably my only regret is that I never totally overcame my fear of public speaking, and it has influenced some of my choices, especially around university appointments. Would life have been better? I doubt it, but you wonder, so practice your public speaking!

2. Don't let money be your main interest or measure of your success. Chasing it is futile. There will always be someone with more.

3. Pick your specialty (including family practice) from what you love doing. Ignore the money and prestige angle.

4. Live where you would want to live if you weren't a doctor. There is always medical work to be done everywhere as long as you can adapt to not having all kinds of exotic tests and specialists immediately available. Family practice in remote areas has great rewards.

5. You should enjoy and get a real sense of satisfaction out of your work tending to people. If not, find out why not and change it.

6. Have fun. My feeling is that, if it's not fun, don't do it anymore.

7. Remember your family is number one in the long run, so nurture your relationship with your partner and children.

8. Stay active physically and mentally; engage in outside activities, in sports, have hobbies, go to groups etc.

9. Holidays are important. They refresh you, and your energy is rejuvenated. I recall a New York City psychiatrist whom I looked after every summer for quite a few years with his family. He maintained that it took eight weeks off every year for a doctor to become normal again. Perhaps he was right.

10. Remember that it is a privilege to be an M.D. I hope every new doctor can enjoy and appreciate the practice of medicine as much as I have over fifty-seven years.

PALLIATIVE CARE AND THE ONE'S FINAL DAYS (ADVANCE DIRECTIVES AND TRANSPLANTS)

We all must die at some time and in some fashion. It would be nice to have some (as much as possible) control over that. By now, we know how we should live and how to try to enhance it. Eating the right food, exercise, sleep, and stress reduction all help, but despite that there is a finish line.

Can we influence that? Definitely, and I wish more people *would* by having advanced directives. Let people know. Write it down. Do you want CPR and under what circumstances? Write it down! Make sure your people, your friends and relatives, know because when it comes to needing a decision NOW, there is nothing worse than a family squabble with gridlock that leads to bad feelings, even resentment, when you need to support each other. You must reach consensus beforehand. If you cannot, then the Power of Attorney is in charge.

An important, indeed vital, part of this discussion is the possibility of a transplant that might save someone else's life. It really is the gift of life. There may be some solace, and some people look upon it as a type of immortality (or at least life after death) in that one part of their loved one is still alive. There are restrictions on age-related body parts, but there is great satisfaction knowing the importance of what you have done.

I had a sister, who never smoked in her life, but she had a very rare lung condition and needed a lung transplant. She was on the list for eighteen months and took an apartment across the road from the transplant hospital, but to no avail. She died waiting. There must've been someone out there that could have saved her. We all tend to agree it's a good idea, and I'm going to sign on for that tomorrow. Other things come up, so it doesn't happen. Please talk about it!

I believe our transplant system needs major changes. Spain and other European counties have a system that makes everyone a donor unless they specifically opt out. It forces you to think about it and provides more donors.

It seems irrelevant, but I recall the time one of my son-in-laws shot his first deer. He brought it around in his truck to show us. Being a naturalist and conservationist I thought, *poor deer*. As I thought more about this, however, I realized that the deer had been healthy, enjoying its life until the time of its sudden death. If it had not been shot, how would it have died? As it gets a little older, not so fast, possibly a little disabled, it probably would've been taken down by a wolf pack or a cougar. It would've died a miserable death, since the wolf packs, for instance, start to eat before their prey is fully dead. It makes being shot look merciful after all. Animals don't get to die in bed surrounded by family.

Palliative care is huge right now, and I've worked as a palliative physician. It's a matter of keeping the patient comfortable during their final days. This, has come a long way and works for *virtually* everyone now, but not everyone! For some people, under some circumstances I think that doctor assisted suicide would be a more reasonable approach.

Beyond that there is euthanasia, which is a very different thing – but I believe has a place nonetheless if life has lost all meaning and importance to people. There will be great debate and resistance, however; so, if you think it might be reasonable for you under certain circumstances, write it down. Tell others.

So, the decision has been made not to have any more active treatment – what *do* you want? What do you *expect*?

Write it down.

Typically, the further a family has travelled to attend a patient, the greater their demands and expectations. Guilt is a major player there because often the patient hasn't been seen for a long time. The relatives who have readier day-to-day access and who are close to the patient will virtually always have more knowledge and understanding of the situation. In the final days, *comfort* is the word that applies to all things that would make you content.

For myself (and we are all different), I would like to be outside in the sunshine or perhaps in the dappled shade of a maple or red oak tree with a warm sun and a gentle breeze just moving the leaves a little. In the near background would be Beethoven's Ninth Symphony, and all my family would be surrounding the bed, my wife holding my hand if that is possible. Beethoven's Ninth would reach the final crescendo as I left this earth.

FAMILY PRACTICE – WHAT'S GOOD ABOUT IT?

I became almost a part of many families, so much so that I became almost that uncle, a grandfather, a best friend, a confidant. In other words, I did sometimes fill a necessary role in some people's lives. I was someone they could talk to in confidence without fear of being judged – at least in the sense that a legal judge could take legal action. My role was to listen primarily, perhaps advise or suggest, or at least try to lead people in a reasonable direction.

I can remember a couple of times having a patient in my office who I knew the police were looking for. My lawyer suggested I not tell the police, and so I didn't.

With their physical problems, if I could not diagnose the problem, then I made sure to have a plan to refer to someone who could. Almost always, I would have a good relationship with my patients. If you have a good relationship, the patient will go along with your recommendations.

I would often, after presenting a patient with alternatives, be asked what I would do in their place.

Understanding that everyone is different, as are their circumstances, it's probably a good idea to preface recommendations with that statement. I was in a much better position to help them with decisions by virtue of the fact that I had known them for a long time – and presumably they had faith in my judgment. Most people, if they have a physician whom they trust, are less likely to spend hours on the internet searching for answers and getting upset and confused.

On the rare occasions when a patient disagrees with you once you have diagnosed their problem and offered a course of action, you can explain your position. If they, are still wanting to go in what you consider the wrong direction, you have a choice of giving them what they want or sticking to your principles, in which case, they might leave. I can think of a couple of examples. Many years ago, a mother brought in a child with measles. She wanted penicillin to cure it. I tried to explain the reasons why it was not a reasonable thing, but she was adamant, so she left the practice. I'm sure it was better for both of us.

Another patient with mechanical back pain insisted on seeing an orthopedic surgeon in Toronto. I could see no reason for that. I told her so and recommended physiotherapy and some other modalities. She was angry enough to write the college that I wouldn't send her. They suggested I just do it. I did. When she saw the surgeon, he lambasted her for wasting his time.

Another bipolar lady had done very well on the drug lithium for ten years, and regular blood tests which were always normal, but then one day she became toxic. There was no change in her dose, so *maybe* she inadvertently took some extra pills. Once settled, she was subsequently very suspicious. When I saw her three weeks later, she said she now had thirty-five side effects of lithium. She had not had any lithium for over a month, so I said I doubted all the symptoms she had were related; however, she was not pleased with my explanation. When I saw her in another three weeks, she was now convinced she had fifty-four side effects. No amount of explanation could change her mind, and she refused any other medication and left the practice. I happen to know that, unhappily, she was never able to settle in with any other doctor despite a few tries so she bounced around the community never really recovering. Was it my responsibility? Should I have forced her to an institution at that time? I didn't think originally that she was a danger to herself or anyone else, but in retrospect she was a long-term danger to herself.

The positive sides of family practice include heartfelt thanks, respect, and genuine affection. Even now many years after I gave up my practice, I get a lot of hugs and handshakes from ex-patients when I see them in stores and on the street. It is very gratifying, and so many have asked if I could just look after them. Your reputation is an important thing, and it spreads to other people. You are respected often by people you don't even know, but they know *you* – or at least know *about* you, which is almost the same thing. It always makes me anxious when people come up to me and insist that they've heard a lot about me.

"Mostly good, I hope."

As I've said, there is so much opportunity to learn from people beyond just their medical history and personality – there are their hobbies, jobs, and interests.

Many years ago the only hangman in Ontario was a patient. He was the guy who knew how to tie the knot. Even his wife didn't know what he did. It's not something you could talk about generally. I was his chance to vent. He has been out of a job for a long time now, and I'm sure he has since passed away. I wonder if he ever told anyone else about his job.

If things are going well, you develop a sense of confidence and satisfaction, but you must be careful you don't become overconfident and too sure of yourself. Realistically appraise your strengths and weaknesses periodically. To be too confident is a trap. You may overstep your abilities. If you don't know the answer, it's okay to admit it. There is nothing wrong with saying, "I don't know but I can find out."

And of course, there is nothing wrong making referrals if you find yourself stumped or out of your depth. In fact, it is the ethical thing to do.

There is a great deal of fun in family practice. Be sure to enjoy it when it presents itself because there are downsides as well.

The hours are long. Sometimes you are dealing with uncertainty, and you must have a mindset that can handle that. You will make less money than your specialist colleagues. The question of prestige is one you will have to decide for yourself. And as a family doctor, you must stay on top of everything all the time which requires considerable diligence.

People asked me why I went to such remote places. I had to think about that myself. A few things are probably involved.

First, I was never fearful of what illnesses might appear because I was around when we had to do almost everything ourselves and before extensive laboratory and testing capabilities were available. My training taught me, to trust my own clinical skills, and that always served me well in remote areas.

Second, I have an interest in aboriginal spirituality and general approach to life. I'm talking about those who are still living "on the land" and less affected by our modern ways that have adulterated their relatively pristine previous existence. They are part of the land, and their spirituality is connected. I have certainly not had contact with all the aboriginals in the world, but have learned a lot from the Inuit, Inuvialuit, and many other First Nation tribes in Canada and the Métis as well; then there were the Māori and the Moriori of New Zealand, the Aboriginal Australians, and some of the tribes of South America. Although they have different stories, their basic concepts are the same. The central theme, with many variations, is their relationship to earth, nature, and their inherent *spirituality* (or whatever word describes to the individual what they derive from that relationship). Perhaps there is no proper word to describe the inner feeling involved, but it seems understood (without argument) by most aboriginals.

Third, I have a great interest and curiosity about nature, so I am particularly looking for rare species and events, which are more likely to be found in remote areas. The black robins, the magenta petrels, the antics of Chatham pigeons, the wolf pack howling in the presence of the northern lights, the Namibian desert dunes at sunrise, the Galapagos cormorants, and so many other life-altering occasions.

RETIRED. SO, WHAT IS AHEAD
TO LOOK FORWARD TO?

My beloved wife Marian arranged a huge retirement party for me that was attended by about two hundred and fifty people – most of whom I had not seen for many years. She did it entirely without my knowledge. The kids and grandkids were all there also, and Stephen, our youngest son, was the master of ceremonies. I was totally surprised. I thought I was going to someone *else's* party. Some of the other family members spoke also and surprised me with their words.

Fortunately, I have lots of hobbies, so I will be at them with renewed vigour now that my days are my own. So much to occupy my time: photography, carving, travelling, paddling, skiing, snowshoeing, nature observations, writing my book, presentations, fixing and fiddling with wood, birch bark, and buckskin, maybe I'll even try my hand at root type furniture.

PART TWO
TRAVELLING

Travelling is something you either enjoy or you don't. Why do we travel? I guess there is an innate curiosity about other environments, cultures, and climates and most of us love to learn about and experience new, different, sometimes exciting, sometimes risky things. I hate to think I missed out on something like a chance to do something different. Does that mean I have to try absolutely everything? No! There are a number of things I have not attempted, and I'm not missing them, for example, skydiving, not on my list at the moment.

A lot of our travels were interspersed with work – although the majority of cruises and lengthy tours were done after retirement from the office at the beginning of 2000. To be truthful, I can't remember the exact dates of some of them before 2000 which is when I started a diary on our travels. If Marian can't remember either, which would be unusual, they will be lost to the mists of time.

As a child, my family did virtually no travelling. We went to my grandparents' cottage quite often and went for Sunday drives. Ostensibly we were looking for a farm property. It never happened.

At the cottage, we did a lot of fishing, swimming, and chasing of frogs and butterflies but no real travelling. We stuck around the cottage and the nearby lake.

I got interested in looking around the next corner or turn in the river. Was there something new and different there? Possibly! I better have a look, maybe there is a deer there or some new butterfly, bird, or wildflower. And so began an insatiable love of travelling because there is always something or somewhere that needs to be discovered.

We have travelled a lot in a lot of countries, so we have a lot of tales to tell, but I will confine the remainder of this book to what I considered to be the more interesting, meaningful, or instructive locations.

As a doctor, I was very sure I would not spend my entire life in Toronto – after all, both the fishing and skiing were poor – so after interning in Toronto, I headed to Vancouver to do a year of internal medicine. A whole new world opened up with mountains, rivers, ocean, new wildlife, plants, and activities. Even the prairies were fascinating, especially the pronghorn antelopes and their speed.

Being a skier who'd never attempted beyond anything more rugged than the Laurentians or New England, I looked to Mount Baker (a magnificent quiescent volcano in Washington State that could be seen from Vancouver) with awe. Whistler was only a dream at the time, so we drove to Mount Baker in July. That was overwhelming for a Toronto boy. Awesome, an overused word, was very appropriate.

We went to Boston next, which was the mecca for internal medicine. Karen was born there, and we carried Karen around in the bottom drawer if we drove anywhere. You could get lobster culls (parts missing – not presentable) down at the dock for fifty cents, so even poverty-stricken residents could afford that. Despite the fact that we were in the Kennedys' hometown – and he was our patient – all of the doctors were Republicans and couldn't understand why we admired John F Kennedy.

From Boston we moved to Orillia for one year in order to catch up a little financially, but I guess I never did because I spent fifty-four years in Orillia doing family practice. Travelling was still a major interest as the family grew to four children. We did a lot of skiing and camping, mostly with a soft-top tent trailer or canoe.

I will try to hit the highlights of our adventures rather than attempt a comprehensive travelogue.

8. CANADA

Vancouver Island off the west coast of Canada has many things to recommend it, and we have spent quite a lot of time there. Victoria is a clean vibrant city with an excellent harbour and great botanical show places.

Cathedral Grove, about a third of the way up-island, has many gigantic old-growth trees including Douglas fir, western red cedar and Sitka spruce.

On the West Coast are a lot of beaches which you can hike into or even camp on. Ucluelet at the south west of Vancouver Island has a lot of rocks and shoals, crashing surf mixed in with some great sand beaches and lots of hikes as well. The one hike right in Ucluelet is especially scenic but also the most used. Tofino has easy road access. It is around forty kilometres northwest of Ucluelet vie Highway 4 and has great surfing and kayaking. Clayoquot Sound and Mears Island are definitely worth the effort in kayaks or canoes.

The drive through the mountains from Port Alberni had some great photo ops, and it's the only way through to the west coast of the island. Further north on the inland side of Vancouver Island, there is whale watching at Telegraph Cove where we were lucky enough to see some of the offshore orcas. The captain was very excited about it. He has only once in thirty years seen them before. They traveled their usual thirty kilometres each day, and he said they would be past the island by tomorrow on their way to Alaska. They were breaching a lot and yet their sonar apparatus picked up nothing. The usual pods that they see almost daily are all known by sight and by sound. He felt that they must be navigating by sight. At any rate, we were lucky again to see such a rare event.

There is skiing at Mount Washington on Vancouver Island, but it is very prone to weather change, so could be ice or could even be without snow. It was icy and foggy when we were there, not a good combo, especially if you don't know the mountain.

Campbell River is famous for its salmon fishing. It also has ferry connections to various Gulf Islands. There are actually quite good ferry connections with many of the islands, Salt Spring, Quadra, Main, Texada, Gabriola just to name a few.

Prairie smoke

Where we live just 30 kms outside of Orillia is on the edge of the Laurentian Shield so that one side of the Lake has the Carden Plain which is limestone alvar and home to many rare species of plants and birds and insects. The north side of the lake is all granite, many islands and bays etc. It is *the edge of the Laurentian shield.* We live at the end of a two-kilometre peninsula in the middle of lake Dalrymple. The peninsula (really a drumlin) was gouged out by the last glacier, and it runs northeast so we get the sunrise across the lake in the morning and the sun set in the evening. It is the best possible situation.

Fall in Ontario

Sometimes we miss the mountains, but then we remind ourselves that the sun didn't come up until about ten in the morning then went behind the mountains again about three, so not much sun really, and you can't have everything.

I've talked about the West Coast and the Arctic (and will cover the Maritimes next chapter). What about the middle? Ontario is huge and takes about two to three days to drive across. It even takes two days from where we live in central Ontario if you are heading west.

Northern Ontario along the north shore of Lake Superior has scattered habitation and many, many rushing rivers and remote lakes. Remember, Ontario has five hundred thousand lakes, and if you are up in a small plane it looks like it's almost fifty percent water. Canada has more freshwater lakes than the rest of the world put together. Just think of the potential fishing, canoeing, and camping possibilities.

The prairies are not totally flat, but some areas such as Winnipeg and Regina are very flat so the most pronounced part becomes the sky, the sunrise, sunsets, and watching the storms move around. A lot of people love the flat lands.

I prefer the rolling prairies with some wildlife. Saskatchewan's Grasslands National Park along the Montana border and, further west, Cypress Hills Interprovincial Park (two protected areas one of which straddles the Saskatchewan/Alberta border) are both great parks full of wildlife. I was surprised to see pelicans in Cypress Hills. Grasslands National had bison, prairie dogs, badgers, and my favourite, the pronghorns. They are so stately looking and can run at tremendous speed, the fastest land mammal in North America they can reach speeds of close to ninety kilometres an hour over short distances.

ALGONQUIN PARK

We spent a number of summers camping at Algonquin Park, mostly at Rock Lake, from whence we would hike or paddle with short portages with the kids. Most often I would take two of them at a time for overnight excursions maybe a lake or two away meaning that some portaging was all part of the experience. I recall one night when we were camping on a little island there was a great clattering of utensils outside. Wearing what you usually wear in a sleeping bag, I emerged to find a pair of raccoons making off with our pots. A chase ensued to recover the pots. I guess the terrifying sight of a naked man chasing them through the bush at night was too much. They dropped the pots. Another night we had planned on fishing in the morning, I left some worms in a can underneath the fold out of the trailer where we were sleeping. At about five in the morning we were suddenly rocking up and down in the bed. The bear was directly below us and enjoying the worms. You learn as you go.

Another evening around the campfire, a bear appeared heading directly for us. He was probably confused by all the food smells and the campfire. My wife wisely got behind me. The bear, vision not being there strong point, came perhaps six to eight feet in front of me looked up and circled around just as if I was a tree before lumbering off. We heard some shots later, so I'm afraid the poor guy met the ministry somewhere. A lot of people had been quite frightened as he had wandered through the campground.

Our annual canoe trip with the boys in the spring was always anticipated. We took different routes over the years including the Magnetawan River, the Black River, and various Algonquin lake and river systems. Speckled trout was a main thrust of the trips, but we had a lot of campfires and fun. We had some bad weather, sometimes pouring rain, even snow – and don't forget the black flies that time of year.

One year we took a lawyer with us who had no experience. He looked up everything he could about canoeing and camping, but he had never portaged. The killer for him, though, were the black flies. It turned out to be the worst year ever according to the Ministry of Natural Resources. I believe they assess them by having a metre square cheesecloth or equivalent over some running water where they breed. I'm not sure how long they leave it there, but we were told there were fifty thousand black flies per square metre. You might as well stop swatting and surrender. You are outnumbered!

9. CAMPING

MARITIMES AND NEWFOUNDLAND
IN THE EARLY SIXTIES

Our first visit to Newfoundland involved driving the south shore of the St. Lawrence and around the Gaspé Peninsula and camping there before catching the ferry from North Sydney over to Argentia in Placentia Bay at the St. John's end.

We saw a number of whales and whale spouts along the way. Since we were camping, we had to buy supplies along the way. At that time, late nineteen sixties, we had a lot of trouble finding fresh fruit or vegetables and milk, but we camped in an excellent campground north of St. John's called Terranova. There was a good trout river close at hand. Many people fished starting at the bridge by the highway. I was determined to go up a mile before starting to fish. About there, I came to some falls with a large pool below. Nobody else had been seen for the last half mile. The fishing was incredible, virtually a two to three-pound trout with every cast. When I was up in the twenties, I believe, I kept one or two and headed back for trout dinner with the family. We did a lot of hiking, including one little lake where the fire warden in the fire tower above it said he had not seen anyone else carry a canoe in there for fifteen years. Great fishing and even managed to land an arctic char. There was just a very short stream down to the Atlantic.

We drove across the island to the Gros Morne National Park which was a very rudimentary setup at that time. Of course, we had to walk into the fjord and climb Gros Morne Mountain. Interestingly the local people have climbed Gros Morne forever, but since it just became a National Park the so-called experts in Ottawa decided where the trail should go using their topographical maps. Unfortunately, the topographical maps don't show boulders, so the trail went up over a boulder field. It was the worst possible route. When we got to the top, the fog moved in, so visibility was limited. One of the kids, Erik, hurt himself in the boulders on the way down. It was a long carry. I'm sure the route must have changed by now.

L'Anse aux Meadows had received a lot of press, so we drove there. It is thought to be the first Viking settlement in the New World, established hundreds of years before the arrival of Columbus. At that time there was nothing except one person with a small spade digging. He could tell us about it a bit, where the old fire pits had been etc. I understand there is a full display there now.

Never having been to Labrador, we went to Flower's Cove and took the ferry over to Blanc-Sablon, which is on the Quebec-Labrador border. The ferry could hold seven cars, all on the deck. You drove up a ramp onto the deck and then a group of men put chains under the car and lifted it sideways, one grunt at a time, to make room for the next car. You then had a choice of staying in the car, which had been secured, or going into a small cabin for the crossing. The kids wisely opted for the cabin. I decided to stay with the car. Another big mistake! I learned something else. Small boats are much more prone to be affected by big ocean waves than larger ones. Each time the boat rolled, and I was looking right into the sea, I was hoping they did a good job of securing. THEY DIDN'T ADMIT TO LOSING ANYBODY.

The Canadian Automobile Association had given us maps and suggested routes. This included driving back from Blanc-Sablon along the north shore of the St. Lawrence River, which I thought was a great idea. We would see more country. The only problem was, there was no road back to the rest of Canada from there – still isn't beyond Vieux Fort. So we drove east instead past L'Anse-Amour, L'Anse-au-Loup, L'Anse-au-Diable, admiring the rushing rivers and wide open and totally unpopulated hills and mountains, very impressive. We crossed the Pinware River on our return where we could see salmon jumping the falls and dropped into a lodge where they were kind enough to put us up for the night. The last time I slept double in a single saggy cot. Slept may be overstating the situation. The kids were happy, and it was Karen's birthday. They even whipped up a cake for her. It was an exciting birthday at a salmon lodge in Labrador. What more could a young girl ask for?

The next day I thought I must fish. For this a guide is mandatory, and of course, a license. The guide explained that the salmon were not hungry. They're going upstream to spawn so you aggravate them by dragging the fly across their nose. There were salmon everywhere. You couldn't miss. The guide and the game warden sat up on the bank smoking cigarettes while I lashed away dragging it across their noses. I only had one salmon on for probably ten seconds before it jumped downstream over a little set of falls and broke the line. The guide at the end of the day, since we had nothing to show for it, caught two with no difficulty. One was for supper and one to take with us. "Fry it in lard" was their advice. It did seem to work. Before we left, he took us to a set of falls about twelve feet high that the salmon were jumping, an amazing sight. There were up to a dozen in the air at any one time. I didn't even own a camera at that time, so no pictures. One man, incidentally, had gone downstream to the area where the river entered the ocean and caught twenty-five trout averaging about five pounds. Most people seemed to think he had wasted his time. I'm not so sure about that.

We had to take the ferry back to Newfoundland so we, drove down to Port aux Basques and took the ferry back to Nova Scotia. , The crew said it was the roughest day of the year. Virtually everybody was vomiting.

Our second trip down there, several years later, we had to sleep on the floor on the ferry. The trip was a month, and it rained every day except one. That day it snowed. Again, we camped around and did some trout fishing, which was always great. The boys especially appreciated that. Gros Morne was much more developed the second trip.

On the way back, we camped at Rivière-du-Loup on the south shore of the St. Lawrence where we met both rudeness and a great understanding of prejudice and its roots, as mentioned earlier. The fun the kids were having, made us see the possibilities for long-term changes in attitude.

COCHRANE AND LAKE SUPERIOR IN THE SEVENTIES

We decided to try different spots to camp each year so one year we went to Cochrane and took the Polar Express to Moosonee and then the freighter canoes (big square ended canoes with motors) over to Moose factory.

I met an engineer from Orillia who explained their above ground heating system by insulated pipes. It seemed to work. It was the kids first experience, I believe, with First Nations kids mostly Cree. In that area the graves were all marked in Cree.

Getting back down to Cochrane, we then continued our journey west along the north shore of Lake Superior, climbed the Sleeping Giant, a giant mesa, in what was then Sibley Provincial Park (now

Sleeping Giant Provincial Park) and then crossed the border at Duluth and continued along the south shore of Lake Superior before crossing again at Sault Ste. Marie. The most notable thing about the south shore of Lake Superior was the flies. They were fierce with long, sharp fangs.

NEW ENGLAND AND CAPE COD

Continuing our attempt to see as many places as we could, we set off for Cape Cod camping via New York, Vermont, and New Hampshire before descending into Massachusetts and Cape Cod. One of the things I envisioned there was surfing with my Sportspal canoe. It was very light with Styrofoam lining. As I approached the beach with the canoe on my head, the lifeguard came to meet me. When I told him what I had in mind, he insisted I do that "down past that post" and pointed where he wanted me to go. I realised that he did not want to be responsible for my demise. I tried it twice, but with the big waves and a strong crosswind, I could not get a decent start and so the results were a great flailing mess with me in the middle of it. I'm not quite sure why I tried it again, with the same result, but at least the kids got a good laugh out of it. We stuck with body surfing after that.

ALASKA (1971)

Having enjoyed our camping so much in Algonquin, Cape Cod, and New England, we decided to go for a big one. Alaska and back! And so, we got what information we could. Remember, there was no Google then, and we knew the Alaska Highway was brutal. It was necessary to have a pan under the car and a screen on the front to try to prevent damage to lights and windshield. Despite that we had ten flat tires, mostly on a tent trailer that we took with us. I was still married to Gigi at the time and she did not want to go, so the four kids and I went with their German nanny Evelyn. She was a great help, never complained, and we still have maintained contact almost fifty years later – she married a Canadian and lives in British Columbia.

Our route was across northern Ontario and the Yellowhead Highway across the prairies. One day in Saskatchewan, a fierce wind blew our trailer over. There was no one in it at the time. We took the Alaska Highway starting at Dawson Creek, British Columbia. It was thirteen hundred miles of brutal stones and gravel and virtually no traffic. We usually camped beside lakes or rivers and as we neared the Alaska border we stopped at Liard River Hot Springs Provincial Park. The timing was just right. We were hot and dirty from the very dusty road, and there were cold springs too. Generally, back then, the further north, the less regulation or facilities. In fact, most of the places we stayed had no office or gate or even a sign. The Alaska Highway book indicated at what mileage to look for them. A clearing near a river or lake was usual. We had a bear family for breakfast one morning. I think they liked my cooking – or maybe it was the bacon. They seemed content once they had that and disappeared.

At the Alaska border, they would not let Evelyn – a teacher from Germany – in without a visa, so we had to wait a day until we got it sorted out. While waiting at the border, we chanced to see a taxi from Edmonton pass with two little old ladies sitting in the back seat. The next day we heard that a taxi driver from Edmonton had been found murdered. Were those *really* two little old ladies in the backseat?

We drove through Anchorage through Chugach National Forest toward Seward (the community not the peninsula). We camped there. I slept in the back of the station wagon. Evelyn slept with the kids in the tent trailer. About four in the morning, I was awakened by a crashing sound. A gigantic brown bear was trying to get at the garbage which was in cans on a large square concrete slab. The cans fit into grooves and then heavy metal bars held them in place. This bear was angry. He turned the concrete slab and garbage upside down and then sauntered away. It occurred to me that he could've turned my car over or the tent trailer very easily. They would weigh a lot less than what he *did* turn over. At any rate, he sauntered away, and the next campsite was maybe thirty metres away. As the bear walked by their tent, a lady stuck her head out. She was still screaming fifteen minutes later when the bear was long gone. She probably scared him.

Another evening, we pulled in late to a rudimentary campsite with no office and no facilities beside a little lake with a point where there had been a campfire before. There were four to five large American RVs already there, but they were asleep. We got the kids into the tent trailer (with Evelyn) and I settled in in the back of the station wagon. Shortly after falling asleep, around two or three in the morning, five carloads of drunken kids drove in, started a fire and began shooting their guns. What to do? Confront twenty-five drunken kids or just hope the bullets were going some other direction. Some of the Americans were getting a little perturbed and had their own guns out behind their rigs and firing them. Where? They were preparing to leave. After a very long couple of hours, the kids jumped in their cars and drove off. In the morning, we saw a sign which read: in case of trouble call the state police at TOK junction. The only problem with that, , was that TOK junction was twenty-five miles away.and the nearest phone

Since Alaska was so remote, the radio reported people who were travelling by canoe or dogsled and where they were going. This was done carefully and clearly and then repeated so the destination was aware of when and where people started out and could be expected to appear. This was all before cell phones and satellite phones. Most of the highway signs in Alaska had the numbers and letters shot out of them. They loved their guns.

It was the radio as well that delivered sad news one night while we were driving towards Fairbanks, Alaska. Louis Armstrong had died. He was my favourite jazz musician. It was disturbing. Now, of course, it provides a ready timestamp on that day: July 6, 1971.

It was a high year for rabbits, so they were all over the place, jumping across the road. It was impossible not to hit a few.

We had just bought some new moccasins for Marla, and she wore them all the time, including on a glacier where she lost one down a crevasse. We could see it in the distance. With my fishing tackle, I was able to hook it and retrieve it. I was a hero that day.

Another day we spent most of a day climbing (hiking) up a mountain. It was great exercise and a great view.

There was a road that ran along the peaks in Alaska called Top of the World Highway on its way to Dawson city. Spectacular scenery, all around, and we saw virtually nobody the whole distance. We camped in Dawson city. The kids got a big kick out of the old-time stage show with dancing girls and old town atmosphere. From there, we sifted down through the Rockies before heading back across the prairies and home, a little over a month on this occasion and only ten flat tires. Fortunately, the stations along the way were well equipped with tires, but they were often up to a couple of hundred kilometres apart, so you had to always have at least two extra with you. Actually, we did have two flats at the same time once.

We did not stop at Cypress Hills or Grasslands National Park in Saskatchewan, but we did another time. They're both great, with lots of white tail deer, mule deer, prairie dog villages, and the those fast, graceful pronghorns. There was also the shorebird sanctuary off Highway 1, with all kinds of shorebirds Avocets etc.

CALIFORNIA (1972)

Our next big trip was across northern states, the Dakotas (badlands, cliff carvings of US presidents etc.) then up from Montana into the Kootenay area of Alberta and British Columbia and through to Vancouver where we camped in Marian's sister's backyard.

One of the places we stayed in Montana was just outside a Wild West type of town; it seemed sort of extra quiet and there were almost no campers. During the evening, however, something untoward happened in town, and whatever it was, it occasioned a police response and t wielding bullhorns.as theyordered people around. We just quietly left the next morning, so we never found out what really happened.

Montana reminded me of another time crossing it several years ago late at night. We had not seen a motel and we were despairing at the prospect of not finding beds. Finally, a barely visible little sign alerted us to a rundown looking place that we stopped at. They had two rooms that shared a common bathroom the doors to which were ragged curtains – one to each room. The price was two dollars for one and four dollars for the other room. No, it was not exactly five-star, but again you survive. You wondered if it might have been the scene of one of those horror movies.

Alberta and British Columbia were beautiful, and we are regular visitors there skiing most years. Heading south from British Columbia, we stayed pretty well along the coastline and usually waited until late afternoon to get a campsite. While we were in Oregon, we visited the beaches, of course, and found quite a few stone and shell fossils.

One day Marian was taking Stephen (the youngest) to the toilet, Walking along the beach. immediately behind her was Stephanie.

Marian returned with Stephen. "Where's Stephanie," she asked.

"She was with you," I said.

"No, she wasn't."

Panic stations. We ran down the beach, and there was Stephanie walking around with a policeman following her step by step. She was not having anything to do with someone she didn't know. She had not seen her mother turn into the toilet with Stephen. She was lost, but not worried. We did the worrying.

We drove on down to California, Big Sur country along the glorious Coastal Highway. I thought we really should camp among the redwoods so we drove into one of the campsites, where the person in charge practically laughed at us. You had to make reservations up to two years in advance. In the middle of this conversation, a man came in and said something had happened at his home and he had to leave. Lucky for us, we got his campsite which had a redwood that was fifty feet in circumference. It was massive. We spent a couple of days there with this immense tree. One of the tallest was right across the river from us. Everything was bigger there. Those slugs that you see on vegetation were seven inches long.

We followed the coast to San Francisco, Golden Gate Bridge, Alcatraz and all its stories, Fisherman's Wharf, the steep hills, streetcars and curvy little streets on the hills. All of this was new for the kids. A trial of swimming on the beaches reminded me of how bitterly cold the ocean was even that far south. In fact, it was quite a lot colder than in British Columbia. Ocean currents I guess?

Eventually we arrived in Los Angeles, where our campsite was a mostly permanent trailer park in a rather rundown area in Long Beach. The tent trailer with seven kids in those circumstances was a little dicey but no problems. We were all day at Disneyland and Universal Studios. We were up until midnight for the Main Street parade with Stephen (our youngest) asleep on my back. They were long days, but lasting memories for the kids

Universal Studios was a must while we were there, so we spent a day there seeing how some of the special effects worked; the parting of the dead sea, a flash flood rushing down the road at you, a gunfight with people falling off the roof, and pictures of the kids' amazing feats of strength. This was July, so we were now heading in land, where the heat was intense, and camped at Needles California – temperature one hundred and seven. We stopped in to get gas. The attendant had a sweater on.

"Why a sweater?" I asked."

"It's a little cool now," says he. "Last week it was one hundred and twenty."

It was hard to sleep some nights, but the kids were adaptable.

The Grand Canyon was the next big item, and again, we were lucky enough to get a campsite and spend a couple of days exploring this spectacular area. Personally, I was particularly impressed with the colours in the Painted Desert. We picked up some souvenirs T-shirts and hats. I wondered how long they would last.

In Utah, the monuments were spectacularly displayed and with virtually no one around it made it almost surreal. We then drove through Colorado and the flat states Ohio, Indiana, and finally home. It was a trip none of us would forget.

We had along with us fifteen-year-old Chris, our friend's son who we knew well, and he was a great help since there were nine of us in one station wagon. The kids arranged the schedule in the back where we kept an air mattress with pillows so that they could play games, sleep, or do whatever they wanted. Of course, this would be impossible now with seatbelt regulations. Still we came through unscathed. We would get out frequently and run around and play tag or climb a hill or something. We had a tent trailer behind us, and a big box on top of the station wagon where we kept all our food and a lot of supplies. Strapped on top of *that* was a canoe that served as the box's roof; I recall people taking pictures of our rig. Almost every night was a campfire with songs and stories – a good time by any standard.

10. CANOE TRIPS

Where we live in Ontario, there are a couple of rivers with some rapids up to grade three that we can access easily on a day trip or even a half a day, so that was our local playground. We also did canoe fishing trips every spring with the boys as mentioned previously. Marian and I made several trips, all mostly after the kids were grown.

One of my favourite pastimes as a young man was to explore new areas by canoe. Looking at the topographical maps, I would see remote lakes and rivers which always intrigued me. What was in there? Certainly, peace and quiet to relate to nature (the great spirit) and beauty. Often there would be superb fishing. One day I caught fifty-five bass good-sized. Another day I caught over one hundred bass. I virtually never took any home. To be that productive obviously means these lakes were very remote, often involving several portages and almost always I went alone. When you are young and strong you are invincible – well maybe not! Most often I didn't even tell anyone where I was going, until one day while bush-whacking from one lake to another with the canoe on my head, I sprained my ankle. It was a real effort to get out of there. If I had broken my leg I would still be there, and nobody would have ever known where. It takes some of us a little longer to learn pretty obvious safety precautions.

What follows are my recollection of a number of trips I've enjoyed with friends and family over the years.

THE NAHANNI RIVER (1988)

The Nahanni River in the Northwest Territories was our biggest canoe trip. We also met Fred Smith who was quite famous in canoeing circles there in Yellowknife. He was going to a different river, however. To get to the Nahanni, we flew to Yellowknife, where we met the group we were going with – the Black Feather Wilderness Adventure Company. From there, we flew to Fort Simpson on the Mackenzie River, and then flew with our canoe to Rabbitkettle Lake, which made for a medium-sized portage from the river. It was a very pretty little lake with all the unusual vegetation of the Arctic: reindeer moss, spongy tundra, many species of wildflowers, and Arctic cotton.

The river itself moved at almost twenty kilometres per hour, so we covered a lot of miles in a day. We were two weeks on the river, often losing touch of what day it was. It didn't seem to matter when we were so involved in nature. We were in magnificent surroundings and tried to pay attention to our paddling techniques. The number of people on the river is limited, so you would likely not see any other group.

The Black Feather Wilderness Adventure Company had guides that were excellent. No-trace camping is very important, so we were very careful about that, and it did look virginal almost everywhere. We happened to be there a year after an earthquake, so there was, funny looking slants on trees and rocks; it was also a time of flooding, so the river was silty and really moving and powerful. The rapids were challenging. Virginia Falls, when we got there, were huge and magnificent. It was higher than Niagara, and the rapids below it in Fourth Canyon had huge standing waves such that, even with spray skirts, we would have to burst through the waves. Everything was wet. We did five miles in fifteen minutes, it really was moving, exciting and threatening. The cliffs of the canyons were very steep and probably twenty-five hundred feet high so don't think about taking a rest part way.

We did see some mountain goats a couple of times and a bear was right behind our tent one morning. We saw a grizzly one day eating some berries and paying no attention at all to us – that was on a little side trip hiking to the Tufa Mounds – big limestone formations where water started from the top in the middle and ran down the sides leaving ridges and pools.

The other side trip was to Sun Blood Mountain which was across the river just above Virginia Falls. A wonderful hike up the mountain gave a panoramic view of the surrounding area. It was customary to leave a rock on the pile of rocks that others have left before, although you do feel like you're the only one who had ever been there. How small you feel in these giant surroundings, and yet somehow, the smaller you feel, the better you feel. Why is that?

One particular rapid was prefaced by a large whirlpool known as Hell's Gate. The guide made it clear that anyone who didn't want to run Hell's Gate wouldn't have to. There were two German doctors in our group, an ophthalmologist and a gynecologist, and they were quite fearful. They convinced Marian she didn't have to do it, so I did it with another man who had dumped on his first try. We just couldn't coordinate, so we dumped also. The water was three degrees celius, so it got your attention very quickly. One canoe dragged us over to the sand beach while the two guides with a lot of difficulty had to catch up to our canoe and pull it back up the river to the sand beach, while the rest of us paddled down to what we called the Nahanni laundromat. It was called that because every branch as far as we could see had something wet hanging over it. A warm fire helped a lot too.

A lot of interesting people do this type of thing. Two American businessmen who did a canoe trip every year said they had been planning Nahanni for twelve years. There was a single lawyer who I think must've had Crohn's disease, and a semiretired nurse with malignant melanoma who said she had wanted to do the Nahanni all her life, a couple from Toronto and he was an accountant, then there was the German couple, and of course, me and Marian. The Germans were amateurish enough that they had to be split up, each one with a guide. We had two young men in their early twenties as our guides, and they were amazing paddlers and terrific with people. There was no other significant event until we got down to Nahanni Butte where a bus was *supposed* to meet us. Several bridges had been washed out because of the flooding so we had to paddle an extra seventy-five miles down the Liard River where the bus picked us up and we got back to a ferry, from there back to Fort Simpson then an aircraft to Yellowknife and finally home again.

We did run into a German Television crew along the way that I guess was doing a documentary on the river. They had at least one male singer with a powerful baritone voice that was so compatible with the surroundings that it gave you a little chill up your spine. We saw no little birds on the river, but some large shorebirds and a great gray owl. There were no bugs either until we got down to Nahanni Butte, where the mosquitoes were suddenly swarming us and very attentive. No doubt they had been amassing and planning their attack awaiting our arrival.

Plans to do the mountain river in the Northwest Territory in 1990 were abandoned when Marla and Stephanie decided to get married that year. Then Krista got married in 1991. Despite my best effort, I simply could not convince them to all get married the same day. Think of the savings! I guess maybe that wasn't the first thing on their minds?

MISSINAIBI (THE LATE NINETIES)

We started the trip from Hearst in Northern Ontario and took the Algoma Central Railway down toward the Agawa Canyon and Sault Saint Marie except we weren't going that far. The train stopped at the side of a little lake (Wabatongushi). We unloaded all our equipment and began our two-week trip. We found some deserted villages along the way. Oba and Peterbell were nothing but ruins, but it's easy to speculate on what life would have been like for the people who lived there long ago.

The first week we spent doing rapids and portages and crossed the Atlantic/Arctic watershed divide. One interesting thing evolved. We were pounding through a remote lake, and we saw a young boy sitting by himself on a rocky little island then another and another all by themselves no book no canoe no equipment. It turned out there was a private boys outdoor school on the lake, but I guess this was an attempt to get them to relate to nature, perhaps learn to "feel the outdoors" and even to philosophise a little. I thought it was a great idea.

After a week, we arrived at Lake Missinaibi Provincial Park which had a road to it and a remote campground which no one was attending at the time. There was no staff seen either. One person in our group, an engineer, spent his lunch making masts and booms for each canoe so suddenly we had sailboats which we sailed the length of the lake lashed together perhaps twenty miles. We were slowed down by a swamp where the next portage began.

Lake Missinaibi had quite a large number of pictographs which were well preserved. There were lots of rapids some of them tough and quite famous – Green Hill was a good one, and we did manage to make it through unscathed, so we were getting better and better at those things. No dumping on this trip, it was just a very pretty river, lots of wildlife (ducks, moose, etc.) and clear, dark water. We found some flints and arrowheads on the sand beach at Missinaibi Park. On the way back, we had to portage the aptly named Thunder Falls. The trip was sort of a loop, and we finished up back on highway eleven not that far from where we started. I guess you could say that we spent two weeks that accomplished virtually nothing. However, anything to get you out in nature for two weeks was certainly worth it

DUMOINE RIVER (2000)

When we did the Dumoine River in Québec, we arranged that through Black Feather the same group that had taken us down the Nahanni in 1988. We had to meet on the Ottawa River and were flown, with our canoes, into the starting point in a small lake. As we were waiting to see who else would come, Marian was concerned because there were no other women at the site. She was right. She was the only woman on the trip a total of perhaps twelve people. The others were mostly lawyers and accountants from Ottawa. The conversation noticeably changed and deteriorated when she had to leave the campsite for nature's call, and then it would calm down when she returned. There were lots of challenging rapids. We spent the first day doing manoeuvres to practice, and then we were into it. We did exceptionally well except for one rapid where Marian misunderstood someone's directions and pulled us onto a rock. Thank goodness for those waterproof camera cases. Other than a sixteen hundred metre portage that was a real grunt, it was a great trip, and as always, you meet new people on all excursions. We ended up having to cross the Ottawa River which had significant current and that day a lot of wind also, so we did it as a flotilla sticking close together to break up the waves. Incidentally, we met the famous (in canoeing circles) Fred Smith who guides on the river. He said it was his seventy sixth canoe trip and that he knew those rapids well and was going by himself.

PUKASKWA PROVINCIAL PARK (2000)

Pukaskwa on Lake Superior was another canoe trip with the same friends. Lake Superior is the largest lake in North America, and the third largest freshwater lake in the world, and when we started there the water was rough and so it sort of made us cautious. The first day we had to hide in a place not very far from where we started. We finally got a little further along the shore, but again, heavy weather set in and we were forced to hide basically from the weather for a couple of days. Lake Superior is like an ocean – in fact, *gitch-gami*, the Ojibwe name for it means "great sea" – it even has a small tide which we measured. I was able to get some people interested in the microscopic world of the mosses, lichens, even rocks with a magnifying glass and a jeweller's lens. It really is quite fascinating to see things from an entirely different perspective. There were fires nightly, of course, gourmet food, and good fellowship. Eventually we were able to return to our starting point near Marathon.

OPEONGO (EARLY 2000S)

The Opeongo River starts in Algonquin Park, we attempted in it September one year with some friends we had canoed with before. It was probably a mistake because the water was very low, and so it made it virtually a rock garden. The first few days were through lakes in Algonquin Park having started up the East branch of Lake Opeongo which was the biggest lake in the park. There were times on the river when you actually had to get out and then pull your way through the rocks on foot. We had to use the ferry to get started down the east wing of the Opeongo and the person driving it showed us the place where a bear had swum over and killed two campers. There was lots of wildlife, lots of moose, deer, beavers, muskrats and some beautiful little lakes with nobody on them. It always makes me want to go back and spend more time on them. Why do we always seem to have a (usually self-imposed) deadline? Another enjoyable trip with good friends and good food, lots of laughs and communing with nature.

KILLARNEY PARK (EARLY 2000S)

Killarney Park off the north shore of Georgian Bay featured quartzite hills and offered some excellent canoeing throughout. A beautiful park established in 1964 in no small part due to the conservation efforts and lobbying of the Group of Seven – A.Y. Jackson in particular.

GEORGIAN BAY (EARLY 2000S)

Georgian Bay from the French River area over to Killarney was a beautiful quiet trip. It certainly required topographical maps because there were so many islands. It is called the Thirty Thousand Islands after all. Georgian Bay is big water, so most of the boats are big, but they must stay further out so in between all the little islands we had it all to ourselves. One morning, we were getting started, having camped overnight, and a fisherman saw us leaving and asked if we had heard the drums beating overnight. He was First Nations and we had camped inadvertently on their property. Topographical maps don't tell you those things. Another night, we had a tremendous windstorm requiring a lot of rocks to hold the tent down near the La Cloche Mountains.

NOTTAWASAGA

We paddled the Nottawasaga River through the Minesing Wetlands one day with local naturalist Bob Bowles. When Marian pointed out a turtle, Bob – who knows everything about nature – was so excited because it was his first wood turtle. We took pictures which were eventually sent to the museum. Imagine anything being a first for Bob.

ORANGE RIVER (2007)

The Orange River runs between South Africa and Namibia, and when we were there, we took a one-day trip down the Orange River in kayaks – vessels I never feel comfortable in. The first set of rapids, were the most difficult.. I think Marian and I were the only ones that didn't dump. Experience is worth something, I guess. So, by the time we got down to take the kayak out, the water was so low that we were practically scraping bottom most of the time. The reason for that was that we were paddling through a wine-growing area. The wineries were all sucking the river dry.

RESTIGOUCHE (2012)

One of our friends who was originally from the Maritimes had always wanted to paddle the Restigouche River. It is a great and famous salmon river which runs between Québec and New Brunswick. We elected to do this at the end of September 2012, which was getting a little late again. We drove down there along the south shore of the St. Lawrence, east of Québec city. We enjoyed stopping at some stores with carvers etc. which was a real treat. We stayed at a quaint little spot on the hill over the St. Lawrence, and enjoyed a glass of wine on their deck as the sun set over the Laurentians across the river. There was significant migration at the time, flocks of snow geese, plovers, yellow legs, sandpipers, and many other shorebirds. The man who was renting canoes for our companions(that is the other people – we brought our own) – was a little reticent because the water in the river was so low; however, it rained the night before, so the water was up enough that he thought it would be okay.

Normally this stretch would have about three to four significant rapids he said. Because of the low water, we had about seventy-five. Some were quite tricky. Incidentally, I was his oldest customer that year. It was cold overnight, so a campfire was mandatory, and Marian was very cold so now she says anymore canoe trips will be five-star only. Surely, she doesn't mean that after all these years of canoe-ing? Maybe I should act more my real age rather than what I like to think I am. We ended up where the Miramichi River runs into the Restigouche. The colour of the leaves was great, and we saw a number of salmon along the way, but fishing was not allowed since salmon camps along the way pay a lot for the rights to fish in their river.

11. ADVENTURES CLOSE TO HOME

Sailing was a sideline for many years and even included some racing. We sailed a sixteen-foot Hobie catamaran. There were a number of them on Lake Couchiching where we lived. We had races several times, especially with other doctors, so it was called the medicat races. We were sometimes successful.

Catamarans are very fast, responsive sailboats. They also tip very easily, so if we were racing we were on the edge all the time often with one hull up in the air and we were out on the trapeze on that same side. Often times both of us would be on the trapeze. It was very exciting – and risky – if you were going as fast as you can. We had a lot of fun over the years, won a few races lost a few races, and had quite a few dumps. Our children stopped coming with us because they didn't like the dumps particularly. If we were on the trapeze, and the one hull dove under the water, the person often swung around the front of the boat and up on the other side. For some reason or other they stopped thinking that was fun.

Actually, Marian and I have begun to think that's not so much fun either, and we have become much more cautious sailors. We haven't dumped in a few years now, and hopefully even though we continue sailing on Lake Dalrymple which is much smaller, we can keep it that way.

Since we lived on Lake Couchiching for many years, waterskiing also became an important part of our lives in the summer, and for Erik, bare-foot skiing was essential to his mental health. To do that you must go fifty miles per hour, so that's what we did with our one hundred and fifty horse power motor. We moved to the smaller lake where we live now, and because the kids were not using the boat, we sold it with the house.

PEMBERTON (1991-99)

We owned a seven-acre farm ten kilometres upstream from Pemberton, which was about twenty kilometres north of Whistler, British Columbia, at the end of the road right on the Lillooet River. It had a huge beach on the river – which was riverbed really but was a lot of open beach when the river was lower. Flooding had been a problem in the past, so you could not buy flood insurance for your home there. There was a house, a cabin, and a barn with a paddock for horses. From one window, we could see Mount Currie, the biggest mountain around – always snow-covered – out the opposite window the Three Sister Mountains as we called them as they looked alike. It was Fantastic really. So, we used it to ski in the winter and did a lot of hiking in the summer including one up over the top and into the Stein Valley. The Duffy Lake Road runs from Mount Curry to Lillooet, so we would take our Jeep up the logging roads that ran off the Duffy Lake Road as far as possible above that and then start hiking. Sometimes there were trails, sometimes not. One time we climbed some steep scree. It was impossible to come down again, so we had to pick another route following a little creek through huge boulders. When we got down a little lower, it was starting to get dark, and since we were following a creek the possibility of bears not hearing us coming was a concern. That particular area was known for its bear population. Fortunately, nothing happened, and we eventually got back to the cabin well after dark.

Then the explosion happened.

Our youngest boy, Stephen, was staying with us there was furious because he didn't know where we were, and it was late – sort of a role reversal. He was right, of course, so we always left word from then on.

Another escapade involved driving over the Hurley pass west of Pemberton (significant enough that folks who had done it had bumper stickers saying so). On the way, there was a road off to the side that found its way to some delightful generally unknown hot springs by the side of Lillooet tributary.

Near the top of the pass was Bralorne, a totally deserted little village with many houses surrounded by vegetation and no signs of recent life. The remains of the top of the mine were decaying in the edge of a stream. Down the other side of the pass was Gold Bridge, a tiny ex-gold mining spot. Next was the return to Lillooet. To get there involved driving through some more mountains, past some gorgeous little lakes, and along a one lane "road" along the edge of a scary canyon. I tended to lean to the inside even though I was in a car and I hoped nobody was coming the other way. We were told that there had once been a sign that read: anyone going over fifteen miles per hour will be fired. It was put up by the mine owners and seemed very reasonable to me.

We fixed up the cabin to our satisfaction and rented the house, and therein lay the problem. The renters, all highly recommended, of course, grew progressively worse. The first one had horses and a series of boyfriends. That's okay, but her son liked old cars, so he soon had the yard full of old derelict vehicles, tires, and car parts. The second young couple were very pleasant we thought, but he had a bit of a temper, and he punched holes in the walls and doors. The next guy seemed to have endless money and a nice new girlfriend; he also had horses and made trails through our surrounding land.

Unfortunately, his wife – or perhaps her lawyer – found him so all that money evaporated. We never did get all the rent. The last renter had the house and a lot of the surrounding property full of marijuana. It was interesting, how the marijuana was planted about every ten feet in the grass. I guess it is not so detectable then from the helicopters flying around at that time. We were supposed to have had a person who was going out to check it out periodically, which we paid for. I can't believe that she ever actually went out, or she would have seen the marijuana. At any rate, sadly, we felt we could not look after it from a distance with any degree of certainty, so we put it up for sale and sold. We were happy to see that the fellow who bought it has done a great job with it. He's expanded on its possibilities in ways that we might've been able to do, had we been able to hang on a little bit longer.

12. SKI TRIPS

We skied regularly at local areas – in our case Horseshoe Valley – since 1962 when things were rudimentary. There was no phone, so as a doctor, I had to leave the local farmer's phone number and pay him if he had to come and get me. The road down into the valley at the time from the Orillia side was along the side of the hill, curvy, steep and twisty and really only one lane, so if it snowed, and someone got stuck, too bad.

Eventually Pine Ridge across the road from Horseshoe opened up. It was a small (one hundred and fifty families) private ski area. Since everyone was part of a family, it was comforting to know everyone at least a little and to know, if something happened to your child, they would find you immediately and vice versa, of course. It was a wonderful family club that ran for many years. In the eighties, at the time of the recession, we had to relinquish it because we didn't have enough families interested to keep it going, but it developed some great skiers. The rules were very loose, and the kids did all kinds of things they could not do elsewhere. They built gigantic jumps, trails through the woods too narrow for adults, and skied down under the lifts sometimes if there was new snow. Our small club racing team won the Ontario Championship one year, beating all of the big clubs from Collingwood including Blue Mountain, Osler, and Georgian Peaks. It was sort of a shock for them because they had never even heard of us. Our son, Stephen, was on the Southern Ontario juvenile ski team for two years, and a number of other Pine Ridge members have gone into the ski industry – have been featured in ski movies, were ski directors, ski pros etc. It was sad indeed when we couldn't keep it going.

One terrifying incident happened to me one day while glade skiing. I guess the snow was a little low, and I was making a jump turn between trees. The tails of my skis caught under the root of a tree as I was lunging forward which pulled me back so that I hit the back of my head on the tree and my neck was hyper-flexed. I was quadriplegic and sliding down the steep hill unable to move or help myself – a moment of absolute terror. After about a minute, however, I felt some sensation returning, and shortly after that I could start to move again. I guess that is called a cord concussion and there are sequelae possible.

Subsequently our local skiing was done mostly at Mount St. Louis which is not the western mountains, but it served as good practice for the big mountains.

Marian and I also did adult racing. Marian was quite athletic and won all the women's races and beat a lot of the men, but she really wanted to beat me. She did one day – by one one hundredth of a second – and stopped racing so I could never get back. It's probably a good thing because she probably would've beaten me by more the next time.

There were many ski trips with the kids to Vermont, New Hampshire, Quebec, and Whistler in British Columbia. All have their advantages and challenges, and we enjoyed them all.

A few things stood out. One time while at Mount Saint Anne, we were in having lunch, when we heard a loud boom, and upon looking outside saw that ice had slid off the roof of the main lodge and absolutely crushed a whole row of parked cars. What a mess!

Another extremely fond memory for all of us was at Jay Peak, Vermont. We rented a small farmhouse near a little village a few miles away from the mountain. It was a quaint little unit in a narrow valley with no television reception and very poor radio reception. What were we to do? Best vacation ever! There were multiple games and musical instruments around, and we all had a great time laughing trying to play musical instruments and playing all the games. Did we really have to have television when we got home again?

Marian and I have skied in Switzerland and Austria and virtually all of the major ski resorts in North America except Mammoth Mountain in California – which is on our list. Colorado has several great areas such as Aspen, Vail, Beaver Creek, Snowmass, and Breckenridge. They were all great, and you can pretty well count on a lot of nice powder snow. As you get closer to the Pacific, the snow often changes to heavy wet snow. Utah has great areas, for example Deer Valley and Park City. Montana has many great areas as well, Big Sky, Big Mountain. Idaho has Sun Valley, which is a wonderful ski area and tougher than it sounds. Wyoming has Jackson Hole in Grand Teton National Park, which is a real challenge. Washington has Mount Baker; Nevada has Lake Tahoe, Squaw Valley, and Heavenly Valley, which are all wonderful and highly recommended – and they were right on the California border so some of those places were actually in California.

Canada's East had Mont Sutton, Le Massif, Mont Orford, Mont Tremblant and other smaller areas which were all great. Calabogie (near Ottawa) was a favourite because we found a motel where all eight of us plus the dog stayed in one room. Air mattresses and sleeping bags did the job. Vermont had ski areas like Jay Peak, Stowe, Sugar Bush, Mad River Glen. Maine had Sunday River; and New Hampshire had many areas.

New York had many areas as well, most interesting of which was I think was Lake Placid. Interestingly I recall being there when they just opened a new run from the top called Cloudspin. Since it was new, never skied, and still had stumps on it, the ski patrol was at the bottom questioning everyone about their ability to ski on this dangerous run. Just ahead of me in line was a slightly obese man who had socks overlapping his ski pants. He did not look at all athletic, but he was certain he could handle anything, so because he insisted, they finally gave in and let him go. He fell getting off the lift. It was a great run if I avoided the stumps, so of course, I repeated and repeated. About three runs later, the guy with the socks had probably covered a total of one hundred and fifty metres. What a waste of his time. Perhaps he learned something that day. He learned that snow plow does not conquer everything. Snow plow is what beginner skiers learn how to do before they parallel.

New Hampshire skiing includes Cannon Mountain, Wildcat, and Mount Washington (with no lift) all great ski areas, but we had to climb up to Mount Washington and it was a long climb.

Another interesting incident occurred while skiing in New Hampshire. Karen, my oldest girl – age seven at the time – wanted to hide on the ski patrol and then ski down after they had "swept" all the hills. We did that, only to come out at the bottom to find our four-year-old daughter Krista on the ground with a broken tibia, surrounded by ski patrollers and her mother. She would not let anyone help her until I showed up. What a great day to play that kind of stunt!

We've skied all over Western Canada of course, starting in Alberta including Banff's Mount Norquay, the Lone Pine run is memorable for its giant moguls. I loved it then, but I wouldn't want to try it now. They also had a run next to it said to be one of the ten steepest runs in America, I think it was called Memorial bowl. It was strictly back and forth thing all the way down. The North American downhill run went all the way down to the highway in the town itself.

Sunshine is another terrific Banff resort, a huge area and mostly above the tree line. The last time we were there it was cloudy and started to snow, I still had my cataracts. I could not see anything. I fell down standing in one place I was so disoriented that one time, even though I was standing, I was sure the trees were moving around and heading towards me. It took me close to an hour to get down, far enough so I could become oriented. We spent the afternoon below the tree line where we could see a great deal better. Now that I've had my cataracts out, maybe I should try it again. Lake Louise is also a huge area that regularly holds the World Cup and has a huge variety of trails.

A little further south, British Columbia's Panorama Mountain Resort is also a giant area we visited to see our daughter Karen who was working there in 1985 during a World Cup event. The day before, the chair had broken down while we were heading up with a member of the Canadian team. We were able to chat with him while they fixed the chair. He used 225 centimetre skis for recreational skiing – very long for most people. In the next race, the next morning, he did not win but he was clocked at 144 kilometres an hour.

The Okanagan valley has a number of very popular resorts from Silver Star at Vernon, which has a sort of cowboy motif, to Big White and Apex. We had bad luck the day we were at Apex, we should have brought our skates, but you never know do you? Kamloops has Sun Peaks which is more and more popular with the easterner's, and don't forget all that powder at Fernie. Revelstoke and Golden also have great skiing with lots of challenge.

Further west in Canada are Grouse Mountain, Mount Seymour and Cypress Mountain in North Vancouver, but Whistler Blackcomb is the biggie. It is judged best in America almost every year by the snow and ski magazines. It's a huge area with well over two hundred runs. Ski runs are divided into green (easy), blue (a little tougher), black diamond (quite tough), and double black diamond (for experts only). We have given up on the double blacks now unless one gets accidentally caught on one, but we still ski blacks and blues. As long as it's fun, I guess we'll keep doing it.

A friend of ours who moved to Squamish so that he could ski a lot got caught in a real predicament last year. He was skiing off the main hills when he skied into a tree well which turned him upside down, skis across the top, head down. Fortunately, he knew exactly where he was, he was unable to extricate himself, but he had his cell phone with him and he was able to call his wife in Squamish – who wasn't skiing – and tell her exactly where he was. The ski patrol saved him, a very lucky fellow; he might easily have been found in the spring.

In Europe we skied at Davos, Verbier in Switzerland, Dachstein and Innsbruck in Austria. I loved the concept of skiing down one mountain up the next one down the next one. One day, we ended up fifty miles from where we started, and it took us over an hour on the train to get back. Skiing through farmers' fields was different than in North America but was still wonderful.

HELI-SKIING (1985)

The big event for us was to go helicopter skiing in the Bugaboos, a mountain range in the Purcell Mountains in southeastern British Columbia. In the morning we spent about, an hour learning about avalanches. We wore transponders, so they could find us if we were buried, so we practised by burying a transponder and then we had to find it and retrieve it. If we needed to, we would turn on the transponder, when we were skiing so they could find us if we were buried. The appeal was deep fresh powder, different run each time. The trickiest part for us was skiing through the trees. The advice given to us was this: "Don't look at the trees, look at the spaces." That was great *theoretical* advice but hard to maintain when they're coming at you or it seems like they're coming after you. Anyway, it was a glorious, glorious day. We think of it often, especially when we hear about those taken down by avalanches every year. We were aware of avalanches when we were skiing, but we had to be optimistic or we wouldn't have done it.

Interestingly while we were heli-skiing, there were two young French-Canadian boys with us who we knew were going further north to ski more powder the following week to an area called Blue Hills (I believe). The following week, while we were skiing elsewhere, we heard that two French-Canadian boys were caught in an avalanche at the area and were killed. We don't know that it was them for sure, but it probably was. If you're going to do risky things, you realize you're taking chances. It has been said no risks, equals no reward, but I guess there are degrees of that.

13. CRUISES AND ADVENTURE TRIPS

BERMUDA IN THE SEVENTIES

The first actual trip by aircraft that Marian and I took together (for reasons other than skiing) was to Bermuda, which had beautiful craggy black rock, pink sand, and empty beaches. We were there in December, rented a moped, and set about seeing the whole island – all forty kilometres of it. Marian's parents had been stationed there with the Salvation Army, so she was interested in connecting with various spots. Because it's in the northern hemisphere (same rough latitude as Savanna, Georgia) Bermudians considered December as winter, so we saw people with hats, gloves, even a couple of fur coats. The beaches were deserted, and no one was swimming except me. Marian felt the cold, which she realized later was because she was hypothyroid and thus not her usual energetic self.

PUERTO RICO (IN THE NINETIES)

Our first actual cruise started in Puerto Rico then went to the Dominican, Barbados, then to some of the smaller islands of St. Thomas, Antigua, and Grenada. We entered cruising rather reluctantly because, being people who are always busy, we were fearful that it might not be enough to keep us busy and interested. Wrong! Cruises have multiple facets as well as great food, nightly entertainment, and lectures on appropriate subjects.In Barbados we did enjoy a submarine trip down about 90-100 feet to see the fish , turtles and coral. Shore excursions were always interesting. Each island was different, but overall, the Caribbean islands have more similarities than differences. Most of the ships have tours arranged, but some people prefer to go ashore and find their own. Take your choice, but be active. There was also an exercise room on board, and it was a ritual for us to go to the gym before breakfast in the morning. We tended to take all the side trips available because chances were we would not be back there again, and ,there's always new places to go.

HAWAII (1998)

Our twenty-fifth wedding anniversary required something special, and Hawaii certainly qualified. We could not say anything negative about Hawaii – unless it had to do with the number of people. It was warm, sunny, beautiful, and the people were so very pleasant. The highlights for us were, firstly, a helicopter ride around the island of Maui, where we spent our first week, seeing all the waterfalls pouring down from the rain forested mountains. Snorkelling and hiking were great, but the bike ride down the volcano Haleakala was super. I believe it was almost sixty kilometres and ended up at the beach where the young bloods were doing all their tricks with their surfboards and sail boards. The weather report each day gave the size of the surf as well, and that day it was twenty-five feet. No wonder they were so airborne and for so long. If only I was two weeks younger! On the bike ride, one of the men missed a corner, fell off the bike, and broke his arm. That held us up for a while, as did the early morning ice on the road at the peak. The second week was at Kauai, the garden island with excellent hikes, mountains, huge beaches, and *fewer* people.

EUROPE BY CAR (2002)

At last we got off to Europe, having put it off for a year due to fear on the part of Helen, my wife's sister, and Helen's husband Peter over the events of 9/11. Helen and Peter would be joining us. We left Toronto overnight above the clouds, so as we approached Amsterdam, the sunrise on the clouds produced a spectacular effect as if cotton balls were floating on an unusually bright red sea. We stayed at a small inexpensive hotel in a cabin out behind the main building. It was one of those places where you say, "Oh well we won't be here for long." A great city; we watched a gay parade with emphasis on avoiding HIV. We rented the car here for our trip.

Bicycles appeared to be the main mode of transportation. We visited the Van Gogh Museum and the Rijksmuseum before Peter and Helen arrived. I guess Van Gogh was bipolar and shot himself. Looking at his originals gave me a little chill because I have seen pictures of them so often. They also had Gaugin, Renoir, Rodin, Rembrandt and many others.

At dinner, we met an ex-pat Canadian who'd had an interesting life here, there, and everywhere. He seemed a little lonely and maudlin and did a lot of reminiscing about Canada. A jazz musician, he also played a local bar.

A canal tour the following day stopped first at Anne Frank's house. The Franks who were Jews hid in an attic during World War II. She kept a diary, and they had to keep very quiet, so the Germans would not find them. It's a good thing, when we are complaining about the little inconveniences in our lives, to remind ourselves how very fortunate we are. Imagine what survivors were forced to endure during those times – not to mention the millions who did not survive.

The red-light district, of course, was fascinating. All the "ladies" with their little closets – and I must say some quite ugly – to each his own. One prostitute did approach me, and when I said that I was married, she replied...

"That's okay your wife can watch."

For some reason my wife didn't go along with that. I didn't ask her to explain.

Germany

The next stop was Bad Godesberg just south of Bonn on the Rhine, an old embassy town. The Rhine was brown and extremely busy with boats, tugs, kayaks with all manner of cargo. We took a boat tour down the river and stopped at Links a quaint little place with twelfth-century gravestones. When we got back, we walked the last eight kilometres back to the hotel. The Rhine had castles everywhere, most of them on top of hills most with walls, some with moats.

Next, we arrived in Frankfurt where we thought we would try to get Czechoslovakian visas if we could so we could spend some time in Prague. We spent what felt like two weeks there one morning trying to find out if there was a Czechoslovakian consulate. Eventually we gave up trying to arrange it and rationalized that we were *glad* we couldn't get it because we might've got into some kind of trouble there or been murdered.

We wanted to see a woman named Christina in Kessel. We met her in New Zealand, Milford Sound, and she was a friend of Evelyn our old nanny who went to Alaska with me. We didn't know at the time, but Christina was telling Evelyn later about this older (what does she mean by *that*?) couple she had met. The world gets smaller all the time. She was an English teacher in Germany, and she had other arrangements that she had invited us to be involved in that day, but we thought better to move on so back on the autobahn to Fulda, a beautiful historical city with the church built in 749. The ballroom of the place we stayed in Fulda was exotic and the breakfast/dining room was the most elegant ever. The décor included teak furniture and was beautiful, and they served food of every description you could even ever imagine for breakfast. Some people brought their elegant little dogs with them. Germany is very neat, very clean, and very organized. The little dogs were treated like royalty.

We tried to go to Dachau, but it was closed that day. The next day we went to the Mauthausen Concentration Camp and Gusen Memorial. That was very emotional. They had a fifty-minute video and you would not believe what men could do to each other. There was still an odour in the crematorium where thirty-seven thousand people died. How could they go home to their wives and children after guarding that place? The whole scene gave rise to a lot of the dark thinking about humanity.

Vienna

Our next stop was Vienna, that magnificent city with its opera house and incredible ornamentation and attention to every detail. A tourist tour which included the Royal Palace of the Habsburg Empire dated back to the sixteenth century. Napoleon married a Hapsburg after divorcing Josephine. The Palace was dripping in finance and money, and everywhere you looked there was gold, and hand-made tapestries. The ceiling was done similarly. Riverside Gardens covered hundreds of acres of pools, fountain statues, memorial arches. On the ground floor there was actually a McDonald's. What was going on?

The next day we visited the Vienna palaces. Actually, it was interesting at the Winter Palace; we went to a concert at the Lichtenstein Palace and heard Mozart and Strauss. It was excellent.

Austria

The Romantic Road along the north shore of the Danube was our next venture. It was rolling and pretty, a quaint country with evidence of recent flooding. All the walls next to the river had water damage halfway up the ground floor. We stopped at Melk, a colossal abbey on top of the hill with monks coming to and fro while the village below looked somewhat impoverished. It seemed to me like all the money went to build and maintain that site. Is that a reasonable use of money? Maybe to them it was, maybe they were fearful of complaining since God might strike them down.

We had a timeshare coming up in in the mountains in Austria south of Salzburg. It was a ski resort, but it was fall now, so it was relatively quiet; it was aged but well looked after little village, surrounded by snow-capped mountains. Many houses were ornate dark wood with white stucco. A lot of rivulets were running down the mountain, and some roads were still washed out. There were lots of lakes and rivers around the lodge where we stayed which was called the Marco Polo Alpena club.

There was September snow in the mountains around Salzburg. Salzburg was great very old, very hilly, and a huge fortress that dated from the Roman times sat atop of the mountain. There were lots of old churches dating from seventh and eighth century. *The Sound of Music* with Julie Andrews was shot there in several places in the city. It snowed and rained and was cold for five days, during which time, we couldn't even see the mountains. There were lots of trails, but with no hiking boots, we couldn't really even walk the lawn since it was so wet.

Venice

We went to Italy next where it was snowing and raining. The dolomites were quite spectacular with new snow on them. We visited Peter's relatives on their one-acre farm in Pease, Italy. It was very clean with a lot of livestock in the form of cattle, pigs – every inch was productive. We stayed near Venice and took the train twenty kilometres to Venice then the gondola through the canals to magical St. Mark's Square, which was awe-inspiring. The gondoliers with their red and black stripe shorts added to the ambience. They used a J stroke to paddle. We ate dinner at a great little restaurant in the street with musicians nearby. In St. Mark's Square, there were five different musical groups playing at the same time, far enough apart to enjoy separately – there was even a jazz combo. They were amazing! I can still see the moon rising and the lights on the canals. I must go back.

Tuscany

On to Tuscany, as I sit on the deck, the sun going down over the rolling hills, I feel so lucky to be alive and experience yet another breathtaking place on the side of the hill: no other resorts or people even close by.

Marian and I have driven all the way taking turns at the wheel, but Helen was terrified and has asked us to keep it at one hundred kilometres per hour or less. That was impossible on those roads where drivers were averaging one hundred and thirty or one hundred and forty kilometres. If we slowed down or left a space in front of us, then someone would pass and cut in – even in the mountains – with their Mercedes and BMWs or Audis.

Some were going two hundred kilometres an hour on the autobahn. Tuscany had an enchanting, sort of orange-coloured atmosphere. Karen made the arrangements there through Linda (a business partner). There was a fine, warm, comfortable feeling there except when driving traffic circles. They often had twelve signs, and no familiar places, and were surrounded by trees, so we had to make a decision in a few seconds about which way we would like to go, and we didn't know any of the names. It kept life interesting, and it was easy to get lost. There was no GPS when we were there. We ended up thirty kilometres away one night. It made us wonder how we would get to Firenze or Roma.

Sienna was nearby, with Piazza El Campo, a gigantic square surrounding a huge cathedral and many restaurants. They actually had an annual major horse race in the square.

Florence

As I sat watching the dusk quietly descend on the Tuscan hills, the mellow warm hue of the buildings gradually turned from orange to blue grey and then went dark. It seemed to cool quickly up in the hills once the sun was gone, and the distant lights started to twinkle. Today we drove down to Botia and then took a taxi into the centre and Piazza Republic of Firenze. There were tourists everywhere, mostly in groups with leaders with little flags running around followed by tourists. The famous *Ponte Vecchio* [gold bridge] was as elegant as expected as befits European women who generally dressed very well. The Florence Cathedral (also known as Il Duomo di Firenze) was gigantic, the third biggest in the world and the frescoes filled up the dolma and the cupola. There were hundreds of characters and biblical scenes painted in great detail. There were also statues everywhere including David by Michelangelo who I think must've been on steroids because he had big muscles but a small penis.

Roma

We drove down the coast to Fiumicino near the airport then took a train into the city. What a city, a dirty city with lots of overdue garbage. It was interesting that the taxi from Fiumicino to the train cost was eleven dollars in the daytime, but when we came back that evening they wanted fifty dollars to drive the same distance about three miles with no stop lights. Peter, being Italian was very, very, angry and he didn't mind venting on the various taxi drivers who, of course, were all Italian. We managed to find someone who would do it for half that price.

In St. Peter's Square we saw where the Pope lived, and we saw the sculptures and then the Vatican Museum and Sistine Chapel said to be the best art in the world. I won't argue. There was work of Leonardo Da Vinci, Raphael, and many others. It had been estimated that if a person looked at every picture in the museum for sixty seconds, it would take twelve years to see it all. It was overwhelming really, and after a while my brain turned to mush and I was really not absorbing very much I think

Heading north now from Tuscany towards Pisa we saw the Dolomites with snow on top, very steep mountains, clusters of mountains villages built high up really steep inclines.

Cinque Terra

Cinque Terra on the Italian Riviera had five villages that you could walk to. We did that another time and there will be some writing on that later. We drove along the Italian coast, Monte Carlo, Monaco, where there were a lot of high-rises against the backdrop of rugged limestone mountains with minimal vegetation so that the houses looked like they were suspended and glued together.

We followed the autobahn to San Bernardino Martinique. Our timeshare in the mountains in Switzerland was called Port d Soleil.

The mountains were magnificent, half lost in the mist sometimes, sometimes singled out in the sun. One looked like the Matterhorn, but it was too small. The accommodation was excellent with the deck out front where one could sit and look out over the mountains. Helen was fearful of getting out the door, so she stayed in most of the time, and Marian and I drove over the top and down the other side into France the next day. We passed a lot of ski resorts and a lot of colour as we descended to Lake Geneva. It seemed like we were going downhill for about forty kilometres. What a bike ride it would have been. There were a lot of beech-like trees with that golden glow surrounding them and many rivers with their falls and rapids. How pretty could it get? Geneva, just as the pictures suggested, was serene with the lake surrounded by spectacular mountains and sunny too.

Heidi must have been around there somewhere in the mountains. The two of us went for a long mountain climb and it reminded me of *The Sound of Music*. There were distant cowbells there in the village below, saw some goats also. It was a wonderful day on top of the world. It was always harder going back down the mountain. I fell a few times, but no problem. We climbed and hiked again the next day, very romantic really.

It was time to move on to France and Spain, where we expected to see all the glorious ladies you see in all the magazines. It must've been their day off. We did run into an older man up high in the mountains standing beside his car looking wistfully over the valley and mountains. He was apologetic for using his vehicle to get up there, but he couldn't climb them anymore because of his arthritis – I assured him I understood, and I did. That was before I had my knee replaced. The next morning was foggy again, and as we drove past Chamonix, it lightened up for a minute. We had a couple of glimpses of the snow radiating in blue sky through a hole in the clouds. We moved on to Albertville and then Grenoble – previous Olympic sites – before heading south to Provence. I could spend days describing the gorgeous country side and the fields of lavender. The town of Nyon was our intended stopover; it was known for being an ancient city, old arched bridges, narrow twisting streets, and almost tunnels from one to another. I expected David Copperfield and Uriah Heap to appear. At night, it was poorly lit and almost creepy. We ate at a place called "the caves" a little restaurant with delicious exotic food. Trying to capture the mood of this ancient place was difficult. It was mostly grey with occasional bright colours so we were looking forward to tomorrow's market and some wine tasting.

One little tunnel sloping irregularly down to the next street which looked empty was suddenly filled with a beautiful female voice singing a melancholic song which seemed to waft up the slope on the morning. We hated to leave Nyon with its warm ambience. We bought some lavender for no other reason than we had driven through fields of it just before getting to Nyon.

We agreed it was time to move on towards Spain, so back to the autobahn. We passed through the rest of France and then into Spain down the coast to Guerra and for Lancia. Fortunately – or unfortunately – we avoided Barcelona, thinking we would be caught up in a lot of traffic, but we may have missed something there. We arrived at our destination Dénia. We had a timeshare there for a week. It was three to four hundred feet above sea level but had a magnificent view of the Mediterranean framed by flowers, multi-coloured roses, and white or yellow stucco. There were no screens on the windows. There were beautiful beaches, lots of markets, but lots of Gypsies (or Roma, but in Spain, Gitano) also. In the harbour were multiple sailboats including some catamarans. There were washrooms where you don't dare touch anything, the door opened and soap for water then the dryer without you touching anything, even the exit door. Next, we drove north and turned at Barcelona towards the Pyrenees and Andorra. We drove past Montserrat's "Sawtooth" Mountain.

Andorra is quite high, with snow-covered mountains, a separate country with border guards etc. It was cold when we arrived as it had snowed the night before. Peter and Helen were highly unimpressed. They were definitely not going to stay there. "It's a dump." You could tell they were not skiers, so we left and headed down to France. It was a long drive into the Limousin region past Doral, and we finally stopped at the Arches Hotel on the River in Braun. We took a long walk by the War Memorial, along a road beside the canal scattered with fallen leaves in the late day sun. It was a peaceful if somewhat melancholic experience.

Paris

On Sunday, October twenty-third, we drove to Paris where we arranged to meet Charles – an egotistical Brit of our acquaintance – at his apartment which we rented for the week. Everyone was very friendly and helpful. The apartment was small cluttered with junk which Charles called antiques, and he bragged that he had taken five hundred trips on the Concorde supersonic jet which was no longer in service. We were located near the Eiffel Tower and the subway which was so convenient. We walked under the bridge to the subway then to the Louvre which was an overwhelming place. It was impossible to absorb even a fraction of all that was there. We managed to take in quite a bit of it, saw the Venus de Milo, various Aphrodites and many mythical Greek gods. When our brains could absorb no more, we left and walked down the Champs-Élysées, toward the Arc de Triomphe with the wind blowing leaves around our feet and hand in hand enjoying the ambience of Paris.

Another day we were off to the Notre Dame Cathedral, it was so impressive – huge, magnificent stained-glass windows. The best thing was a choir of six professionals and fifteen boy sopranos; with the fantastic acoustics, a song resonated from the hundred and fifty foot high ceilings. If you could hear that every time you went to church, you might be there quite often.

However, we then ventured to the left bank, a great place which had either a little or a lot of just about everything. It had many unique bright coloured stores, restaurants, and shops stacked floor-to-ceiling with wares. There were many little tangled streets, a couple of nice squares with fountains gargoyles, and of people all shapes, sizes, colours and languages all in one place.

Everybody buys their baguettes fresh every day. The bakery on a corner next-door to our apartment was busy, and people often would be triple or quadruple parked in front of it picking up their baguettes before they went home. The Eiffel Tower gave an almost complete view of Paris with the River Seine below.

Versailles is a must to do when you're in Paris, so we took the train to get there. Opulence is the only word for it. In the famed residence of Louis XIV "The Sun King", everything was gilded with gold and covered with beautiful paintings, tapestries, and fabrics. All the walls were marble and there were chandeliers everywhere. In the gardens, even that late in the season, were still great flowers. Our plans to see the opera house were mostly foiled by rehearsal. We managed some quick peeking out over a wall.

We had to go shopping at Les Galeries Lafayette, which was full of sidewalk vendors, restaurants etc. Marian bought some brand-new perfume, so she would be one of the few people in the world with it and probably the first Canadian. Overall, Paris was a special place for its own ambience with stylish ladies. Our car had been on the street in the same place for a week with cars touching front and back, so we couldn't move even if we wanted to. Finally with a lot of pushing, pulling and some cursing we were able inch by inch extricate ourselves We had a rain-soaked ticket on the windshield which some how we forgot to pay. We drove back through Belgium, Antwerp, then to Amsterdam then flew home.

BALTIC CRUISE (2005)

Our next big adventure was a Baltic Cruise which started in England with a view of the famed white cliffs of Dover. We spent a few days in London, doing the town. We visited St. Paul's, Westminster, Harrods, Trafalgar Square, Buckingham Palace, and Fleet Street. We strolled along the Thames and saw the Parliament buildings. We went to see a production of *The Lion King* which was extremely well done. We visited Piccadilly Circus and rode a double-decker bus around town passing Trafalgar square three times and eventually went to the Black Lion pub for supper, trying to soak up more real English atmosphere – and we definitely did that. A visit to the Natural History Museum revealed an ape ancestor that looked a lot like Peter; I could hardly wait to tell him.

—

Oslo, Norway, was next, the site of the annual presentation of the Nobel Peace Prize. First impression was that it was a lot like Canada, particularly Muskoka. We took a train up to the top of a mountain and then walked back down with the guide who showed us the trolls, the Holmenkollbakken (the Holmenkollen ski jump) and we saw several little lakes as well. It was a nice hike and gave us a feel for the place.

—

Stockholm, Sweden, was marvellous. It is an archipelago of the thousand Islands and is often called the Venice of the North. It had narrow cobblestone streets and inviting little shops. Marian bought a leather coat there. They had some interesting underwater sculptures that could just be seen, an ear, a hand and some other parts.

—

Tallinn, Estonia, had a wonderful colourful older section – a lot of which was on a slope. It was populated by a lot of very attractive blonde women, and there were a lot of churches and cathedrals in Kesklinn, the Central district of the city. How do women in high heels walk on cobblestone streets without breaking an ankle? Determination and practice, I guess.

—

Helsinki, Finland, on a sunny day, was enchanting. A bus tour accompanied with music from Sibelius gave us a good view of the city. Apparently, it was Putin's old hang out.

—

In Moscow and Red Square, they were preparing for the anniversary of the deaths of children who were killed in the Beslan school siege the previous September – an incident precipitated by *alleged* Chechen separatists and brought to its bloody conclusion by government forces. We also visited the Metropole, a gigantic store several stories high. The KGB building was rather grave and somber – and a little bit frightening even now. The subway in Moscow was extraordinary with marble floors, gigantic chandeliers, and escalators. We had to be careful somebody didn't run over us. We had to stay to one side because people ran up and down. Lunch was borscht (a sour beet soup) and vodka in a beautiful room of multiple magnificent carvings. This was the Writers Club (The Central House of Writers); they had a Tolstoy room, a Dostoyevsky room, and rooms dedicated to several other writers. A four-piece string quartet added to the ambience – a great "classical" day. Our guide spoke very good English and she toured us around Red Square, the Kremlin, St. Basil's Cathedral with its vivid colours and spiral towers, and the oppressive KGB building. The aircraft that we took from Moscow to St. Petersburg was hard to recommend. It may have been very old, but the seating was very tight. We noted one large man who could not sit down with his knees touching the seat in front of him his buttock was halfway up the back of his seat. Nobody said or did anything.

St. Basils

—

The next day in St. Petersburg, the equestrian statue of Peter the Great in *Senatskaya Ploshchad* (St. Isaac's square)] its magnificent bronze horse reared up on on two legs and the Church of the Resurrection standout in my memory. The Hermitage Museum in front of the Winter Palace is a huge famous art gallery and noteworthy – also noteworthy were the miles of cranes in the harbour. We were unable to visit the Hermitage Museum, unfortunately, because there was a long lineup and not enough time.

—

Berlin was a two and a half hour train ride, but worth the trip. There was so much history there starting with the Berlin Wall of infamy; they have left evidence of where the "wall' was lest they forget. There were only few sections of actual wall left, but I found them quite dramatic. There were paintings on it, but the many handprints told such a story. The Brandenburg Gate symbolizes triumph and the freedom of East Berlin. There was a holocaust monument right next to Hitler's bunker, Checkpoint Charlie, the memorial church bombed during WW II that has been left as a reminder.

Berlin is at the junction of four rivers and it had sixteen hundred bridges

—

Copenhagen was a beautiful city, and it seemed as if everyone was on a bike. We took a three-hour bike ride – not so great on the cobblestone – and Marian fell off but took no damage fortunately. We saw the famous statue of the *Little Mermaid* down by the water. It set the tone for the city of many parks a nice market, and there seemed to be a lot of talk about the Russian invasion and occupation.

SEDONA, ARIZONA (A TIME SHARE; 2006)

Everything was red, sculptured, and dramatic. The land was mostly desert-like, but there was some vegetation and some rivers and streams. There were many hikes and trails through the mesas gullies and arroyos. There was a surprising amount of wildlife including birds, snakes, mammals, and lizards. There were rattlesnakes also, so we had to be aware. Sedona was a very photogenic place with an adventurous atmosphere. If you go there, go with the intention of being active.

Very early one morning, we met fellow adventurers and, as arranged, climbed into a hot air balloon which was a first for us. They were a little noisy, but the glorious views of the sun rising over the already red desert, lighting up the canyons and painting everything a rusty orange, was certainly worth the early rise. Being presented with a glass of champagne when we finally landed in a farmer's field rounded off the morning.

SOUTH AMERICA (2006)

Ecuador

We flew into Quito, the capital of Ecuador, via Miami. We had been booked to stay in the best hotel, but Alfredo Palacio, the president of Ecuador at the time, was making a visit so we had to go elsewhere. Quito is almost three kilometres above sea level, and we ended up almost another kilometre higher than *that* in the mountains in a place with fireplaces in each room. It was apparently an old monastery. The problem for me was altitude sickness, even with the pills. Taking the suitcases up a trail of probably only one hundred vertical feet just about did me in. I couldn't eat dinner. Marian was fine. We moved around Quito the next day. The drivers were scary. Red lights were of no importance it seemed. It was a very historic city and full of old South American architecture.

We went to the equator which was fascinating. You cannot walk a straight line on the equator. Water swirls differently if you're one side or the other. If you're right on the equator water flows directly down and out of the funnel but if you move only a couple of feet each side and it goes the opposite way.

We got up early for birdwatching then drove to the Otavalo market said to be the best one in South America. It was huge, and the prices were unbelievable. Marian bought a multi-coloured jacket, spring or fall type, just great, for twelve dollars then on to the neighbouring town of Cotacachi for leather goods. We couldn't believe the prices there either, but we controlled ourselves.

Galapagos

The main event for us on this entire trip, were the Galapagos Islands. Once we were flown out from Ecuador and landed on the little island, we knew we had to get out to the boat, so we were to meet in a certain place and, lo and behold, there were sea lions sleeping on the bench where the zodiacs met us to take us to the ship *MS Islander*. There were birds everywhere. The ship was mahogany and teak. There were forty-six of us on the trip that we booked through Adventure Canada. We started with a swim in the ocean. Some hard-core birders were discussing eight different types of storm petrel to the exclusion of everything else. Over our time there, we saw all kinds of wildlife, birds of all kinds, marine and land iguanas, seals, sea lions, and sharks (while snorkelling). We were told the sharks don't like humans, I guess that means we don't taste the best.

The blue footed boobies were a never-ending source of amusement. They had bright blue feet and they dove into the ocean from a great height, like a spear, after fish.

When trekking around the islands, you must have your naturalist guide and stay on the path. The animals and birds don't have access to the rules, so they may lay their eggs right on the path. There was no fear of humans. Everyone has likely heard about the different finches in different sites on different islands as pointed out by Darwin on his visit – one of the influences for his theory of evolution. They have developed differently on different islands over the long term, adapting to their particular circumstances and being separated by ocean. If ever you have doubts about evolution, you will see it all there. One of the most striking things for me, were the cormorants with only tiny vestigial wings. There were no predators they needed to escape from in-flight. The water was an endless supply of food and left them with no need to fly. Just lean into the water and there's lunch.

I was surprised to see that there were penguins at the equator. I always thought of them as further south. We saw magnificent frigate birds with their ballooning red chests and little crabs that could race across the sand beaches faster than you could run. The giant tortoises were incredible to see. They were higher than my knee and lived in the Highlands. We saw nineteen one day. They live a long time, may be up to four hundred years. Shearwaters, redheaded tropic birds, flying fish, whole school of dolphins, and Byrde's whales up to fifty feet were all seen.

Florian Island was the whalers' post office. It was still active and had been working for centuries serving the needs of whalers who were often out to sea for over three years. There was a mailbox there, and if you put mail in it designated for some special place, then if somebody else came along and was going somewhere near the posted destination, they would deliver it personally and the other way around, so that people who were going there could bring mail and leave it in the post office with no attendant and so, hopefully, you would be able to pick it up.

It was albatross mating season, and we saw some action in that regard. There were other birds as well in all stages of development. On one island they had a goat skull mounted, thought to be the last one on that island. Originally brought by the explorers looking ahead so they would have meat or whatever they needed when they came back later. The ecological result, however, was devastation of local species. Cats were the worst of the invasive species, but rats, sheep, and goats were not far behind.

Galapagos was a life-changing experience; we saw the origins of so many things and understood in evolutionary processes better. It's all there for anyone to see. No one surely could doubt it having been there.

Peru

Lima was our first stop in Peru. The capital was a big city, and we were there only briefly, waiting to travel to Cusco. There we met other people travelling with Gap Company that we had engaged for this part of our trip. There were two Austrians, one Spaniard, two Brits, two Bulgarians, and two Americans. I was probably the oldest there by about thirty years.

Noticeable in South America was the fact that (theoretically) the people were all Roman Catholics, and they often attended church, but the younger ones were questioning and drawing their own con-clusions. Several said to me they had "mountain religion" and (like many First Nations for instance) held their relationship to nature and mother Earth as sacred. Cusco was at 3,400 metres and surrounded by mountains – quite beautiful.

One day we were hiking up in the Andes when we could hear a flute playing higher up. As we approached, we realised it was an older man all by himself surrounded by the mountain peaks. Magical; even spiritual

A street vendor was selling alpaca sweaters with sleeves for four dollars each, so we bought a few of them for the male members of the family. They were good quality, and we're still using them many years later. It gave me some idea of the different values of items in other countries.

Machu Picchu was, of course, a very important part of this trip. We were part of a small group, and we had to take first a bus and then a train to get to the Patchtech hotel in Machu Picchu. We did not do the hike because the mountains were quite steep, and they may have not been a good idea for a person of my tender years. Machu Picchu was built by Incas atop a mountain ridge in the mid-fifteenth century prior to contact with the Spanish, an incredible feat of engineering and precision involving huge polish stone blocks. It was really beyond imagination even how they would do that today, but they did it several hundred years ago. And the stone came from elsewhere and they had to get it up there. How could they have done that without major help? And if so who? It's easier to understand the pyramids than this. Then they all left – deserted it perhaps because of the advancing Spaniards. They were small people, but very strong I understand, for some of these blocks were quite large.

On the return, the train ran out of power, so we were left sitting in total darkness for maybe two hours while we waited for a rescue engine to show up and push us back to where the buses were waiting for us. It was fascinating to listen to the sounds of the jungle at night, the screeches, the howls the grunts – it felt very real and gave me a feeling for what goes on out there that I might not see otherwise.

The sacred valley was all about the Inka tribe – up to ten million people at one time. Pizarro raped the land and the gold and the people. They had guns while the Incas did not.

Amazon

After waiting through some weather delays, we finally got to fly into Puerto Maldonado. It was really interesting to fly in over the Andes Mountain and see the devastation of the Amazon forest. It had been cut right up to the very edge of the protected area and a lot of selective illegal cutting was going on within the protected area also. In Puerto Maldonado, we had to buy some rubber boots for the jungle. Then we got into dugout canoes. The motor had a really long shaft, so it could run in shallow water. The Rio Madre de Dios, a branch of the Amazon was quite high, and the water was very muddy with significant current.

Incidentally, when we arrived at the airport originally, there was no one to meet us, and we all spoke only English, except one Spanish lady, very fortunately because Spanish was needed. She phoned around, and eventually a guide showed up about one and a half hours later. He was a nice fellow, but if I asked him a question, he would probably answer inappropriately because he didn't really understand me, but he tried hard. We got to the lodge by going up the river and walking into the lodge called Intova. It was quite rudimentary – open concept with the roof and walls and the usual mosquito netting because of the chances of malaria. Interesting to note that one morning when we woke, up there was a little pile of stool right beside the bed on the *inside* of the mosquito net, so some animal had been in there and done his business and we had been unaware of it at the time.

There was an interesting American couple with us. She was reasonable. He was a bull rider and, according to him, the world's best big game hunting guide – I guess that made him a bull shooter as well. Unfortunately, he had never been out of Montana before, and he was busy telling everyone they should do this and should do that the way they do it in the United States; in fact, they should take this place over and teach them how to run a country. He had no idea that people might like the country just the way it was. One night at Pepe's Bar, he got a little drunk and confided to me that he hated killing animals. He should try a different line of work, I suggested. He also had a chronic sore back.

Our first night on the Amazon we were awakened very early by a horrendous roaring sound that seemed very close, actually quite scary at first. It turned out to be a group of red howler monkeys enjoying themselves. Pepe, the namesake of the bar, was also a howler monkey, and he lived in the bar. He had himself a little place up above the bar where he spent his time. He was a cute little guy, and he loved women. He was not interested in men at all, so of course, the ladies all loved to hug him, and he loved to be hugged.

We got up early in the morning to see the clay areas frequented by macaws and parrots. There was a blind so that we could watch the very commonly seen ones. There were also many other species of birds and plants. The jungle was very luxurious, lots of vines completely unknown to us. We heard the large river otters, but we did not actually see one, nor did we see a jaguar. We did some fishing and caught some piranhas, a little change in the usual perspective – you think of them as eating *you*; we ate them for supper, and they were quite good. Our guide was quite good at going over all the birds that we got to see out of a bird book, and he pointed to the ones we had seen, and I have a list of some of them. On the way back to the coast, we stopped in at Arequipa, which was very high in the mountains surrounded by snow-covered peaks

MEDITERRANEAN (2007)

This cruise started from Rome, and our first real stop was Messina in Sicily with Mount Etna looming over our heads. It had been quite an active volcano and erupted not that long before our arrival.

There were several Greek islands on our itinerary. Santorini was one that had six hundred and ten steps, which Marian and I climbed – Helen and Peter took the gondola up. On the way back down, we decided to take a ride on the donkeys which most people took up. That was not a good idea because the way the donkeys lurch back and forth with each step, they felt like they were going to fall over the edge. Fortunately, that didn't happen. The other Greek islands were idyllic and beautiful with exposed rocks, blue skies and the azure waters of the Mediterranean.

Mykonos was where we learned a lot of Greek mythology. We bought a painting from a local artist of the white cupola-shaped buildings most of which had windmills on top.

We spent a couple of days visiting Athens and all its many attractions – the Parthenon, the Acropolis, and the Panathenaic Stadium etc. You could almost feel the history

Then we sailed to Turkey. Ephesus, one of the oldest cities in the world (and once part of the twelve-city Ionian league), was a huge ruin which, even now, revealed what a wonderful place it must've been in its glory days. It even had a plumbing system of sorts and a very elegant architecture (based on what's left of it).

Apparently, it was built on the coast though now it lay several miles inland.

On our way back to Rome, we stopped at Naples in Italy, which was a rather forgotten but apparently crime-ridden city, and we witnessed an active volcano spewing some lava and smoke, which was quite a sight at night.

UNITED KINGDOM (2007)

England and Wales

London was the first stop in the United Kingdom – and a great place to start. One of the best cities in the world, I believe, but maybe because we speak English. Paris was also great; however, we had just come from Rome to London by Lufthansa Airlines, and they lost some of our luggage. They did get it back to us within a day, so we went down to Brighton, having rented a car. Peter and Helen were spending some time in London first, and we had been there before, so they wanted to meet us the next day or two. We were impressed once again that the Brits drive on the wrong side of road, but perhaps they may eventually learn. Brighton was on the south coast. It was a university town and so there were a lot of very young people around. We stayed at the Royal Albion Hotel which was over a hundred and eighty years old. We were met by a dour lad that surely made us think that he must be related to Uriah Heep of Dickens fame – a close cousin perhaps.

We drove to Hastings and then to the site of the Battle of 1066. Seven thousand people died brutally that day, and an abbey was created on the spot run by the Benedictine monks.

When Peter and Helen arrived in Brighton, we departed for Stonehenge. Three thousand BC was the noted estimated date for the erection of the stones which were brought hundreds of miles. It was very impressive, and a number of them denote astronomical events apparently, for example, the summer solstice. In those days, religion and science were opposites. That hasn't changed really over the centuries, has it?

Wales was on our list since Helen and Marian had a connection, so we drove to the town of Gewnbr and took them to Trinity Church Cemetery looking for the grave of Rachel Alexander. No luck, but a lot of it was overgrown with brambles and weeds.

—

A bed and breakfast at Morecambe in the southern Lake District was very nice. It was a beautiful area with lakes, mountains, stone fences, and hedges. It was like stepping back in time and right into some of the pastoral paintings by one of the old masters.

Having never had a Guinness beer I felt I ought to try it. Surprise! I liked it.

Scotland

Next, back on the M5, we crossed the Firth of Forth over the huge suspension bridge and stopped at Kinross which was ten to fifteen miles north of Edinburgh, having spent some time in Edinburgh walking in the downtown area exploring the parks, Edinburgh University and the impressive local architecture.

Being anxious to see Balmoral, we drove north through Cairngorm's National Park. We followed a very old Rolls-Royce with panel doors for a long way – even the driver and his partner were old, maybe in the late seventies at the very least. Oops sorry, that is not old! There were lots of rivers and lakes that looked like they would have trout or salmon in them. The vast hills with the remaining heather gave me a sublime peaceful feeling.

The queen was in residence at Balmoral. We had not let her know in advance, so the guards at the gate wouldn't let us in to say hello. She is such a nice lady, I'm sure she would have invited us in for tea, if only she had known it was us.

The River Dee, running through Cairngorm, certainly made me want to go fishing.

We stayed at a little town called Aviemore and climbed the ski hill the next day, which was said to be four kilometres uphill; locals claimed we could see the north of Scotland from there –maybe the eagles could.

The following day we took a Highland Discovery tour which included Inverness and a lot of local history, then a cruise down Loch Ness where we did *not* see a monster, but of course, you should worry that it might come up and swallow the boat or something. I guess we were just lucky we had an uneventful trip. We stopped at Urquhart Castle with its own long history of different families. Later, we visited Culloden Moor where, in 1746, the English responded to Prince Charlie who had come back from Italy to take over Scotland.

Following the Scottish tradition, the next day we went "hill roaming" which really was a joy across the open spaces and ancient trails. There is a "right to roam" in Scotland, which means you can walk anywhere you want. It is colliding somewhat with the privacy that some people think is very important. They're busy sorting that out still I believe.

The Scottish Highlands were stark, lots of old crofter's huts out on the moors, mostly deserted. It happened a long time ago when they raised the rents and the crofters could no longer afford to pay it. Most of them left and they went to either Canada or Australia.

The Isle of Skye was very scenic, but the Scotch whiskey we tried there was not nearly as appealing to me even though we tried several types (maybe too many?). We circled back to Edinburgh and the Royal Road, followed by the famous Edinburgh University and tried Haggis for supper. I actually liked, haggis, the trick is not to think about its components. Evidently you must find the right place for good haggis. I guess we were lucky.

Ireland

Ireland was next on the agenda, so we flew from Edinburgh to Dublin via London then drove to Killarney. Why should we feel a connection? It probably has a lot to do with the history and old stories surrounding it – the lilting Irish songs. There were a number of famous drives, meaning car drives in Ireland, and the Ring of Kerry was the most famous. It circled a peninsula starting and ending in Killarney, the roads were very narrow and were really only one lane. The dwellings were small, often stone and many looked in need of repair. There were many seabirds along the way as well. The Irish pub with Irish music was crowded and lots of fun. Marian Andretti (Hall) drove the next day along the coast again. The scenery was amazing, with the old stone fences and buildings. We noticed a lot of the signs in Gaelic only, and we were not too fluent in it, but I guess they were trying to maintain tradition. It was a foggy day helped by the presence of many fuchsia hedges. We were reminded of the Irish poets and writers – Wilde, Yeats, Joyce and others. We went to the Grand Hotel, an Irish pub for Irish music and fun and heard mournful but romantic songs like "Galway Bay". There was virtually no traffic on the road. The Mahar Cliffs were a major item, and it reminded us a lot of the Chatham Islands actually.

The Blarney Castle was a must, of course, so you must learn to establish the difference between Blarney (subtle flattering for mischievous purposes such as seduction) and baloney which was an outright lie. Marian kissed the Blarney Stone. Thanks anyway. I climbed up to where you were to bend over backward to do it, but I didn't feel the need to kiss the thing. Who knows who just slobbered on it? Later we drove to Cork then flew to Heathrow airport and home.

ASIA (2008)

The trip started off as a medical cruise starting in Osaka, Japan, so we flew in to what was a very industrial area. It seemed like we were passing maritime cranes for miles before reaching Osaka. The next day the cruise went to Nagasaki, where there were statues about the atomic attack and hope for peace, there was a zone ceremony; the religion of the region being Shinto and Buddhism.

—

Busan, South Korea, was the next stop. The second largest city in South Korea, it was very impressive with fruit trees and blossoms, huge markets, and obviously a very civilized, high-tech country.

—

Our first stop in China was Dalian in the north near the North Korean border – and where I actually considered working at one time. Interestingly, in Dalian, we got to meet a family with eleven children – so this was obviously an older family because that's not allowed anymore. The tradition in China was for the oldest boy to look after his parents. The place they lived was sort of an old, grey building lacking colour or personality. I would call it uninspiring. I asked the father about religion, and he said he now believed in the great God money. They had a small apartment, the kids are mostly gone, and the one son was staying and expected to look after them.

We did see a woman police force, and they were all tall, pretty, and expert horsemen. Interestingly one of them, who was quite pretty, came up to Marian and told her how pretty she was and wanted her picture taken with Marian, so we have one, and they have one. About three percent of the people had cars, but we saw Mercedes,

BMWs, and Audis. Virtually everyone lived in an apartment. The average salary was about two thousand yuan a month (a little over $400 CDN), so they couldn't afford much so where did all the big cars come from?

The next port was Tianjin, the maritime gateway to Beijing, a gigantic port city of nine million people, but it seemed like nothing but ships and cranes.

Beijing, China

We then went on to Beijing, a city of almost 17 million (or about twice the size of New York City in 2008). What a place; smoke and so much smog. Driving around in a bus with the guide, thousands of trees were being planted along the side of the road. It seemed to us to hide the poverty, and pollution from the eyes of world; the Beijing Olympics in a matter of months.

The Temple of Heaven was a magnificent building. A round, brightly-coloured three-tiered temple built in the early 1400s. A pit stop made there was evidently horrifying for most of the ladies. Tiananmen Square brought back many memories the massacre of students there in 1989. It was the biggest square in the world and featured a huge picture of Chairman Mao. Next to the square was the Forbidden City, a massive palace compound that covers 180 acres and contains close to 1,000 richly appointed buildings with ornate carvings in evidence. There were three million cars in Beijing, and *theoretically* they drove on the right side. Did anybody pay any attention to that? No!

We noticed security was evident everywhere.

We had Peking duck for supper (appropriate don't you think), and the following day we went to see the Great wall.

The Great Wall of China was an amazing engineering feat. It was thousands of miles long and varied in the height, but it was virtually unclimbable anywhere from the sides. It took thousands of Chinese people and slaves to build it over many years, supposedly. I believe it was built as a protection from the hoards to the north, who, might attack. It had steps on it so that we could climb it. The section that we did had over fifteen hundred steps up to a little guard post up near the top, but we could see it ran over the hills and mountains in the distance. I'm sure it must have cost many lives building it.

Some of us flew to Xi'an the capital of Shaanxi province to see the amazing Terracotta Army. Each of the 8,000 terracotta warriors was unique; some stood some rode, and they each had their own expression on their face. There were apparently more that they have found, as well, which will be dug up sometime in the not too distant future. Apparently, Emperor Qin Shi Huang (247–220 BC) wanted to have his army with him to protect him in the afterlife as well. We had dinner at a place called Tang Dynasty where the after-dinner show was spectacular. The outfits, the choreography, and the music were all extremely well done.

A word about religion surfaces – but only occasionally. Communism is totally against religion, but there is an undercurrent of a mixture of Buddhism, Taoism, Confucianism, and Greek philosophy; Taoism and Confucianism were complementary. Taoism was all pervasive and relates to the natural order of things.

We were off again, this time to Shanghai, with a population of nineteen million people. The average apartment was nine hundred square feet and cost about three million yuan.

There was a history of colonization in Shanghai by the British, the French, and the Americans.

We took a ride on the maglev train which went from Shanghai to the airport in eight minutes at a speed of 431 kilometres an hour. It felt like it was floating, and I guess it really was because it used magnets to keep slightly above the tracks.

We went to see a new building eighty-eight storeys high with a one-hundred-plus-storey building going up close by. The elevator took forty-five seconds(?) to get to the eighty eighth floor but there was no feeling of movement, and when the door opened, and we stepped out, we could see down the inside of the building to the lobby. The smog was so thick, that we couldn't get a very good view outside. We had the same lack of sensation on the way down. A British tourist next to me said, " if you knew it was made in China you wouldn't buy it would you?" We don't know how they did that, but it was quite remarkable.

Across the Pudong River, Pudong had been built in eighteen years – almost 1210 square kilometres of gigantic high-rise apartments built by the hundreds. They just moved all the area farmers out and moved them to apartments further away from their neighbours and friends. The all-powerful government could do whatever it wanted, and it was a very impressive" progress" in a very short time. Human rights were not mentioned. There were pockets of poverty right beside the massive buildings – laundry hanging out the windows sometimes on racks or spools. Our guide told us a downtown apartment with a view of the river and the nightlights cost an impressive $1,000 dollars a square foot. Next day we were stranded in Shanghai because of the fog.

China had apparently fifty-six different nationalities, but ninety-four percent were Han.

The Olympic stadium did not look finished, and the Americans in our midst were sure they would not do it in time for the Olympics. They did, of course, to no one's surprise.

A lot of people wore surgical masks, and some believed the smog was sand blown in from the Gobi Desert (a government suggestion).

The Silk Road was a major trading route for a long time from Europe, starting in Turkey, I believe, and heading right through China. We visited a couple of the outposts on the route. We finally got going, but we were late getting to Hong Kong so would have to tell our new guide from Goway that we would be late. We passed through the Taiwan Straits but could not see Taiwan because of the fog and smog.

Hong Kong

When we talk about shopping opportunities it was probably impossible to be in any better spot. The ship was only two blocks from the main street. We walked a few blocks to the Harbour City which was four floors of stores, over a thousand apparently. Marian visited some women's shops and couldn't find what she wanted to buy. I visited one camera store and bought a 100–400 mm hundred Canon lens with a few accessories. I love the lens image stabilizer and automatic focus, but it is heavy. Nighttime was very busy in Hong Kong – lights everywhere and crowds of people off running around (some in boats), and it seemed like the oceanfront was several million people all in one square block. It may be not quite that bad. I got some pictures of the juxtaposition of poverty and wealth on the waterfront.

Next morning was a flight to Vietnam

Rich and poor

Vietnam

Again, we were delayed by the weather, but when we arrived, we stayed at the Riverside Resort about fifty kilometres from Da Nang. There were a lot of motorcycles and scooters and the way people drove I don't like to think about how many fatalities there must be on a weekly basis. The average wage was $150 per month, and they must pay for their education. The resort was old but recently refurbished; it looked like you might see Ernest Hemingway lurking somewhere there.

Da Nang was 1.2 million, Hanoi 7.5 million. I felt like a giant because the average man was five foot four and the average women, five feet. Marla, our shortest daughter, would feel big there. Our guide Tony took us to the World Heritage site that was bombed and left as a reminder of what war was like. Two million Vietnamese died during the war, and 60,000 Americans. I didn't see evidence of either pro-American or anti-American sentiment – they probably realized that tourism was their future, and the Americans were the richest. We went to a market which was almost impossible to believe, and I bought a silk shirt for fifteen dollars. Marian bought some clothes for what seemed like very little money, and they did some tailoring right on the spot.

We then took the *Hải Vân* [Ocean Cloud] Pass and looked out over the beaches from a little site at the top of a mountain on our way to Saigon. Vietnam had a population of 85 million people. There were very few cars, but a lot of bicycles and motorcycles that were whizzing in all directions. I asked how many cyclists got killed every day. The answer was about thirty at one point, but since mandatory helmets, it was down to about five. There must be *some* rules of the road or they would all be dead. The roads were choked.

Apparently, they throw old tires in the ocean, and when the oysters attached themselves folks would bring them up and put them on the highway, and cars would drive over them, which dislodged and broke the shells so the oysters could be retrieved.

We drove for a while on a four-lane road next to the ocean. There was really no one else around. They can't afford cars or gas. We noted there were no American tourists at the site where we stayed in Saigon. There were Europeans, English, and Australians.

We visited a place called Marble Mountain where they carved marble with hand tools. While Marian was in the store buying small articles, I got to liking an eagle sculpture I had seen in the yard. The price kept coming down, and they promised to cover insurance and transportation and everything else, so we finally agreed on a price and bought it. It's white and orange marble and weighs five hundred pounds. It took about three months to get home, but now that we have it on our front deck at home, we love it and it is a fine memory of one of our trips. Despite communism, prosperity was very gradually improving. Everyone was very thin and ate lots of rice, of course. Who knows what else they get. The only problem with Vietnam, a beautiful country, was that the motorbikes were everywhere, and they were constantly honking. They claimed they learned that from the French.

Bangkok, Thailand

Bangkok held 10 million people and all of Thailand accounted for 68 million. Thailand was much more affluent than Vietnam. There were a lot more cars. To our surprise, April 13 was Songkran (their New Year) and so from ancient stories, came the art of throwing chalk and water on people – including us. Many were driving around in trucks throwing buckets of water on each other. At the end of our tour, the guide pulled out a water pistol and sprayed us with it. It was all good fun, but we didn't have a weapon to respond.

It appeared that everything was gold-plated and spires were everywhere.

We went to see the floating market approximately 130 kilometres from Bangkok and saw some beautiful carved rustic furniture. It was truly an adventure floating up and down the little channels crowded with people in boats. In the markets, all along the sides, we could pull up if we saw something that we liked and deal with the proprietor from our boat. It was an unusual but great outing.

We were not allowed to go to Tibet because in March of that year there had been a great deal of political unrest and China was still responding; there was a lot of persecution of the monks, and the

Tibetans were being suppressed and diluted with mainland Chinese. Some were killed, and so no one was allowed in at the time, so we missed out on that, but another possibility was a flight to Chengdu, China, which we accepted. It was the highest (altitude-wise) major airport in the world.

Chengdu, China

We left Bangkok at three a.m. and arrived at Chengdu at 5:38 in the morning. Since we had been in China already, and our visa said one admission, we had a major problem. Our guide, Panda Jim, was waiting for us at the gate and could see us from a distance. Since our Chinese was extremely limited we were fortunate they were able to get Panda Jim, and he explained that we had to buy another visa, which we did. There couldn't be many tourists in Chengdu because people were stopping and pointing at us. Some were asking to have their pictures taken with us. One night at dinner there were six or eight of the waitresses that stood around staring at us.

"Why?", we asked.

Marian's eyes were extraordinary in colour for them, so they all wanted to see.

We visited Mount Qingcheng a UNESCO World Heritage site considered to be the birthplace of Taoism. It was a very beautiful mountain under the sun, one of four mountains sacred to Taoists in China. A large temple at the top had a lot of steps to get up. There was incense burning everywhere and lots of monks around. There were lower cast slaves carrying huge bundles of something up the stairs strapped to their back with tump lines. The muscles in their legs were immense.

It is also where all the pandas in various age groups were kept. The mother pandas were only allowed a certain amount of time with their babies each day. The babies were trying to get into all kinds of activities, and their mothers may not approve, so they attempted to stop them. The babies then tried to escape and hide on their mothers. It's all fun to watch and so universal. You could have paid to have your picture taken with a baby panda. There were red pandas also, which really looked a lot like big red raccoons, so they're not nearly as popular as the black and white ones of all ages. As we were leaving the zoo there were a couple of classes of children coming in. They were curious about us and were practicing their English with enthusiastic, well-pronounced *hellos*. They wore big smiles and were incredibly polite.

Incidentally the parks were very good and used heavily by individuals and groups, for example, there was a singles group, a ballroom dancing group, even a group doing the tango. There didn't seem to be much interest in democracy there.

"We have always been ruled by somebody else," said Jim. "So the Communists are just one more."

They were aware of all the political graft and corruption in the government, but they were better off than they were a few years ago, so the idea of doing something about free speech or about the corruption seemed foreign to them. They were quite used to being dominated by someone or some group.

Our driver was scary. He would be up on the sidewalk or anywhere. Jim said he was good. I shuddered to think of the others; actually, we did see a lot of others. One time, a bunch of school kids were crossing the street, and the driver headed straight for them with his horn blaring, kids scattered in all directions, big smile on his face. We told him in Ontario he'd probably be in jail for that.

We next flew back to Shanghai for a few days to get more involved in the city. They had a huge area where there were no cars allowed, and there were many hawkers out on the street pushing anything you can imagine so there were many small businesses on many floors of many shopping complexes. So if someone talked to us in the street about buying a watch, suit, or something else, and we were interested, he would take you up to the shop which might be on the twelfth or twentieth floor, and it would be a small shop run by some local people. There were no big box stores like Costco or Walmart around, or at least we did not see any. What a shame!

Suzhou was the Venice of China only two hours from Shanghai – a series of interconnecting canals with some shops that ran right to the water's edge but not nearly as much fun as the floating market in Bangkok.

—

On a side note: On May 12, 2008, not long after we left, the Wenchuan earthquake struck northwest of Chengdu killing an esti-mated 69,000 people. Mount Qingcheng was affected and killed a number of schoolchildren (and a couple of pandas as well). We phoned Jim to see how he was, and he said that no one would go back in their apartments, as they were fearful of the aftershocks. So, ten million people in Chengdu were living in the street and in the parks. He was out of a job because no tourist would go there for a while. He was in a tent with his parents and girlfriend.

SOUTH AMERICA AND ANTARCTICA (2009)

We started our voyage in Rio de Janeiro where we stayed at the International Hotel on the beach. Looking down the beach, we saw all the suntanned tourists. If we turned our eyes left, however, we saw rows upon rows of houses that looked like they were on top of each other. The *favelas* [slums] crowded the base of the mountain known as *Corcovado* [hunchback] with Christ the Redeemer atop looking out over the city. Poverty and wealth side by side, separated by a highway.

We visited the iconic statue and the Sugarloaf Mountain the next morning before proceeding to Buenos Aires via the Holland America ship Amsterdam From there we flew to Iguazu Falls on the border of Brazil and Argentina. Next was Montevideo, Uruguay, where we spent a day with the gauchos on their 3,065-acre estancia. The Falkland Islands followed, and then Antarctica. From there we slowly returned to Tierra del Fuego, Cape Horn, The Beagle Channel, Magellan Strait, and Patagonia (including Torres del Paine National Park and finally Valparaíso and Santiago before flying home.

I won't give you a comprehensive list of all the wildlife we saw but will mention quite a few with whatever stories of interest that went with them.

Rio de Janeiro, Brazil

Rio was a gigantic city, so it was hard to see much wildlife other than kelp gulls and magnificent frigate birds (the ones that puff their red chests up). One night, the sky was full of hundreds (maybe thousands) of them flying several hundred feet above the sea. Since they were sea scavengers, one wonders what attracted so many to that height that night.

—

It was interesting to note that the further south we went, the more sea life was evident. The basic food for many species – unless they eat each other – was krill, a small crustacean that was more plentiful in colder water. Even when we were hundreds of miles from land, we could see lots of birds which reminded us, once again, that sea birds don't need or even care about land except to lay an egg and have a chick – every three to four years for the albatross.

Iguazu Falls, Argentina

We flew to Iguassu Falls which had to be the most beautiful falls in the world. There were probably two hundred separate falls cascading down both sides of this gorge. The falls were surrounded by lush vegetation and rainbows were plentiful. An amazing sight! We saw caimans, hawks, turtles, and cormorants all enjoying themselves only a very short distance above the falls. Did they know how close they were to disaster? Coatis are a raccoon-like animal that were common in the area also.

Montevideo, Uruguay

The next day at Montevideo, we were transported to the working *estancia* [ranch] with 650 milking cows plus wheat, beef, and potatoes. They also grew a lot of Australian eucalyptus because they had good hard wood, grew fast, and had a pleasant odour. The gauchos spend so much time on horseback that they almost became one unit. They all wore the long boots and most wore berets, occasional flat-top cowboy hats. It must be a good life. They all seemed happy and eager to share their experiences. We saw lapwings, green austral parakeets – hated by the ranchers because they eat everything – a great egret, southern martin, and an austral thrush.

The next two days were at sea en route to the Falklands. Right whales and southern minke whales were seen, and some people thought they saw orcas. There were Atlantic petrels, Wilson's storm petrels, giant petrels, and our first sighting of the legendary albatross – these were black-browed species (relatively small with a wing span of just over two metres). We also encountered sun fish which looked like big blobs with huge dorsal fins and no visible tail; they seemed to just sit in the water even when the ship was close to them. How do they move?

Falkland Islands

Some people found the Falkland Islands desolate and did not appreciate them as I did. I did feel sorry for them if they couldn't see and feel the beauty in the vast open spaces with the volcanic peaks poking up through the peat, which Falkland Islanders cut, dried and burned. We took quite a long hike along the windblown shore and saw several rare species that live only there. Kelp geese, Patagonian crested ducks, oystercatchers, Falkland thrushes, skuas and, Magellanic flightless steamer ducks (which spoke to the lack of predators on the islands). Our guide pointed out that there was a certain lack of imagination there. They had two types of ferns, small and tall. They had a meadowlark with a bright red chest which was called a long-tailed meadowlark. The plants were unusual as well – sea cabbage, scurvy grass, and diddle dee a small bush with red berries that made good jam. There were also multiple cormorants and Magellan penguins on the island as well as king and rock-hoppers

A lot of the huge sand beaches could not be used because there were still a lot of landmines out there from the Falklands War – intended for invading British soldiers, the penguins weren't heavy enough to set them off and so didn't seem to worry about them too much.

There were many rusted old ships in the harbour, remnants of that brief conflict between England and Argentina. The people seemed very British and many spoke with British accents. The homes were all painted bright colours, yellow, blue, red, and green, which lightened up the landscape.

Antarctica

Next stop was Elephant Island, Antarctica, a rugged mountainous terrain featuring glaciers that flowed down to the sea.

We saw a number of whales (mostly humpbacks), Weddell seals, sea lions, and many species of birds, including skuas (both brown

and Antarctic), fulmars, prions, and petrels (blue, cape and giant).
Only a few sooty shearwaters were seen, which was surprising since it
was the most common bird in the world. Cormorants were common
(rock, imperial and blue-eyed).

Penguins, of course, were everyone's favourites and were quite
common in those icy waters. They swam, dove, porpoised (which
is to say leapt from the water like a porpoise), and slid on the snow
and icebergs. They looked like they were having fun. They left red
trails where they climbed the mountains (remember that krill was
their staple). It was humorous to see them slide down the snow if they
slipped trying to climb up. They just got up and kept on trudging in
their comic waddling step. For some reason the Gentoo penguins
liked to nest several hundred feet up the slopes. We also saw Adélie
and chinstrap penguins; the latter seemed to wear a bow tie with
their tuxedos.

The heroes for me and a new love affair were the royal albatross
(wingspan of three metres) and the wandering albatross (with a
wingspan of up to three and a half metres). I watched them for hours

as they soared effortlessly, drifting with the wind, first up then down almost touching the waves at times. They occasionally tilted even at right angles to the sea. We witnessed them come from behind the ship which was doing about 22 knots (40 km/h) and pass it. All of these maneuvers without ever flapping their wings. Masters of the wind, they gave new meaning to the word graceful. The researchers even suspected that they may be able to sleep while soaring. Apparently, with implanted devices, they found that they may go twenty-four hours without landing on the sea. They also were apparently able to lock their "elbows" so there was no strength required to keep their wings extended, the perfect flying machine. What a fantasy to be able to do something like that.

The cape petrels with their white patches on blue wings were quite dramatic as they swooped and dove, often in flocks of forty to fifty.

Since it was summer, fog was not unusual with the ice all around and the relatively warmer air. Mystical lighting effects were common as the sun broke through the clouds and reflected off the glaciers and the dark water sparkled amidst the icebergs. Most people, including me, considered it a spiritual experience. If you are not affected by these incredible displays, you must need to turn up the volume on your sensitivity apparatus. Hours were spent out on the deck as this panorama evolved before me, ever-changing and entrancing. Almost totally silent except for the background droning of the engines, it was occasionally ruptured by the roar of an avalanche or the thunderclap as the ice split off a glacier and crashed into the sea, sending waves out into a semicircle from the point of contact. I was glad I was not in a canoe close to it.

—

Reflections on Antarctic Ice

I have to admit that, before our trip to the extreme south, I was slightly cynical about what we would find that was so different from the Canadian Arctic. I knew, of course, that Antarctica had penguins that the Arctic did not, and that the Arctic had some land mammals that the Antarctic did not. Other than that though we'd spent quite a bit of time in the Arctic and had seen the magnificent mountains and fjords of Baffin Island. How different could Antarctica be?

Our doubts were soon gone even as we first approached Elephant Island which lay just off the tip of the Antarctic Peninsula. The mountain range was really a continuation of the range that started in Alaska and came down the west coast of the Americas, except that, south of Tierra del Fuego and Cape Horn, the tectonic plates have pushed the range in a bulge eastward before appearing again in the Antarctic Peninsula.

Ice was everywhere from the glaciers, to the ice shelves, to the icebergs. From the practical point of view, there were two types of sea ice: *tabular* ice which was flat on top with sharp sides and *non tabular* ice which came in a myriad of sizes shapes and hues of blue white and grey. We had onboard several very experienced geologists, naturalists, historians, and an ice captain whose job was to advise the ship's captain about the ice and where it was safe to venture. Apparently, they never argued with him. He had been there over one hundred and twenty times. The three main terms they used to describe the ice were *tabular*, *growlers* – which were less than a metre high – and *bergy bits* which was everything else. Growlers and bergy bits may be from glaciers. The tabular bergs have broken off the shelves which are along the coast and the bays. The first one we saw, we estimated at between three and five kilometres long. It was very hard to estimate the height of them because you don't want to get too close, considering that most of the ice is underwater and therefore dangerous, and so it was hard to get a sense of scale. Some of the ones we got close to seemed to be over a hundred metres high.

Some of the icebergs had a bright and brilliant blue-turquoise colour which evidently meant the ice was older. Some of them had blue lines on various angles so they must've tipped over during their lifetime, and if they got any vegetation in them or touched bottom, they could have some amazing designs and colours.

The steel hull of our ship was less than two centimetres thick so not really prepared to meet up with any collisions. The Russian icebreakers often used as tour boats now had hulls five time that thick. It reminded me of the fate of the MV *Explorer*, a 2,400-tonne tour boat that sank in Antarctica waters in November of 2007 when a hole was torn into their hull – they felt that it might have been a growler. One of the icebergs we saw looked exactly like a ship with decks funnels etc. Was it the ghost of the lost ship? Another berg seemed to have horns and cloven hooves. Perhaps it was the devil? Did that have anything to do with the ship that went down? A little imagination can lead you a long way – there were icebergs of all shapes and sizes so lots of room for it.

We were very fortunate to get into some places that had been impossible for some time. Paradise Bay was well described by its name. We were surrounded by mountains and glaciers, the sea was calm, and without the omnipresent wind, there was a great silence descending upon us, one of those moments.

Another incident quite the opposite occurred while attempting to circumnavigate Paulette Island in the Weddell Sea, close to a huge Adélie penguin colony of about 100,000 – and yes, they *did* smell, but they sure were cute.

There were four of us on the top open deck when a sudden severe wind almost blew us right off the ship. We were forced to crouch down behind a metal barrier and crawl along to the steps to safety. Marian was blown *across* the deck before she got down. This was a katabatic wind which is about 150 kilometres per hour. The Floridians told us this was equivalent to a force two hurricane. It felt like it. These types of winds start suddenly coming down a mountain slope then accelerate for some reason. It was all very exciting for us, but the ice captain told us later that he was terrified as the ice was starting to move and we were not prepared to meet it. We escaped while the penguins were enjoying themselves in that fierce wind and waves, surfing and porpoising. We were able to get in behind an island so that we were not in any a danger once we were there, and the winds went away eventually. When we got down to the next deck, we found that all the furniture had been blown overboard, so we were very fortunate that our ship was not damaged.

We had to cross Drake Strait, this time going north, and for some reason a lot of people developed white spots behind their ears. These are gravol patches for nausea. Do you suppose it has anything to do with this being one of the legendary roughest spots in the world? It helped to shorten the lineup for meals too.

Cape Horn

The land loomed through the rain and mist as we were welcomed to the most southern tip of South America. Ushuaia in Argentina, which is not that far away in the Beagle Channel, claimed to be the most southerly permanent habitation in the world – Chile disputes that.

The fascinating history of the area boasts explorers such as Magellan, Drake, Darwin and many others.

The Beagle Channel is a narrow strait, two hundred kilometres long, which cut across the tip of Tierra del Fuego and southern Chile. It was full of mountains, glaciers, waterfalls and rich with wildlife such as seals, sea lions, shags (cormorants), petrels, geese, and gulls.

The following day, on the west coast, we arrived at Punta Arenas on the Magellan channel. From there we flew to Puerto Natales where we took a bus for two hours – through the rolling hills of Patagonia – to Torres del Paine National Park. There were magnificent tall, steep, stately, cliff-like mountains that looked as if they had quietly exploded from the surrounding grasslands. They were not the tallest mountains I have ever seen but were certainly the most dramatic. Unfortunately (or maybe fortunately), it was foggy and rainy that day which obscured the view somewhat but gave it a surreal, otherworldly feeling as they appeared and disappeared. They are the mountains we have all seen in ads for Patagonia and Chile.

Once again, we were lucky with the wildlife. We saw Andean condors, guanacos (similar to llama), rheas with chicks (rheas are like emus), and a South American gray fox that wandered by. The guanacos were left wild because, apparently, neither their hide nor meat was considered valuable.

Further north, along the coast and the Darwin Channel, were many glaciers, fiords, waterfalls, rushing rivers, and volcanoes. Chile has about 500 active volcanoes, sixty of which have erupted in the last 450 years. Interestingly the southern Chileans considered themselves as almost a separate country, since there was no road to the northern part without detouring through Argentina.

Puerto Montt Chile, was our access harbour to Petrohué Falls and Volcán Orsono, a huge stratovolcano that we climbed part way up. It was our last highlight before arriving at Valparaíso, the Chilean "bohemia" and the nearest port to Santiago from whence we returned home, inspired once again by visiting another part of this wonderful planet..

NEW YORK CITY (2009)

Cities are not my favourite places. I generally prefer remote rugged places, but three cities that I actually liked were Paris, Prague, and New York – I suppose Shanghai could be a fourth.

New York had an ambience all its own. It was full of life twenty-four hours a day and came with a lot of history: the Statue of Liberty, Central Park, the Ground Zero and the World Trade Center site. We had been up in the World Trade Centre before they were destroyed, so it was very meaningful to us.

The people in New York were friendly and obliging. The shows were great as were the restaurants and the food.

We toured the various areas, Harlem, Brooklyn (and the bridge), Carnegie Hall, and the American Museum of Natural History off Central Park. We stayed in a timeshare only a few blocks from there. It had one window which looked at a brick wall, but if you got down near the floor you could see the sky. The Empire State building at night was impressive. We got into the swing of New York and were constantly busy for the week we spent there. We took a horse and carriage ride in Central Park and saw absolute no sign of crime even though we were out late every evening.

CENTRAL AMERICA (2010)

Panama

We flew to Panama via Mexico City and Mexican Airlines. We were met at Panama City by Jose, who drove us to the Gamboa Rainforest Resort. It was a wonderfully ecologically aware and sensitive place with fine accommodation and food. The birding was incredible, and the noise of the jungle and songs of the birds were all so different it seemed surreal, even right in the resort grounds. There was a huge amount of wildlife. We saw twenty-eight species new to us the first day and twenty-two the second.

The visit included a boat ride to Barro Colorado Island in Gatun Lake – which is the artificial lake created during the making of the Panama Canal – where a white-faced capuchin monkey jumped on board stole somebody's camera and jumped back into the tree. A trip down to the end of the canal in Al Capone's old rum-running yacht, the *Isla Morada*, to the Miraflores Locks on the Pacific was educational.

We also visited the RiveraIndians to see how they lived. They were content although they led rustic lives. What's it all about anyway? They used dugout canoes. Their biggest problem had been the natives from Columbia, which is across the Darian gap – several hundred miles of dense swamp with no roads or recognised waterways. They attacked often, and they were impossible to control. Despite no roads through the swamp, they still managed to show up.

Asking my usual spiritual questions, I was told they believed in the land and the river and that is where the spirits were – which seemed similar to other aboriginal responses I have found.

The negative side of Panama was a lot of garbage all over the place – none in the resorts of course – but along roadsides and in the cities. Following the Gamboa Resort week, we stayed at the home of Connie Cochran and Jack Siegel. What a beautiful mountain home, a stream running right beside it, and a large deck surrounded by bird feeders and many species of birds present. We had a guide, Davis, who worked for *National Geographic*. On arriving, we were told to meet May Jean at her house for she had the keys. Her house was very small and made mostly of tin and looked quite rundown but suddenly emerges May Jean, a beautiful looking young lady, very well dressed. I've forgotten how many people lived in that house.

Davis, age twenty-five, was May Jean's brother and a wonderful guide and took us several places. We saw legions of exotic birds including nine Quetzals, four together on the first day. They are probably the world's most beautiful bird – red chest, long scissor like blue-green tail. I actually got so I called a couple of them in.

The price of food was unbelievable in markets or roadside stands. The prices made us think returning there would be very inexpensive.

We also visited an orchid farm where the owner had 2,500 species of orchids and 850 hybrids (mostly of the *Dracula* genus).

We saw a prong-billed barbet, which Davis assured us was more prized than the Quetzal by most serious birders. We also saw a turquoise-browed motmot which was Nicaragua's native National Bird.

Costa Rica

Next after missing a flight we flew to Costa Rica and drove to the resort. I guess we didn't really need a guide there but there was one there and he was very good on the birds and he took us walking a couple of times even in the extreme heat. They had had some flooding recently so the swimming pool was full of mud. We have a long list of the birds we saw which I won't put in the book but they're in my diary, if its important to someone some day.

Nicaragua

One day we drove over to Nicaragua mostly to see Masaya Volcano. At the border were trucks lined up both going and coming. We just drove past them all. Apparently, it can take three days to cross the border, so some of the drivers were asleep and had hammocks under their trucks. The volcano is within *Parque Nacional Volcan Masaya* [Masaya Volcano National Park]. There was no one else at the volcano, so we had the whole place to ourselves. The first smell was foul and sulfurous, and looking into it was impressive since it was continually active smoke and red hot in the bottom. Incidentally, sixteenth century Spanish conquistadors thought the devil lived deep within the volcano and they planted a cross at the top to keep him from emerging. While we were driving back to Costa Rica, we decided to count the trucks waiting at the border. There were 276 trucks lined up. While we were in Nicaragua having lunch, we needed to use the washroom. The cost was fifty cents, and for that, you got a trough and a barrel of rainwater to wash your hands. Fifty cents seemed like too much.

—

Back at the lodge in Costa Rica, a group of coatimundis (a Central American member of the raccoon family) came to dinner and were climbing up on the adjacent unoccupied table as well where there was no food. They were just looking – perhaps studying the menu? Subsequently, we went to Santa Rosa where there was a beautiful beach where we went swimming and body surfing.

GREENLAND AND THE NORTHWEST PASSAGE (2010)

We had just finished our third trip to the Arctic, but our first as a tourist, which was quite a different perspective. We flew from Toronto to Kangerlussuaq, Greenland, via an American company that usually flies military personnel around. The view the last twenty to thirty kilometres over the fjords, bays, and little isolated turquoise lakes was so outstanding that no one said anything. There really weren't words to describe it anyway, so an almost reverential silence in awe was most appropriate.

Shortly after customs, we took off to find some muskox and were fortunate enough to find some (a first for us) prior to boarding the ship. There were eighty-nine people and a crew of seventy-two. Do you think we may have been spoiled a bit? These ships were mostly Russian icebreakers, converted to a luxurious state. A ten-centimetre-think steel hull helped with the ice a lot. The captain was Swedish, and he had been sailing in the Arctic for thirty years. It gave one confidence.

Incidentally, Greenland was mostly green or brown in the Kangerlussuaq area – although there was a gigantic ice cap that covered almost the whole island up to three kilometres thick and actually sank the middle of it a hundred and twenty metres below sea level. It was considered ground zero as far as earth warming was concerned.

The next morning was foggy, but we saw a whale from our port-hole (probably a bowhead). We visited a small settlement, Aasiaat on an island that was apparently used as a summer retreat by some Europeans, mostly from Denmark. There were about eighteen to twenty small picturesque little buildings on the rocks, and it was absolutely deserted, a little eerie, which fit with the fog and the mountains. The grasses, sedges, lichens, mosses, and wildflowers were spectacular. There were some remnants of sod houses on the island also.

The origin of the Inuit people was from Siberia across the Bering Strait into what is now Alaska, gradually spreading across and reaching Greenland about five thousand years ago. As our on-board archeologist said:

"If anyone had asked the Inuit about the Northwest Passage it would have saved a tremendous amount of work and saved a lot of lives."

Why didn't someone think of that? Once again, we were caught up in our idea that we know so much more that we can't learn from others.

Ilulissat the next day was commenced with zodiac rides amongst the huge, multi-shaped icebergs. This was the largest source of bergs that ended up further south along Labrador and Newfoundland. We also took a helicopter ride to get a feeling of the size of the icefield. It was extremely rugged and extended as far as you could see. It was very impressive even after seeing the display in the Antarctic the previous year.

The icebergs came in all shapes and sizes. Let your imagination run wild. There were whales, buildings, sunken ships, the devil, and I'm absolutely sure I saw *Neptune*.

The following day crossing Davis Strait on our way to Baffin Island and specifically Qikiqtarjuaq, we encountered two polar bears (a mother and cub) swimming one hundred and twenty miles from shore and no ice floes in sight. The naturalists with us thought they didn't have a chance, but the Inuit aboard thought they would make it. More and more birds were seen even when we were far from shore but more as we got closer. Northern fulmars, dovekies, thick-billed murres, guillemots, black-legged kittiwakes, glaucous gulls, Thayer's gulls and at least one ivory gull were seen. Eider ducks were in large flocks.

Each day's activities were dictated by the ice, which was very thick in some places, so the ship could hardly move. Some places could not be reached because of it, but we did get into Pond Inlet and Resolute as well as Qikiqtarjuaq.

Qikiqtarjuaq felt strangely like a home coming, since I had worked there previously and recognised the whole village – even though the staff of the Health Centre had changed.

We'd maintained contact with the Australian nurse and her husband who were there when we worked there, as we'd done with other people we met during our various endeavours.

One memorable day, we spent in zodiacs close to a cliff where there were five hundred thousand birds nesting. The air and the sea were full of birds. The largest group were the thick-billed murres estimated at four hundred thousand by our experienced arctic bird researcher. The chicks, apparently, were nudged out of their nests, which might have been one thousand feet above sea level by their fathers (mothers have taken off). They fluttered all the way down and were met by their fathers on the sea if nothing happened to them on the way down. Jaegers, falcons and some gulls would try to pick them off. What a scary day for them.

We also visited Bylot Island, Devon Island (said to be the largest uninhabited island on earth) and Beechey Island where the graves of the Franklin crew were discovered. While we were there they (Canadian Archeologists) found the remains of one of the ships sent to look for Franklin. An abandoned old RCMP cabin with a sad tale involved was also visited on Devon Island.

We saw at least eight polar bears, ten walruses, lots of seals, several muskoxen, two whales, thousands of birds (including shearwaters) and many Arctic plants, including, Arctic cotton, Arctic avens, dwarf fireweed, moss campion, wintergreen, and countless others.

I believe I saw a narwhal. It was in the area where they had been sighted before, and it was a large animal on top of the water for a few seconds only before submerging. I did not, however, see the tusk. The only other person on deck at the time was one of the guides. He felt it probably was one, but it was hard to confirm without that tusk

In Pond Inlet, the ship staff had their annual indoor soccer game with the local Inuit. The Inuit won. We witnessed some of the winter games events such as the high kick and throat singing competition

Overall, we were constantly busy in zodiacs, hiking (always accompanied with guns, can't trust those bears), listening to lectures on everything pertaining to the area, eating five-star meals, or observing from the deck. With twenty-four hours of sun, it didn't seem right to spend much time sleeping.

The scenery was larger than life with vast spaces speckled with bright colours of flowers, mosses, and lichens. Ice was a constant feature of our days – from giant icebergs and miles of sea ice to massive glaciers. The sea was mostly calm, but there were some rough days and some fog as well. In a word it was wonderful.

We must put in a plug for Adventure Canada, organizers of the trip. Everything about it and them was first class.

INDIA AND SOUTHEAST ASIA (2011)

India

After finding our way through Heathrow Airport, which was a chore in itself, we finally got to New Delhi, and our Goway guide was there and took us around telling us the subtleties of the Indian nation. They were mostly Hindu, and eighty percent of marriages were still arranged. His girlfriend, who was a doctor, was Sikh, so there could be a big problem with her parents. The first impression of India was that it was hot, humid, crowded, and busy. Even at one in the morning on the way to the hotel, there was heavy traffic, and people were everywhere even dodging cars on four-lane roads.

The British took control of India about 1858 and ruled for over one hundred years. Independence occurred after the Second World War in 1947.

Motorbikes were everywhere, often with four or five people on a single motorbike. Some wore helmets but not all. The literacy rate was sixty-four to eighty-four percent (seventy-five percent men) most had post-secondary education. They had Medicare and had public and private healthcare. Apparently, there was significant waiting in the public system. We visited the Rashtrapati Bhavan (presidential residence), some government buildings, and the Red Fort, a gigantic fort made of red sand stone with a huge moat. We visited Ghandi's Funeral Pyre platform; the India Gate, a freestanding arch which was a war memorial for ninety thousand soldiers, looked a lot like the

Arc de Triomphe; and a memorial of Mughal Emperor who commissioned the Taj Mahal. The streets of Old Delhi, were probably the most interesting part of the day; traffic beyond belief, people walked by taking chances, leaping between them. Beggars were everywhere at stop lights even four- to five-year-olds. The density of people was staggering, people crawling over each other practically, but one can grow accustomed to anything, I suppose.

The subway system looked modern, and it was often elevated down the main streets. Do not rent a car in India if you don't want to drive where there are no written rules apparently. Vendors were everywhere – along the highway, in abandoned buildings and lots. Wealth and poverty existed side by side. Beside the luxurious hotels were absolute slums with broken down and crumbled buildings. Cows are sacred, and they were all over the road, lying wherever they wanted. Brahma type I believe. I'm not sure why there were not more accidents or deaths. Is anyone keeping statistics? Our driver said that, in India, you need three things in order to drive: a good horn, good brakes, and good luck.

Camels pulling material, were seen frequently, flocks of goats or sheep were not uncommon and occasionally crossed a very busy highway. Camels or donkeys may be seen even in the middle of a three-lane highway, and of course, cars coming the wrong way down the highway, was a common occurrence. Passing on the outside of the curve on hills was expected if there was no car in front of you. If someone came the other way, you just jumped on the brakes and squeezed by them. They don't even appear to get angry – I guess, because they expect the unexpected, you must be super alert all the time. Cars passed on either side, frequently within inches, and then cut in quickly. Horns were constant; in fact, trucks had signs on the back telling you to use your horn because they counted on that rather than looking to see where the cars were. Sometimes it was such a chaotic scene that it was hard not to laugh. There was absolutely no sense or order to it, and yet they all did it. Do I sense any rules? Perhaps whoever gets an inch on the other guy has the right of way? Are there speed restrictions slow or fast? Certainly, they were not apparent if there were. Despite all this, we got to Jaipur alive but had many scary incidents.

We stayed at the Country Inn Suites in Jaipur. As I looked at the traffic again, I'm not sure why everyone was not dead, especially the motorcycles which must be more than fifty percent of the traffic. We went through the pink city that day, everything was painted a terracotta pink – and then went for an elephant ride which was a little rough walking, of course. There was a snake charmer playing music for his snake. We noted that the salesman and the hawkers were very aggressive, more than we were used to in North America. Jaipur was a city of 1.6 million people. They lived in such elegance, with many wives and concubines, rooms full of artwork, and very precise buildings. How did they manage to bring stone for hundreds of miles before modern transportation? There was a palace (Jal Mahal or "Water Palace") in the middle of a large man-made lake. Man Sagar Lake had lots of fish and cormorants although it was warm and sluggish. There were a lot of feral dogs around as well. They all really looked related.

For scaffolding, they were still using bamboo tied together with ropes – and claimed it was safer than steel. Garbage was every-where, piled high in places, no one seemed to notice. I guess it becomes normal.

Road construction (and destruction) was everywhere; it was rare to see a stretch of clear road or highway. There were very many small stores along the sides of the highway everywhere. It was part of how they lived, I suppose; people have to eat and with such a dense population retail finds a way. The women generally were very cheerful in their saris. Crowding appeared quite normal – swarms of people like an ant hill or beehive. We saw twenty-five people in a regular

Jeep; fifteen to twenty in a three-wheeler, whole families (four to six) on a one person motorcycle; and as many as ten people *on top of* an SUV (usually jeep) speeding down the highway, weaving in and out. Maybe this was encouraged by the government as a method of population control. (??)

We went to a government jewelry store for tanzanite, emeralds, and rubies. Marian had some earrings made back home out of the stones. The next day, we left Jaipur and drove to Ranthambore National Park, where the road was worse than awful, full of construction, potholes, cattle, sheep, goats, and camels. It was a national nature reserve/park, and we had arranged safaris in hopes, particularly, of seeing a tiger. Our first trip we saw many animals – snakes, monkeys, hawks, different types of deer, but we had to be out by five pm. Suddenly just as we were heading for the gate to get out before the time limit, another truck passed us and said they had seen a tiger. With that, our driver turned and drove like fury down to see the tiger. The magnificent creature was lying on top of an old unused dam and looked even bigger than we expected; they can be up to 360 kilograms. Terrific, except that the truck got stuck, we had to get out and push, and that's when the tiger stood up and took a few steps along the dam. I'm sure everyone's anxiety level went up until she lay down again and watched us. She could have been on us in seconds if she had been inclined. We drove out in a big hurry; branches were flying, and we ducked the big ones – all worth it to see a tiger. We also saw some rare rose-ringed parakeet, two baby crocodiles, a peacock, and a three metre cobra.

The next day we were up early again – Muslims chanting about six thirty in the morning – and off to another safari in the park. We saw a lot of deer and different types of antelopes, but we did not see a tiger. We did the same thing again the next day, but still no tiger. The tiger that we'd seen was the first one that had been seen that year – the park opened only a few days before we got there. We saw many types of birds, including a white-breasted kingfisher, egrets, peacocks, peahens, lizards, gray parakeets, and a gray partridge. We visited the ghost city of Fatehpur Sikri which was n other UNESCO World Heritage Site, on our way to Agra.

The Taj Mahal was reached by catching an express train from Ranthambore to Bharatpur – rapid and precise, but the station was vile stinking mostly of the cattle and pigs feces which were all over the place.

The Taj Mahal near Agra was a magnificent white building. It was crawling with people all trying to beat the system by ignoring rules pushing into line etc. Interesting that the entrance to the Taj Mahal had an entrance for "high value people" and we used it; I guess that meant we were worth something. There were some narrow stairs that we had to walk up to get up on the level with the Taj Mahal, and I lost a couple bottles of water out of my pocket from pickpockets, of course. They just picked the wrong pocket. It seemed that everyone in that area was used to lineups. That's just normal.

The following day we went to Agro Fort which was yet another UNESCO World Heritage Site. It has a huge moat, sloping bales for pouring boiling oil down, holes for cannon and guns. It was never conquered.

One day we were confronted with a huge truck that drove the wrong way down the passing lane on the freeway. Of course, lots of motorcycles and three wheelers did it also. Everyone seemed to adapt quickly and just got out of the way.

It seemed that a lot of the Indian people were always pushing or ignoring rules and limits. That was an everyday experience, the prevailing sentiment seeming to be "get away with it if you can." For example, in the airport, the aircraft stopped and several Indians were up getting their luggage before the safety belt sign was removed, despite attendants asking or telling them to stay seated. I suspect they may push the limits of a lot of rules, certainly some do.

Thailand

Kingfisher Airlines flew us to Bangkok to visit an old friend before moving on to Rangoon – a place that evoked visions of smoke-filled bars and mysterious characters that appear at clandestine meetings during the night only to disappear in the morning mist.

In Thailand, we met up with Bill Beamish now a Professor of Biology at Burapha University but also a friend of more than fifty years, having been a schoolmate in high school and university, a teammate, and a fraternity brother. He seemed happy in Thailand.

He was still involved in research with fish. There were so many unanswered questions that he would like to see answered. He had a series of projects queued up ahead of him, for a long time; he was doing what he liked and making a contribution to science. There were 45,000 students at his university. Professor Beamish always had a graduate student around.

We noted that Thailand seemed much more affluent – and generally much cleaner – than India. There was much less garbage on the streets.

Myanmar

We took Thai Airways to Rangoon City. The old Rangoon was always considered colonial. Apparently, Myanmar was the name for the country since the eleventh century. The British changed it to Burma, and in 1989, the local people (and military government) changed it back to Myanmar. The following morning, as we looked out the window, our first impression was that it was old, gray, and run-down with areas of opulence in between. We noticed that all the local men wore longyis which are long wraparound skirts, seemed a little strange at first. I saw some old apartment buildings from the 1920s and '30s, which represented past opulence. Plant life and fungus was everywhere – trees grew in the low spots or in the cracks in the cement, roots crumbling walls, buckling sidewalks everything seemed slightly skewed or uneven. We noticed that the Burmese (or Myanmese, I suppose) drove within the lines generally and didn't honk.

We talked about the Karen people, and what we had heard previously. Our guide said that they were used politically when it was expedient to pit Thais against Myanmese. Where is the truth? Following that, we went to see the Aronpura monastery with the monks and novices. Some had come from orphanages, and when that happened, the monks became their family. They may start at age five or six, but when they were about fifteen or sixteen they had to decide whether to stay in it or proceed further in school. They had their own bowl and plate, which they carried into the dining room. They lined up outside in single file and walked to the dining room. There was no talking at all.

We noticed no motorcycles downtown, it almost shocked us. We attended a wonderful market comparable to Otavalo in Ecuador we thought. Lastly for the day, we went to Shwedagon Pagoda, fourteen acres of gold spires, temples, and various idolatry – very impressive. Think of the money involved that could have been used for something else. We drove by a lot of people who were praying and meditating all over the various artifacts

They drove on the right side of the road, but the steering wheel was on the right side also, didn't make sense. We were up again early the next morning to catch an Air Bagan flight to Mandalay on a Fokker 100 aircraft that was quite smooth. Our guide picked us up and drove us down the road to Mandalay.

The first stop was Shwenandaw Monastery that housed 1,500 monks. All had shaved heads, there were young boys to men of forty-five, and all stood, totally silent, in line for food during their eating time which was twice a day. Apparently, every boy from Myanmar who is Buddhist must spend at least a few days in a monastery. It was a discipline most parents enrolled their kids in. The monastery was connected to a huge pagoda.

We had a Thai lunch, which was very nice, and then we went on to the Kuthodaw Pagoda associated with the world's largest book comprising 729 "pages" carved into large, freestanding marble slabs. After that we headed for the Mandalay Hill to watch the sunset over the Irrawaddy River. And later, from the *Irrawaddy Princess* (a river cruising boat), we saw the moonrise in the east. We could see many pagodas glinting in all directions, kind of romantic, especially since we were the only people on the cruise. We had a Burmese dinner, followed by a walk through a joyous, raucous, colourful festival – there was lots of food cooking and smoking bamboo.

We were up early again the next morning to see how gold leaf was made. From thirty grams they made 460 gold-plated pieces of gold that they still hammered out by hand with a small sledge. There was a religious market at Mahamuni Temple that we saw as we drove along a road towards Mount Popa. It was a good highway, with no traffic. There were some motorcycles, some horse-drawn carts, but a lot of ox-carts the characteristic huge wheels used mostly by farmers. There were rice fields aplenty, a lot of fields still full of water, plowing was done with oxen where feasible. For lunch we were at Mount Popa resort where we could see the pagodas and buildings built on top of what looked like a volcanic cone since the thirteenth century. We had an absolutely spectacular setting for lunch, and there was virtually nobody around, it was once-in-a-lifetime place. We got a price list and saw that the most expensive room was $180 a day. Following that lunch, we drove to the village at the foot of Mount Popa. From there you could mount 777 steps to the top of Mount Popa. Marian and the guide did it. I stayed and stopped at the 100-step mark to amuse the local tourists. Finally, we drove to Bagan and a hotel right on the Irrawaddy River.

Next day, we started with a superb breakfast by the river under a huge tree. It started with climbing up a very steep pagoda with an overview of other pagodas some dating back to the tenth century. There were 4,000 pagodas in 42 square kilometres. Most were grey brick and in a state of decay, vegetation growing on them, mosses and bushes (even trees) and great streaks of fungus. The painting and stone and woodwork on the inside, was outstanding. Flying back from Bagan to Yango (Rangoon) on Bagan Air, our flight made a stop to allow a group of people to get off and hike in the mountains surrounding a lake – then we were back in the air and Yango-bound.

From Rangoon, we flew to Bangkok, and from there onto Cairo, Egypt[1]. I guess it had something to do with American feelings on the changing politics of the area, but overall, Myanmar was recovering from long-term military control and seemed to be doing well. The people were content, even happy, as they slowly got back to their traditional way of life.

Egypt

Arriving in Cairo from Myanmar via Bangkok, we were met by our guide, a man named Mohamed Sally. He took us to the Hotel Sofitel where we would be staying. It was at the southern end of Gezira Island in the middle of the Nile between Giza and Old Cairo. We needed a rest day because we had been up since five in the morning the previous day with air traffic from one place to another. Our guides were wearing shirts and ties.

We woke up three hours later to the sound of *adhan* [the Muslim call to prayer]. Ninety percent of Egypt's population was Muslim, which meant that in Cairo there was somewhere around 18 million followers of Islam. We went out for a walk by the river. We met a man whose son lived in Ottawa, so we struck up a conversation, and he took us to a store not far away, thatwas run, I believe, by another of his sons and his nephew. We ended up buying three paintings on papyrus and some perfume oils, which because they have no alcohol in them, should last forever.

We met a young man who was getting married the next day to a woman who had a good heart but maybe not so good-looking (said he) but would be a good wife in the long run. He needed money

---

[1] Note: I will be keeping all our African adventures together in the next chapter of the book.

to go through with it. I think he needed running shoes to escape, or perhaps he needed them in case she tried to get away from him.

There was a lot of garbage around the streets and in the Nile river, it seemed it was a convenient spot even for construction companies to dump their excesses.

There were a lot of young men hanging around, and we found out later that thirty Christians were thrown off the bridge just around the corner from our hotel. We knew nothing about it at the time until we got on our cruise on the Nile where some Canadians, who had seen it on CNN, told us about it.

The pyramids were built by the Pharaohs so their dead bodies would be safe, so the soul had to check up on the body. The ancient Egyptians made a very precise science of preserving the bodies as mummies including removing the brain through the nose which was then thrown away. The heart was more important.

I found it actually quite emotional to see the pyramids and Great Sphinx of Giza. They were wonders of the world, and there was virtually nobody around, so we got lots of pictures. It was known that thirty percent of the population was not educated, and that unemployment was at seventeen to twenty percent. Tourism was down eighty percent, as a result of the recent riots and the fear amongst other Muslim people. The public education system was poor. Many people smoke shisha (hookah) through a long plastic hose replenished periodically by someone swinging a smoking pot. While we were sitting in the lounge of the hotel, there was a man sitting at the next table who was visited very frequently by young men, and there seemed to be money changing hands? The hotel was full, but there were no women to be seen. We wondered if it was a gay group, but this was apparently a normal Egyptian Saturday night when all the men went out and the women stayed at home.

Following a trip to the museum where we saw a lot of papyrus, it was time for our plane to Luxor to begin our cruise up the Nile to the Aswan dam.

Our first stop was the Valley of the Kings and the tombs of Ramses III and IV. It was one hundred steps down to see the various grades. No cameras were allowed. Surprisingly, the colour remaining in the detail alabaster palace after all these years was sort of unexpected. This was followed by the Valley of the Queens where some of the work was quite exquisite, sitting in the ground through four thousand years. We viewed the original Egyptian calendar of three hundred and sixty days.

In 2011, the Aswan Dam provided fifteen percent of Egypt's power through hydroelectric generation. It is 3,830 metres across, 980 metres thick at its base, 40 metres thick at its crest, and 111 metres tall. It took 35,000 men (and 481 deaths) to create it and Nasser Lake which formed behind it. At the dam, Nassar Lake is 98 metres deep, and freshwater motor boat rides were available.

Along the river we met our table mates and guide Osama. The first stop was the Karnak Temple Complex with its huge columns and statues of Ramses II. He had been a victorious king and treated like a "God King."

Next, we were onto the Luxor Temple which was smaller but more definitive. There were a lot of carvings on the sidewalls of the temple. With the lights on them at night, they looked glorious with the golden glow.

All along the river within the first few yards were palm trees and habitations in places, but immediately behind that were sand dunes as far as the eye could see. We got to see the famous Unfinished Obelisk in an ancient quarry near Aswan. One night on the boat, we were asked to dress up in Arab costumes and had Egyptian food. It was good fun. We had a short boat ride to the Philae Temple which had to be moved inland because it was on an island and would have been submerged by the dam. Aswan was the home of the Nubians, who kept to themselves we were told.

We also spent a delightful afternoon on a felucca, a small sailboat which had room for maybe eight or ten people but only one sail., a ,During that time of sailing back and forth across the river we passed the Aga Khan Mausoleum which was in the process of being repaired so we couldn't visit it. We had a Nubian night on the boat prior to discharge, and we were impressed that there was a lot more staff than was necessary. That was because there was so few people on the boat due to the tourism downturn, but I guess they were trying to keep people employed. Apparently the return voyage up to Luxor only had a very few people booked also. I'm sure that Egypt was hurting a lot without their tourist trade.

At a market one day, where they sold and traded everything, I was offered two young Egyptian girls as a trade for my wife Marian. I demanded three, so the deal fell through. I thought I may have to shackle her.

Tutankhamun and his display,was exceptionally well done, especially with his gold mask.

He was apparently only nineteen years old at the time of his death.

We drove through Tahrir Square, which had been the site of the recent uprising. It was calm the day we were there

ICELAND (2012)

We visited Iceland in from August 8 to August 21, 2012. We arranged to have a four-wheel drive vehicle in order to drive around the whole island. Part of our arrangement included Bed & Breakfasts in advance along our route, so the only expense was dinners and gas ($2.50 per litre). We flew Iceland Air directly from Toronto to Reykjavik, where we stayed one night and picked up our vehicle the next morning. We drove up the west side across the north, down the east and across the south back to Reykjavik – two weeks total. There were occasional forays into the interior also. The four-wheel drive was a must.

I will generalize rather than talk about specific areas along the way.

Iceland had virtually everything you could hope for in a northern country. No palm trees. It had multiple fjords (some totally uninhabited), huge beaches (also mostly uninhabited), and towering cliffs (mostly covered with nesting birds). There were multiple volcanic cones, some black, and some red, gigantic lava beds that covered hundreds of square miles, hot springs, geysers, lots of glaciers, and lots of icebergs in the glacial lakes. Only one eighth of the country had snow.

Perhaps the most outstanding physical feature were the "ten thousand water falls" that fell often hundreds of feet, contrasted against the black lava and bracketed with bright green moss that surrounded the falls – quite impressive. There was, of course, pounding surf and crystal clear turquoise lakes and rivers.

There were only three hundred thousand people in all of Iceland. They all spoke English, which was a good thing because their language was difficult to read and all but impossible to pronounce. Can you say *Eyjafjallajökull*? That was the name of the volcano that paralysed European air travel for two weeks in 2010.

Wildlife in Iceland was quite limited. The arctic fox – we saw only tracks and that only once – was the only wild mammal present, a polar bear rarely floated over on an ice floe from Greenland. They were usually disposed of rather quickly since people felt quite threatened.

Whales were not rare, however; and we did see a few one night from shore; Humpbacks are what we saw, but many species frequented the waters – some blue whales (largest living mammal) were seen in Húsavík the week before we arrived.

Fishing was the main industry, and so there were many fish dishes in the restaurants, including char, salmon, and minke whale, which we tried one night and found it a quite tasty reddish meat; to me it tasted closer to venison than anything else I could think of. Marian had horse meat which she said was like beef. Incidentally they have 40,000 horses on the island, Icelandic horses are shorter and stockier than most breeds and have thick double coats developed to help them face the cold Icelandic winters.

Are there frogs or snakes? We did not see any, but perhaps.

Birds were plentiful, especially the sea birds, and some of *our* rare birds were not so rare there. For example, one of the earliest birds I saw was a purple sandpiper and I had only seen one before in Ontario, but they seemed to be fairly common there. Whimbrels and curlews were seen not infrequently. Golden plovers were not uncommon and seen even up in the mountains.

We were fortunate to get very close to a red-throated loon that was in a smallish pond near the foot of a glacier with this year's chick.

The puffin was a favourite bird, and though they had largely left for the south, they were still relatively plentiful – apparently eighty percent of the world's puffins go through or nest in Iceland. Black guillemots were also common as were kittiwakes. Furthermore, we saw a number of great and Arctic skuas, nasty fellows, but they had to eat like everything else. Whooper Swans (white) were often seen and looked spectacular framed by calm water, blue skies, and black surrounding mountains.

White-fronted and pink-footed geese were sporadic, and there were a number of ducks especially in the Mývatn area which was in an old lava area near Krafla volcano. There was lots of geothermal activity in the area, lots of hot baths, lava caves etc. European widgeons were the commonest type of duck although scoter and scaup were seen. There were many types of gulls to be seen, including, black-headed gulls, Bonaparte's gulls, Iceland gull, and glaucous gulls. Arctic terns also were present. Ringed plovers and oystercatchers were seen also, a surprise to me since I think of the oystercatchers as a more southern species.

Overall, it was a beautiful, variable country. The roads were excellent for the most part and well paved but with virtually no shoulder, so we didn't try to pull off to look at something. A lot of the time there was so little traffic, we could stop on the road for often five to ten minutes before another car would appear – this was especially true the farther from Reykjavik you drove. The four-wheel gravel roads were often quite steep, with a lot of switchbacks, limited visibility, and some scary drop-offs without any barriers.

There was virtually no garbage anywhere, and the houses were generally very clean and neat with lots of flowers. We saw no drunks, no vagrants, and the people (virtually all except for a few tourists) were tall, blonde, and very attractive; they were also very friendly and helpful when needed.

I highly recommend Iceland for any adventurous souls who like dramatic scenery, serenity, and natural wonder.

DANUBE CRUISE NOVEMBER (2012)

River cruises were a novelty for us, so we thought, *why not?* It would give us a chance to see a few more countries, and the timing was perfect for the Christmas markets, which Marian was quite excited about. We had to go via Frankfurt to Budapest, and the brief layover there allowed us to check out the origin of the many international flights. In two hours, we counted aircraft from forty-eight countries.

Budapest

We travelled with Viking River Cruises. We met our Viking Longship Njord in the river between Buda and Pest. The Budapest Parliament buildings, which probably were the most beautiful in the world, were enhanced by the reflection of its lights across the river. A tour of the beautiful old city was arranged the next morning. Most folk were Christian, but they were considering their choices. We saw St. Stephen Basilica, *Hősök tere* [Hero Square], Franz Liszt Square, and an old building full of bullet holes as a reminder to all.

Along the shore of the canal, there were quite a number of shoes cemented in place. They represented the remains of Jewish people, even children, who were shot and had their bodies dumped in the river during World War II. The 1956 revolution was commemorated by a remarkable memorial, erected in 2005 as the fiftieth anniversary approached, consisting of iron bars set in an enormous triangular wedge that comes to a steel point. St Stephen's Basilica involved the origin of Good King Wenceslas, then a quick visit to the Christmas market, where Marian only bought a couple of *small* items... so far, so good.

Bratislava

Bratislava is city of approximately 500,000 and is the capital of Slovakia with a total population of 10 million. Slovakia was the smaller remnant of Czechoslovakia.

I generally slept well, but the constant chugging of the engines was a minor problem on the ship. Fog the next morning made it look, like a setting for a murder mystery.

There were two Christmas markets that were both very good. Slovakia had free education even for university. Medicare had a monthly premium, but it covered *everything*. Hockey was a big sport there, and they were so proud that they beat Russia in the world championship one year.

Vienna

Vienna had, at one point, 7 million people. It was the home of Strauss, the world's oldest German university (Universität Wien), Lipizzaner stallions, Schubert, Christmas markets, and the Hapsburg dynasty. We went to a concert of Mozart and Strauss.

That night on the ship, they had some dancing. We started by jiving and even got some applause. For us, we wanted to waltz to the Blue Danube waltz on the Danube. We were able to do that, and I guess no one else knew how to waltz because the floor cleared, and we had it all to ourselves. Great! Afterwards they called us the champs.

—

Durnstein and Melk were next on our trip. There was a gigantic cathedral and monastery on top of a hill, while down below the area looked rather impoverished. All the money went to the church?

—

We stopped at Linz, and a bus trip got us to Salzburg, but we had been before, so we climbed up to the abbey and atteded a Mozart concert that was excellent with some exceptional voices. Passau in Germany was our last cruise stop before a bus ride to Prague.

Prague

During our last evening, a young woman came over to tell Marian that she was the most glamourous woman on the ship.

Prague was a glorious city to celebrate our anniversary. We walked a lot to the various concerts, restaurants, and the many Christmas markets

The ceremonial lighting of the Prague Christmas tree, along with several thousand people, was a major event. The city was very old, very musical, and very proud of their historic architecture. One thing that bothered everyone was a large communications building built by the Russians during their occupation. It did not fit with anything else. According to the locals, there was one good thing about it. You got good views of the whole city – the only view not marred by the building itself.

HIMALAYAS, TIBET, NEPAL, BHUTAN (2014)

From Toronto we flew to Beijing over the North Pole. This was very interesting to me because I'd spent time in the Arctic previously, and the pilot named some of the places we flew over which were familiar to me and some of which I had visited. The last of these in Canada was Resolute because west of that, in Canada, there is very little habitation. We must have flown over at least a corner of Russia to end up in Beijing, but there was no mention of it as we did it. Seeing the full moon over the Arctic panorama was quite dramatic, we could also see some major cracks in the ice.

Tibet
The next day we flew to Lhasa in Tibet which sat at an altitude of 3,656 metres – altitude sickness was a problem for some people, including me. During our one-hour drive from the airport, Tensing (our guide), mentioned that Tibet was the source of three major rivers two of which were the Yangtze and the Yellow. We noted that the

mountains at this altitude had very few trees except in the occasional valley on the north side facing south.

We stayed at the Four Points by Sheraton We noticed they had oxygen in every room.

Tibet has had a long, contentious relationship with China. This came to a head in October of 1950 when People's Liberation Army of Mao Zedong invaded, and there have been one million dead since as a result and a lot of suppression of monks and Buddhism. Virtually all of the monasteries were closed . Infiltration by mainland Chinese now outnumbered the Tibetans, which made it very unlikely that they could ever mount any significant resistance to China.

Although there was a lot of resentment of the Chinese, there was also hope that, someday, the Dalai Lama would return. The legal status of Tibet, according to its government-in-exile (the Central Tibetan Administration, based in India), was one of an independent state under illegal occupation. The Chinese perspective, however, was that Tibet was an integral part of China.

The Tibetans had a lot of highly skilled artisans who were being swallowed up by the Chinese dilution. The Dalai Lama was seen as a traitor in China, but the Tibetans themselves were still hopeful of his return someday.

Our first venture in Lhasa was to the Potala Palace, which had been the home of the Dalai Lama when he was there but was now a thousand-room museum. It took a lot of stairs to get up there, and I couldn't do it, but Marian could and did. We agreed with the guide to meet at the other end and I was to sit at a certain place. I sat there for quite a while until people started feeding me and feeling sorry for me.

I thought I would move down to the area where I knew they had to come down from the palace. I sat there and waited and waited and waited and waited. No show!

A group of oldsters who were sitting around started to wonder what was happening with me and offered me their cell phones and everything, but I didn't know who to call or where to call, and eventually when the place was getting ready to close, they took me down to the gate and hailed a taxi. At that very moment, a rickshaw appeared and the fellow riding it said what I thought was *Maryann*. I presumed that he meant that my wife, Marian, was down at the next gate, so I got on board.

We rode down to the next gate but he kept going.

I thought, he probably knew another way that I didn't. However, shortly we were out in traffic dodging buses and trucks, and I had no idea where we were going – and I don't think he did either.

Since my Tibetan was somewhat lacking, we eventually found someone who spoke English, and I was able to tell them the name of the hotel that I had come from. He then was able to take me in his rickshaw to the hotel where we were met by the staff, Tensing, Marian, and a lot of other people all of who thought I may have been lost. I had never been worried myself, as I had a general idea where I was, and where I had to go. However, our guide was very upset because he said, in thirty years, he had never lost a customer, and he'd thought maybe this would be his first.

The following day, we climbed some other stairs to some temples, but by then the altitude sickness was better andI was capable of doing it. The guide kept a careful eye on me, however.

Yaks are used for everything from meat, to animal labour, to milk. Their meat is *okay* in burger form, but not particularly exciting. We noted that there were a lot of people with prayer wheels that they carry around with them, and there was incense burning in a lot of places. We learned also that women who wore aprons were married.

Nepal

The next morning, we flew to Kathmandu having flown over Everest (or very close to it) but we didn't know it at the time. It was not mentioned by the pilot, but I supposed that's his routine flight and that he passed over it probably two or three times a day, and it was not a big deal to him. The population of Nepal was 27.6 million and Kathmandu accounted for 3.5 million of that. Eighty percent of people were Hindu. The unemployment rate was at forty percent, and most of the young people went to either South Korea or Dubai for work.

The traffic was fierce, and there did not appear to be any rules that we could understand. Motorcycles were everywhere, and the way they drove, there must have been several people killed every day – the roads were full of potholes, and there were piles of garbage all over the place.

Stupas (dome-shaped structures containing relics and used for mediation) meant for Tibetan Buddhists, were everywhere. There were lots of Tibetan refugees in Nepal.

Sharish, our guide – a man who won an award as the best guide in Nepal no less – took us to our hotel which was called Crown Plaza. It was elegant and well maintained, with pools, restaurants, manicured grounds, quite different than the rest of the city.

We visited the so-called Monkey Temple (Swayambhunath) on top of a hill in the Kathmandu Valley. There were monkeys everywhere and many crafts and a lot of Buddhist statues plus a significant number of Buddhist prayer wheels. The Buddhist statues had a third eye for looking inward while the Buddha watched you with the other two.

Patan Durbar Square a UNESCO World Heritage Site – which has since been destroyed in an earthquake – was very interesting. We saw the Royal Kumari, a nine-year-old girl who was imbued with godliness until she reached puberty. She appeared at a window for a few moments only.

We actually purchased a painting of Everest done by a local artist there too.

Nepal is 800 kilometres long 279 kilometres wide and is mostly situated in mountainous territory.

We went to the Pashupatinath Temple another UNESCO World Heritage Site, where there were a lot of elderly men with long grey beards and orange outfits. They were all covered with ashes. Apparently, they lived on the grounds there and may have used a significant amount of marijuana and perhaps other drugs. There were funeral pyres on the property right next to the river, and there were some immolations going on while we were there. Other families were waiting for empty spots. The ashes were swept into the river after the immolation ceremony.

Boudhanath was a gigantic stupa, and it may have been the largest one anywhere.

The following day we were to take a flight to Everest, but due to a monsoon swooping in from India, and the ensuing storms, that was unavailable, so we started on our way to Bandipur and Pokhara. The mountain pass was absolutely full of trucks and cars going both ways, and it took several hours to get over the pass. The rain was torrential, but we took a temple cable car up to Manakamana Temple. Coming down the steps from the very top, the water was more than ankle deep, and the current was running down the steps like a set of rapids. Eventually, we were able to backtrack a bit and go up to Bandipur, which was a small very old village, probably fifteenth century, up quite high in the mountains. It was quaint and very wet. There were no screens or glass on the windows of our hotel. It was still raining so hard we could see very little if we looked out the window, and some of the rain was getting in through the windows. Since there was no glass in them, it was a cool night, but we managed to get some sleep.

The next morning was quite foggy, but all that rain of the day before had fallen as snow at higher altitudes, and when the fog cleared, the Annapurna Mountain Range was in front of us in its magnificence covered with snow. As the day went on, the news came of the absolute disaster up above amongst the trekkers on the mountain. There were a lot of avalanches and deep snow. Each day we heard more about the number of deaths and missing up above. When we last heard there were forty-two deaths and still something like one hundred people missing. After the third day, we couldn't get any more news about it, so we presumed that the trekking companies were trying to suppress the news since, obviously, it would not be good for their business.

The next morning, we travelled to Pokhara. We stayed at the Fishtail Lodge, which required crossing of perhaps two hundred metres of water. This was accomplished on a barge by a man pulling on a rope which he expertly twirled into a circle on the floor.

It was a beautiful resort and had a lot of birds around, and across the river looking north we could see *Machapuchare* [fishtail] Mountain which was considered sacred and had never been climbed. It looked a lot like the Matterhorn and was beautiful in the evening with the alpenglow. If we looked west from the resort, we looked down a series of small waterways with mountains at the end, a very pastoral scene.

We were paddled down there to another little temple on an island.

They paddled four strokes on one side and then four strokes on the other side. I really felt the urge to teach them the J-stroke, but I stayed quiet. They had been doing that I guess for a very long time.

Next, we travelled back towards Kathmandu a certain distance then branched off along a river valley heading for Tigerland Safari Resort in the Chitwan area.. Once again, the driving was incredible, buses roaring around on the outside of mountain curves several hundred feet above the river below, *hoping* that somebody would let them in and someone always seemed to. We did see one bus burned out on its side and one truck turned over in the middle of the road. We could not see the ones who had gone over the edge and were down in the river. There must've been some. It was the only road that went through to India, so it did limit your choices. Our driver fortunately was quite a conservative fellow.

When we arrived in Tigerland, an elephant safari was waiting for us. We got very close to a black rhino, probably twenty feet, but the elephant and the rhino didn't seem to have any problem between the two of them. It was most interesting to see how the driver controlled the elephant with his feet on their ears and through a few verbal commands. Once there was a branch that looked like it might decapitate us, and the elephant grabbed it with his trunk and tore it off before that could happen. We saw many birds, including, peacocks, storks, bobos, and eagles. There were crocodiles and deer. There were no trekkers this time.

The next morning, we started off early to a nearby aboriginal village. The walls were straw mixed with dung, and the rooves were rice, straw, and bamboo. It worked well. There was no odour, the place was very clean, and they had more than one room in each abode.

It's hard to believe these warm, polite, considerate people were the same maniacs charging around on the roads, but they must be. Our last morning in Tigerland, we went birdwatching with an excellent guide, and we probably saw twenty new birds, but it was quite foggy, so we couldn't see very well.

The trip back to Kathmandu was only 137 kilometres and took seven hours! The roads were paths really; there was occasional pavement between the potholes, and again, the drivers were all over the place.

The next morning, we took a flight to see Everest. You're not allowed to fly within ten miles of it, and you cannot fly over it. It was quite emotional for me to see those mountains you have heard of so much of your life, and we had a beautiful clear day, so lots of pictures were taken.

Bhutan

We took Drukair – Royal Bhutan Airline and flew to Paro. We saw Everest again along the way. Bhutan was very different. There was no garbage, there was less traffic, drivers were less aggressive, the buildings all seemed to have a lot of carvings on the exterior, and everyone was Buddhist. We drove to Thimphu, the largest city in the Kingdom of Bhutan, following a pretty river valley.

The four principles of Buddhism in Bhutan were, first gross national happiness based on one's respect for nature, respect for others, and good governance. The men wore skirts to their knees called Ghos and long socks. Women wore long skirts to the floor.

They were building a grand Buddha on the mountain. At fifty-one metres it would be one of the largest Buddha statues in the world. Their hope was that it would become the eighth wonder of the world.[2]

Sangay, our guide, stopped to pray periodically. I asked what he prayed for and he said he prayed for everyone, for understanding, and peace. Everyone can become a Buddha by reaching enlightenment, and then you don't think about yourself. To do this you must conquer greed so that you stop thinking in terms of yourself; anger must be controlled, and ignorance must be cured.

We went to the zoo to see a Taki which was a 160-kilogram mixture of goat and cow which was the national animal of Bhutan.

We also saw the King's Palace (Dechencholing Palace), which was incredibly ornate and filled with art work. It actually reminded us a lot of the Sistine Chapel in Rome.

The health care system covered everyone. Education was covered to grade nine, but if students wanted to attend university, for now, they had to travel to India. They were working on that, however, and hoped to have a university before too long.

---

2 This work was completed in September of 2015. The largest Buddha in the world, however, remains the Leshan Giant Buddha in China; it is 71 metres tall.

The people loved their life and had a respect for life that went beyond the walls of life – beyond the material. There was no immigration. You cannot go there and stay unless you were born there. They had a tax on smoking.

Paro Taktsang, also known as the Tiger's Nest, is an old convent on a cliff, built in 1692. It is perched more than 900 metres above the floor of the Paro valley. We climbed several hundred stairs as well as up and down hills in order to visit it. We lit a butter candle in each temple and we took our shoes off, and the guide prayed in each one, asking for enlightenment. The legend was that the Buddha, in his conquest of evil, had a tigress subdue the evil spirits in the locality. Marian walked all the way up, I stopped across a gully from the final destination, but I got some good pictures of it from there with my big lens.

Overall, Bhutan was a great country, full of wonderful people (only 750,000) who had a wonderful outlook on the world and other people. They plan to keep it that way by not allowing significant outside influence.

From there we travelled home via Dhaka (in Bangladesh) then Bangkok (Thailand) and finally to Tokyo Japan.

MEXICO (MULTIPLE TRIPS OVER MULTIPLE YEARS)

We have now been to Mexico several times and have visited many terrific locations including, the Mayan Riviera, Puerto Vallarta, Nuevo Vallarta, and most recently Los Cabos. All were beautiful and exceptionally well appointed with excellent service and every conceivable amenity – shops, beaches, swimming, gym, entertainment, and many restaurants. Very noticeable is the tight security. There were also local differences, of course, and they were all developing and changing. The Mayan Riviera has a show put on by Cirque du Soleil accompanied by dinner that is superb. There was also Chichen Itza, which had many other historic temples and the cenotes which are wonderfully cool, vine-covered, cave-like natural pools that you can swim in.

It was along the beach in Puerto Vallarta at the Mayan Palace Resort that we had our first taste of parasailing. You are suspended by a parachute and towed by a boat as you pass along a few hundred feet above the hotels and beaches.

Nuevo Vallarta is developing Cirque du Soleil theme park that will be bigger than Disney World evidently. It was in the process of being developed when we last visited and current estimates have pushed the opening back to 2020. I have gone birding twice at Nuevo Vallarta and have seen many birds (usually about sixty) that we don't see up north at all.

Los Cabos

There was an estuary about two blocks away from our resort which was full of birds, a lot of them migrants from Canada but lots of birds that I had never seen before. We had a peregrine falcon, which was new to me, hanging around the resort, and we would see him picking apart his latest prey up on the roof quite often.

We went fishing there as well, but the initial results were less than dramatic until we were heading back to the harbour and a sea lion jumped up on the back of the boat with quite a large fish in his mouth. I didn't have time to make him an offer before he was gone; perhaps another time. There were also some very dramatic rock formations at Los Cabos, and seeing them at sundown was quite enchanting. There were also many good restaurants in the area. Since we were staying at a timeshare, there was a major grocery store just a few blocks away, which was very convenient.

They also had an art festival while we were there which featured a huge array of different types of paintings – some of which were difficult to understand in my way of thinking.

The weather in Mexico, of course, was idyllic at least at the time of year that we were there – always between late November and early December . Temperatures were usually in the low eighties, so sunbathing was excellent if that sort of thing interests you. All in all, Mexico was a great place for a warm vacation or to break up winter if that is important to you. Although we hear frequently about the crime in Mexico, we have never seen any sign of anything illegal, and I believe it is mostly with the drug cartels in the larger cities

CINQUE TERRA (2016)

The five little villages along the northern Italian Riviera has long been a place we wanted to visit and to hike.

We flew first to Amsterdam and then it was a short hop to Milan, Italy. Upon arriving, since we had a reservation at a hotel, the question was how to get there. There was a bus, and for five euros it would take you to the central station in Milan, where all the trains converged, but of course, we didn't know how to get to our destination from there. We were advised, at the information station in the airport, that it would take at least two buses to get there, so a cab sounded like a good idea.

The cab stand had two prices United States $55 for area A or $65 for area B. That seemed a lot to me, and I said so. The short overweight man turned red, was quite angry, and stomped off. Marian began to laugh. I was quite amused myself but said nothing. Another cabbie came up and showed us over to his cab. It was quite a long way for $55. Interestingly on our way back, two weeks later, we had to take the reverse drive from the central station to a hotel near the airport. With the meter, running it was $18.50. It does make you wonder if you are being scammed and how many other people were scammed every day. It turned out we were within easy walking distance from the central station to the first hotel, so we could easily have taken the five-euro bus to the central station and walked the short distance. All these things you learn as you go, too slowly unfortunately. Flying into Milan with KLM showed a lot of lakes and mountains in Northern Italy – quite an introduction really.

Next, we took the train from Milan to Levanto on the Italian Riviera. The train was rapid, efficient, and went along the Mediterranean coast the last third perhaps of the voyage. Levanto was at one end of the five villages that are perched along the coast on rocky bluffs or protected bays. For a long time, there were no roads to the small areas, and still some of them don't have any; railway, the Mediterranean, or your own two feet – take your choice. We were there to hike, so that was mostly what we did almost always, but we also used the train and the ferry that goes along the coast. It was an excellent way to get a quick look at the villages with all their colourful buildings on the water and cliff edges.

The hiking was quite strenuous at times, and since I was much older than everyone else, sometimes I fell a little behind. Emilio, our Italian guide, had an Aussie accent and a few strange idioms. He was very skilful in how he divided the group so that everybody was hiking while some – okay, mostly me – were doing less strenuous routes. Balancing along the edge of cliffs is not something I should probably be doing now although I hate to admit there's anything I can't do.

The little villages were picturesque in the extreme, with little winding alleys and staircases and bright coloured buildings contrasted against dark rocks. It was an artist and photographer's delight. Many very large houses belonged to some rich and famous people who were seen along the way. They're probably all unhappy for other reasons? Or maybe not! We did a lot of hiking, some swimming, but we also had time for some great meals in the little restaurants, and of course, we had to visit markets periodically.

Interestingly there were three young Aussies – currently diplomats in London – who sort of adopted us (don't know why), but we ended up going to bars and had some good fun with them a couple of times. They, of course, were young and vigorous and in their forties (very similar to us).

Our last stop was Santa Margherita Ligure, and we had been warned about pickpockets. We were getting on the train, and I had to lift my heavy suitcase up that steep stairs on the first car. There were two young girls about fourteen or fifteen standing there, and as I turned with the suitcase, I realized my wallet was half out of my pocket. I quickly pushed it back in, of course, realizing in five seconds it would've been gone. Of course, they jumped off the train just before it took off, so there was no catching them or reporting them. I guess they'd just wait for the next train and try again.

14. AFRICA

Africa is a life changing experience. We have visited three times, and I have collected them all together here as they form their own narrative – as you will soon see.

AFRICA, OUR FIRST TIME (2006)

Our first trip to Africa was with a company called Wonders of Creation, in Arusha, Tanzania. It no longer exists. Our guide was Humura and we had him and our Toyota Land Cruiser (which seated seven) to ourselves. He was extremely knowledgeable about the plants, animals, and the birds. He seemed invested in our interest in seeing *everything* not just the so-called big five most people want to see – the big five are generally recognized as lion, leopard, rhinoceros, elephant, and buffalo. We actually saw the big five our first day, and we saw a lion hunting and chasing a boar. Fascinating! The boar ran a zigzag pattern, so the lioness missed at first, but she'd wounded it, so after that, it was easier for her, and once the boar succumbed, the family appeared to dine. The lion eats first, if they are present, even though the lioness was the successful hunter.

Another time, in Ngorongoro Crater, we watched a cheetah hunting a gazelle. He was sneaking through the grass about fifty metres away. Suddenly the gazelle saw the cheetah but did not run. The cheetah just lay down. I guess they both knew that, with a fifty-metre head-start, the gazelle would make it. A couple of minutes later, a boar family walked right beside the cheetah, no response. How did they know it would be safe?

It was quite a fantastic time! We saw so many species of all kinds – almost all the antelopes, twenty-two lions in one day, eight cheetahs including three brothers lying down together, hyenas, bat-eared foxes, hippos, elephants, giraffes, cape buffalo, ostriches, leopards, jackals, zebras, and thousands of wildebeest. There is a symbiosis between zebras and wildebeests in their migration. It is felt that one knows the way, and the other can find water along the way. All kinds of birds including storks, swans, hawks, eagles, and some wildly coloured smaller birds. I've got pictures of weavers, bee-eaters, swallows, stilts, and many others.

The Serengeti seems like, an endless grassland, and it is incredible in the sheer volume of wildlife it supports. We were in five national parks each a little different.

At Lake Manyara, we met Tumaini, who worked at the lodge. He accompanied us with our Maasai guide down to the lake. He seemed to know more about the local flora than the guide whose English was limited. I assumed he came along to practice his English. We were impressed with him; he struck us as a bright young kid. We were able to talk to him again for quite a while the next morning and got his name and address.

We spent a week with Humura and stayed in beautiful lodges every night. The food was great, and we were able to meet other people on safaris. Following Tanzania, we flew Air Zimbabwe to Harare. We had arranged to stay overnight in a hotel before proceeding to Victoria Falls for a week in a timeshare that we had arranged by ourselves.

Harare

The capital of Zimbabwe was very quiet and run down – almost spooky. Big opulent homes were decaying. It seemed such a shame. We did not learn until later that, on the very night we arrived, the opposition leader was beaten and jailed. In the hotel, Marian wanted some bottled water, so I went out on the hunt. It was very dark, even in the courtyard of the hotel. A couple of ladies of the night were professionally friendly with me and extremely good-looking. We didn't get around to price, but the people were so desperate, I'm sure almost anything would've done. I finally found some water and returned to our room.

We were awakened about five the next morning by a loud noise – shouting the source of which we could not see because we were on the inside courtyard. It probably was rioting because of the night before. We were very happy to leave Harare because we had a really uneasy feeling about it. You will recall that Mugabe, the president, displaced all the white farmers with black people to farm except they didn't understand how to do it., t So now this country – which was once the richest country in Africa – was now poverty-stricken. The black people were good workers but had no experience with administration. Most of the Whites had gone to Zambia next door.

Malawi

We made a brief stop in Malawi en route to Victoria Falls.We were there only long enough to see some farmers trying to scare off some elephants that were trampling their crops.

Victoria Falls was a timeshare again – a very nice lodge with individual thatched cottages and lots of wildlife close at hand. There were monkeys and boars right outside. Talking to one of the staff, he said they didn't use local money to buy things, they traded things. He was married and paid his rent with bags of cement. The *official* bank rate at that time was 1 US dollar to 250 Zimbabwe dollars, but on the street and in stores the exchange was actually 8000 to 1. While we were there, an American arrived for a few days, went to the bank, and got some Zim dollars at the official rate of 250:1. When he came to the lodge, he couldn't afford lunch. He was caught off guard, poor guy.

They had a lot of excellent woodcarvers. They approached us with a piece for $25 dollars. We said no. They followed us down the street lowering the price as we went. They're pleased to get anything – even five dollars – for all their work. I am a carver, so I can appreciate the skill and the time involved. It's a shame that they couldn't reach a larger market.

Victoria Falls

The falls were in flood, and we were told it was the highest it had been in thirty years. It sure made for a dramatic sight anyways. Some people were actually bungee jumping off the bridge across to Zambia

– which is just below the falls. We fought back the urge to try it, with great difficulty. It might damage my artificial knee, right?

Our next guide, Johan, was to meet us in Zambia, so we walked across the bridge with our suitcase and met him at the appointed area. Johan was white, an Afrikaner from South Africa. He took us through Zambia across the Chobe River, also in flood, by barge. For the first night, we stopped at some small individual cottages on the riverbank. One of the staff had a serious snake bite which she had not reported and was now very ill and needing evacuation, so we had a substitute who drove us up the river in a boat where we saw some birds and a lot of hippos. They can be very dangerous, so he was very careful getting by them. Hippos are quite aggressive and have been known to tip boats over – in fact no animal kills more people in Africa every year than hippos.

It was quite apparent right away that Zambia was much better off than Zimbabwe even though there was some flooding.

Namibia

From Zambia, we travelled to Namibia, including the Caprivi Region (since 2013 known as the Zambezi Region) which had only recently been reopened after the killing of the French tourists apparently. We were back and forth, into and out of Botswana before getting to the southern end of Namibia and entering South Africa.

Those few weeks of our trip, we mostly camped in tents on sponge mattresses. Was it comfortable? Not unless you dug a hole for your hips and shoulders in the sand. The camping was mostly inside enclosures, so theoretically, animal free. Jackals are not stopped by anything, they are as brazen as mongooses; they would often be, almost at our elbows while we were eating. They never went for the plate, but we didn't dare turn our back or they would jump up like they do with the lions.

—

One night, in Namibia's Etosha National Park, a warden came to tell us there was a lion inside the compound and last seen about one hundred metres from where we were. There had been one family camping slightly closer but they had moved, leaving us the closest to the site. The warden assured us that they had given the lion a zebra and expected it would keep him happy.

"But best not leave your tent during the night."

Can you imagine telling two older folks not to go to the washroom about fifty metres away all night? The thought of a lion present didn't make holding it any easier. They were patrolling all night with guns ready, and of course, we had to make the necessary visit, but fortunately nothing happened.

—

Another night, besides some very odd squeals, squeaks, and screeching during the night, we could hear lions roaring. They sounded like they were right outside the tent. In the morning, we found they had killed a zebra right outside of the campground, so they were probably one hundred to two hundred metres from our tent. Some nights we slept better.

Another night, a group of baboons were running through the campsite trying to get into the garbage receptacles. Still another night, we could hear a bunch of hooves running nearby. In the morning we found a bunch of tracks – identified by our guide as belonging to kudu, a type of antelope – just a short distance from the tent.

One morning, we were invited to go on a hike; walking with no truck which was considered suicidal by some. We had a guide with his gun ready, and he assured us he was a good shot. At one stage, we could hear a distant rumbling which grew louder and louder. We hid behind a little hillock and saw a herd of probably fifty Cape buffalo stampeding by just on the other side of the little hill. Early on in the expedition, a Cape buffalo stared us down. They are considered quite dangerous, so our guide instructed us to walk *slowly* away so we did. Nothing happened – other than an adrenaline surge. We saw so many birds of all kinds most of them new to us.

—

We visited with a group of indigenous OvaHimba. It is estimated that the Himba people number approximately 50,000. We were led to believe that they meet the modern world and disappear frequently. The women cover themselves with red clay and animal fat to look pretty and to get rid of body hair. They use smoke to clean themselves. The chief had several wives in different villages. We were told there was no jealousy. The women had their four lower teeth removed, and it was considered a sign of beauty. Almost all of them were totally naked except for the crotch area. They believed in a single God and in their ancestors – whom they attempted to contact for important decisions.

—

A caracal ran in front of the truck at one stage, and a desert elephant was seen one day. Both are rare. A caracal is a medium size African cat – the approximate size of a bobcat – that lives in the desert in rocky or mountainous locales.

Morning in the Namibian Desert was a spectacular scene. We got up early and climbed the dunes so we could be there at sunrise. The dunes were a brilliant red which faded as the day went on.

The temperature reached fifty in the desert that day. I melted. We northerners can't handle that kind of heat, but the locals could.

Botswana

In Botswana, we visited the Okavango Delta for a day of poling through marshy areas in dugout canoes. You tend to think of a delta as a place where a river spreads out as it entered an ocean, like the McKenzie or the Mississippi, but in Botswana the Okavango is landlocked and fans out into the desert. Apparently, the lions there could swim from island to island because it really was a huge marsh with a few islands in it. We did see some red lechwe antelopes which were very rare and some very unusual vegetation in the delta.

We entered a church in Botswana while the choir was singing. There was a boy of about fourteen with a spectacular bass voice. He stood out in the choir. We were hoping someone with a musical bent could lead this boy to where his voice would be enjoyed by many. It's not likely that it would happen, but it was a wonderful voice.

Another tribe we saw were called Herero, the ladies stood outside in full colour skirts and dresses and double peak hats. I'm not sure the significance of that. We stayed at Brandberg White Lady Lodge that night, which was a nice change from camping. They had individual cabins in a beautiful oasis in the desert. The food was great, and there were some pictographs there also in nearby rock formations, depicting the local fauna – giraffes, lions, and hippos.

We travelled next to the Skelton Coast Road; it was a salt road (which is to say *made* of salt) along the coast up to Cape Cross. There were thousands of seals, a lot in the water, where evidently, the sharks and killer whales picked them off on the outer side of the group.

Following that the Fish River canyon was dramatic. We watched the sun go down, but it can't be compared to the Grand Canyon; very remote and there was no one around. There were some quiver trees around which were poisonous, and according to Johan, some visiting athletic team used one for firewood, and the whole team died.

We said goodbye to Johan and started our next journey to Cape Town on our own.

Cape Town

We drove to the beach across from Cape Town where there were plenty of windsurfers jumping off waves. We found our way to Hawkes Bay and the home of John Thompson. John was a friend of our son-in-law (Krista's husband), and he was letting us use his place for a week. It was like security overload. Besides a spiked fence and locked gate, there were keys for every room –meaning to go from one room to another *within* the house, you needed keys.

We had not made reservations, so we could not go to Robben Island and see the prison where Nelson Mandela had been held for eighteen years until he'd been transferred to Pollsmoor Prison in Cape Town itself.

Table Mountain, reached by gondola, was amazing with the tremendous view over Cape Town from the top. We also visited Desmond Tutu's church, and the Kirstenbosch National Botanical Garden was great. When we were driving back from Cape of Good Hope at the tip of the peninsula we saw four blesbok antelopes (*Damaliscus pygargus phillipsi*), which were very rare, but so beautiful. We also saw some jackass penguins too on our tour of Cape of Good Hope. We drove through some poverty-stricken areas where everybody seemed happy enough. It was hard to believe that the Blacks were not allowed to vote until 1994. It seems unthinkable now it is so recent.

We spent seven glorious weeks in Africa and spent time in seven countries. The people we met were so kind and appeared happy. Most of them would never have been out of their country, so they did not know how the rest of the modern world lived.

—

Upon returning home, we contacted Tumaini, and discovered that his father had died of malaria at the age of forty-nine. The oldest of four boys, Tumaini became responsible for the two of his younger brothers –his mother had moved to Lake Victoria with the youngest. He had, therefore, been unable to carry on with his education. We offered to pay for college, an offer he was most happy to accept. He decided to take wildlife management since he was always interested in wildlife. First, however, he had to upgrade and then took the course at Moshi College at the base of Mount Kilimanjaro.

AFRICA, OUR SECOND TRIP (2011)

This African excursion followed, directly on the heels of our 2011 Southeast Asian trip (see chapter 13).

Tanzania

We flew EgyptAir to Dar es Salaam, then on to Kilimanjaro International Airport in northern Tanzania near the Kenyan border. It was there that Tumaini picked us up. We'd returned to Tanzania for his graduation from college after four years. We had provided the money for him to attend college, so he was so thankful. He was very excited and ran to see us and took us to the Arusha Hotel.

We went to the market, and Tumaini drove us around through the suburban areas including some of the poor areas where the road was more of a cow path than anything else. It's interesting that people probably don't think in terms of rich and poor, but by our standards, almost everyone there would be considered poor. I'm sure they don't look at themselves that way because they always lived how they are living and assume that that is normal. They seemed generally content, even happy, as they related to each other. They appeared to smile a lot and laugh.

The exchange rate for US currency was running at 17:1 at that moment, and they had an election coming up. The present leader had been there for ten years, and folks were starting to grumble about him.

They were virtually all Christians there, and most went to church. We noticed drums in his church and apparently music was a big part of it. Tumaini is Anglican.

The next day we went to Kisima Ngeda on Lake Manyara. The lake was in the Rift Valley, and we stayed at a beautiful tent camp, but the road getting there was brutal. Thank goodness for those Toyota Land Cruisers. The place was run by a German who grew up in Tanzania and his Argentinian wife. They had been there for fourteen years and seemed very happy.

Later in the day we went to see the Datooga people. They lived in thatched homes made from dung and sticks and were surprisingly cool inside. While we were there they were milling the maize, rock to rock, with the maize in the middle. We then watched them build a forge and melt some old metal they had found into arrowheads and spearheads which were very sharp. They grew most of the onions used in Tanzania, and they also grew some corn. We saw a lot of interesting birds – a sacred ibis, swallows, bush babies, and a kingfisher. This tribe were traditional enemies of the Maasai tribe. I'm not sure how far that goes currently.

Hazda

The following day we went to visit the Hazda(?) people. Differentiating them from bushmen is difficult because of many similarities. The difference seems to be in location. We were able to find some about two kilometres from the nearest village. They had their own language. They stayed in small family groups between six to fifteen people usually. They lived outside except in rain, at which time they make a frame with branches of palm fronds. If they can find some, they top them with plastic. Most don't live past five years of age because of malaria. The men and women stay separately during the day. They were quite a small people and lived by hunting. While we were there, we saw a young boy, probably eleven years old, with a bow and arrow who shot a pigeon on the wing. He brought it over to show us with the arrow still in it. He finished it off by biting its head.

They used a lot of marijuana starting at age ten. They were busy passing some around while we were there. We noticed pieces of meat drying on the branches and on top of their shelters. They were nomadic, so if they killed a large animal, for example a buffalo, it was easier to move the whole village to the animal than trying to bring a buffalo back to the camp. They were singing and dancing and enjoying themselves and very friendly, but of course we couldn't communicate with them in terms of words. A trial with their bow and arrows proved far less accurate than they were.

Serengeti

The Serengeti was our next stop on the trip. The word *Serengeti* translated means "endless plains", and travelling through it the name seems apt. We saw all the animals: baboons, wildebeests, ostriches, hippos, lions of course, impalas, lilac-breasted rollers... the list goes on and on. The following day we saw a leopard walking along and he happened to be going the same direction we were, so we drove along and he gradually crossed right in front of us so that he was then on the other side, and he was so close to the vehicle, I could've touched him, but I decided maybe that wasn't a very good idea so I didn't. We saw lots of hyenas. The hyenas like to play games with the lions. They lie in wait for the lions and if the lion steps away for any reason, then they are right on to whatever the lion was eating. Of course, they *can* also kill their own food, so they're not totally dependent on the lions for food.

Subsequently we revisited the Ngorongoro crater and saw several kills. Lions were eating all manner of other animals. In the afternoon, we watched the black rhino for quite a while. They are not very common now, in fact, they are classified as critically endangered. All in all it was a great day – a total of twenty lions and a lot of other animals and birds.

Tumaini's graduation was coming up, so we had to get back to Arusha and Arrow Merrill River Lodge where we changed for the party. We then had to go to Moshi, where the college was, and the graduation. It was a long tedious ceremony as usual, but Tumaini was really excited, and we met several members of his family, Ezekiel, Emanuel (his two younger brothers), another Emanuel (a cousin), his mother Angelina, and her sister Mary. They were all very thankful for what we did for Tumaini, but his mother could not speak any English. His cousin Emanuel, however, spoke English very well. They laughed a lot, and they had fun with each other, so we see them as a new part of our family and we are part of theirs.

The following day we went to Arusha Park and saw all sorts of birds: tropical boo-boo. , helmeted guineafowl, a pink-backed pelican, collared sunbirds, golden palm weavers, a black-bellied bustard, African canaries, and so many others.

When it came time to leave, Tumaini's mother was very emotional and insistent on thanking us, saying that we had done a much better job as a parent for him than she could have, so she was very thankful indeed.

From there we went to Kilimanjaro Airport and then on home via Amsterdam.

AFRICA, OUR THIRD TRIP (2016)

This trip followed our time in Cinque Terra. We first had to fly back to Amsterdam from Milan and then a lot of walking to change gates, but it was well signed. From there we took the plane to Kilimanjaro International Airport in Tanzania.

We were going this time because Tumaini was getting married to a woman named Pamela.

Kilimanjaro is a small airport, so stair ramps are used to deplane and then a long wait for regulatory process. Tumaini was waiting for us when we finally emerged and drove us to our overnight accommodation. Several dik-diks (a species of tiny antelope) were running around the property

Next morning, we were picked up and taken to see baby Marian; she was the daughter of Tumaini and Pamela and named after my wife. Baby Marian, surprisingly, was not afraid of us, despite our strange colour (or lack thereof), and both Marian and I were able to hold her without any fuss whatsoever.

Pamela was, for all intents and purposes, already Tumaini's wife they simply had yet to be churched. She prepared lunch, and we were on our way to our safaris. We stayed at Lake Manyara Escarpment Luxury Lodge the first night. It was a super accommodation with our own separate unit with a huge wraparound deck looking over Lake Manyara. The view from the lodge was incredible and took in not just the lake but part of the legendary Rift Valley which stretches from Tanzania through Kenya up to Ethiopia and was the original source of humankind as far as we know. It was wonderful. The profound silence punctuated only occasionally by the sound of a bird. We were able to sit on the deck and sort of half dream about the beginnings of mankind in this very area.

Next day in the Lake Manyara National Park, we saw all kinds of lions, monkeys, birds (everything from warblers to eagles), giraffes, hippos, wildebeest, and several types of antelopes. We went back to our new accommodation at Gibb's Farm near the edge of the Ngorongoro crater. It was another beautiful place , it even had an outdoor shower in a rock grotto.

Tumaini insisted on buying us a painting so we picked out a colourful one with a zebra central. The painting looks great in the study. Tumaini has been so grateful for what we have done for him, and he wanted to give us a gift, so this is what he bought. We kept telling him we are so proud of him and the only gift we wanted was for him to succeed and be happy. Every time we talk to him or see him, he keeps thanking us. When we got back to Arusha, we went to the African Tulip which was a five-star Arusha Hotel. We stayed there before and after the wedding.

The wedding of Tumaini and Pamela was a joy –singing, dancing, everyone moving except for the minister, a man with a constant smile. He was a little long-winded, and of course, he spoke in Swahili. Fortunately, Tumaini's cousin, Emmanuel sat behind us and explained what was being said. –It was, all the usual things about marriage.

There are many tribes in Africa. Pamela is a Maasai but grew up in Arusha. The tribal rivalry is becoming less and less pronounced, but Tumaini still had to pay a penalty of a goat because Pamela was pregnant before being married. They are Christians, and there was no alcohol and no drugs in the celebration. I didn't know they made non-alcoholic champagne, but we had some.

As they started clapping and moving from foot to foot, you got a sense of the joy they derive from music. I can't move my hips the way they did, but I sure could feel the music, rhythm, the emotion of it all as they sang often with their eyes closed so intensely. It seemed like they were always in rhythm even when moving from one area to another. They wanted to think of us as part of their family, and we were (and still are) honoured by that. We sat at the family table for the reception.

Tumaini's mother, Angelina, thanked us again in Swahili for being better parents for him than she was able to be. We were thanked by all the relatives, and we were told that we raised them all up. Two of Pamela's siblings are in law school, and they have all generally moved upward in the world. They gave us the credit. We were happy to make a difference, but we weren't aware how much difference we had made. It's very gratifying, more than we expected and is a constant source of happiness.

The wedding was a joy from start to finish. The reception was in a gorgeous setting halfway up a mountain. Everybody was happy; everybody was relating, and we saw the interrelationship of these families. They do everything together, for example, Tumaini's wedding was paid for by a group of his relatives, and they all stood up and were acknowledged. What a great way to do things rather than having one person with all the expense.

The following day, we were invited out to meet Pamela's family. We met her mother and her siblings. One brother is in law school, and his wife is in law school as well, and another is already a lawyer, but he's making cookies and selling them there as well as bread. They were both very tasty, and we had some tea as well. Then it was on to meet the rest of Tumaini's family for lunch – there were seventeen or eighteen and they were also thankful. He kept telling us how we helped them all really. It was an overwhelming feeling.

The following day we went back to Arusha National Park, which was a smaller more wooded park. We saw more animals and lots of birds; there were no lions this time but there were thousands of lesser flamingos around the middle of the lake that might've been four or five deep in places. Following that, we went to the airport, having a shower along the way, and then back to Amsterdam after a sad farewell.

We'd had a wonderful time, and were so happy that so many people were happy as well.

15. WHERE THE HEART IS.

It seems we have spent a lot of time in travelling to other places.

We have a small A-frame cottage on a small lake just off the edge of Algonquin Provincial Park (which is bigger than Prince Edward Island). There is no road, no Hydro, and boat is the only way to get there. There are only twelve cottages on the Y-shaped lake. Most of the time we are the only ones there, so complete silence is usual except for the occasional bird.

Every morning I go out in my canoe to feel the ambience of the place. Paddling slowly, I notice the flowers growing, the birds nesting, and I marvel at how some trees seem to have grown against impossible odds. Their roots are in a crack in the granite rock or under an overhang where they would never get sun, and yet they flourish. The different types of lichen are amazing. Why did they pick the places they do? Every possible spot spawns some sort of life – wildflowers, ferns, lichens, cedars that hang out from cliffs – and I wonder what keeps them there. As the sun rises, I feel warmth on my cheek.

Is that a heron in the bay? I will see how close I can get before he notices me.

I paddle in the water with virtually no movement above water level and moved very, *very* slowly. It is surprising what I see and how close I can get.

Next a quick run up the river to see what the beavers are up to now. Their dams are almost down to the lake now. I wonder if the speckled trout try to navigate them still. They may be very persistent too.

An evening bonfire as the moon rises across the lake completes a great day. Now that we have solar power – and therefore a pump and running water including *hot* water – we have the basics of home while immersed in the woods.

There is no part of Canada that doesn't have something extraordinary to offer if you look for it. Politically we are quite stable, and most people are proud of how multidimensional, multicultural, and tolerant we have become.

Having travelled most of the world, there is no better place to call home.

I wish you best of luck with your travels. Be daring, but not foolish. There is a lot of wonderful world out there and endless opportunities to learn about other people, their cultures, and nature in all its diversity.

If only everyone had that chance to appreciate others, perhaps we humans could learn to get along as a species rather than always emphasizing the differences and being willing to hate and even kill because of them.

May we all learn to live in good health. May we be appreciative and supportive of others and their differing views. And may we remember that we are all members of the same human family.

ACKNOWLEDGEMENTS

I would like to thank my wife Marian for her never ending support and encouragement and my children who always kept life challenging, ever changing, often rewarding, and their spouses and families. They always kept you on your toes (and sometimes on your heels)

I thank Friesen press for guiding me through the unfamiliar territory of the publishing world

Special thanks to my sister Lynne and some friends as well as my son Stephen (computer expert) and daughter Karen (world traveller) for their suggestions along the way. For a neophyte author that is important

CPSIA information can be obtained
at www.ICGtesting.com
Printed in the USA
LVHW070019090219
606807LV00002BA/3/P